First Workshop on Matching from Unstructured and Structured Data (MATCHING 2023)

Toronto, Canada
13 July 2023

ISBN: 978-1-7138-8229-9

Printed from e-media with permission by:

Curran Associates, Inc.
57 Morehouse Lane
Red Hook, NY 12571

Some format issues inherent in the e-media version may also appear in this print version.

Association for Computational Linguistics
209 N. Eighth Street
Stroudsburg, Pennsylvania 18360

Phone: 1-570-476-8006
Fax: 1-570-476-0860

acl@aclweb.org

Additional copies of this publication are available from:

Curran Associates, Inc.
57 Morehouse Lane
Red Hook, NY 12571 USA
Phone: 845-758-0400
Fax: 845-758-2633
Email: curran@proceedings.com
Web: www.proceedings.com

The First Workshop on Matching From Unstructured and Structured Data (MATCHING 2023)

Proceedings of the Workshop

July 13, 2023

Order copies of this and other ACL proceedings from:

Association for Computational Linguistics (ACL)
209 N. Eighth Street
Stroudsburg, PA 18360
USA
Tel: +1-570-476-8006
Fax: +1-570-476-0860
acl@aclweb.org

Introduction

Welcome to the inaugural Workshop on Matching from Unstructured and Structured Data - MATCHING 2023!

Matching is a fundamental task with wide-ranging applications, encompassing search, recommendation systems, and data integration, among others. Given the proliferation of social media and e-commerce platforms, the ability to match information from both structured and unstructured sources has become increasingly crucial. At its core, matching aims to identify pairs of entries in two collections that share common properties. For instance, in the realm of HR platforms/services, matching resumes to job descriptions plays a pivotal role. Similarly, online booking platforms/services strive to match customer preferences with suitable businesses, such as hotels, restaurants, and real estate establishments. Beyond these entity matching examples, matching techniques find frequent application in various domains, such as matching customer reviews about a product to customer queries, aligning snippets of web documents with search queries, and matching user responses in Q&A platforms to new questions, etc. Consequently, matching tasks can take diverse forms based on the type of input source (structured vs. unstructured), the downstream application (e.g., search, conversation, recommendation), and ethical considerations (e.g., bias and transparency).

The primary objective of this workshop is to facilitate collaboration between research communities in academia and industries related to several domains, including natural language processing, language generation, deep learning, conversational AI, information extraction, data integration, knowledge graphs, and human-centered computing. For this inaugural edition of the Matching Workshop, we received 15 original research submissions and 12 application of papers that were accepted as Findings of ACL2023. Thanks to the diligent efforts of our Program Chairs and Program Committee members, we were able to curate a collection of 9 original research contributions (with an acceptance rate of 60%) and also 5 findings papers to be presented during the Workshop's technical sessions.

In addition to the research papers, the Matching Workshop will host an exciting lineup of four distinguished invited speakers and a panel discussion, providing participants with an opportunity to engage with leading researchers from academia and prominent industries.

Keynote Speakers. We are pleased to have the following invited speakers: William W. Cohen (Principal Scientist at Google Research), Ndapa Nakashole (Assistant Professor of Computer Science at the University of California, San Diego), Alan Ritter (Associate Professor in the School of Interactive Computing at Georgia Tech) and Sameer Singh (Associate Professor of Computer Science at the University of California, Irvine).

Panel Discussion. In recent years, large language models have emerged as influential forces driving both research and development. However, the impact of these models on downstream tasks remains uncertain and inadequately understood. As exemplified by numerous events publicized in the media, the embedded bias within these models can lead to catastrophic consequences. Consequently, we aim to foster a robust discussion on this topic by inviting researchers from academia and relevant industries. The panel discussion will count on six panelists and will revolve around the theme Matching in the Era of Large Language Models: Assessing the Good, the Bad, and the Ugly. The panelists are Renée Miller (University Distinguished Professor of Computer Science at Northeastern University), Niket Tandon (Senior Research Scientist at the Allen Institute for AI), Barbara Plank (Full Professor and Chair for AI and Computational Linguistic at the Ludwig-Maximilians-Universitat Munchen and Full Professor at the IT University of Copenhagen), AnHai Doen (Vilas Distinguished Achievement Professor in the Department of Computer Science at the University of Wisconsin) and Lei Li (Assistant Professor in Computer Science Department at University of California Santa Barbara).

We extend our congratulations to the authors of the accepted papers and express our gratitude to all authors who submitted their work, members of the Program Committee, Mentors and Mentees who participate in the Matching Workshop Mentoring Program and the entire ACL main conference organizing team. We would like to specially thank Megagon Labs (http://www.megagon.ai) for supporting our workshop and hosting the website of this event: https://megagon.ai/matching-2023/

First Matching Workshop Organizing Committee.

Organizing Committee

General Chairs and Program Chairs

Estevam Hruschka, Megagon Labs
Tom Mitchell, Carnegie Mellon University, USA
Sajjadur Rahman, Megagon Labs
Dunja Mladenic, Jozef Stefan Institute (JSI)
Marko Grobelnik, Jozef Stefan Institute (JSI)

Program Committee

Program Committee

Abdus Azad, UC Berkeley
Bosung Kim, UC San Diego
Chen Shen, Megagon Labs
Evangelos Papalexakis, UC Riverside
Farig Sadeque, BRAC University
Grace Fan, Northeastern University
Hannah Kim, Megagon Labs
Jeniya Tabassum, Amazon
Jun Ma, Amazon
Nedelina Teneva, Megagon Labs
Nelson Ebecken, Federal University of Rio de Janeiro
Rahat Rafiq, Grand Valley State University
Sara Abdali, Georgia Institute of Technology
Sara Tonelli, Fondazione Bruno Kessler
Seiji Maekawa, Megagon Labs
Thom Lake, Indeed.com
Tianyu Jiang, University of Utah
Vishwas Mruthyunjaya, Megagon Labs
Wasi Ahmad, UCLA
Yusuke Watanabe, Amazon
Yutong Li, Apple Inc.

Mentorship Program - Mentors

Andrii Krutsylo, Polish Academy of Sciences
Pouya Pezeshkpour, Megagon Labs
Sairam Gurajada, Megagon Labs

Keynote Talk: Invited 1

William Cohen
Google
2023-07-13 – Room: **Room 1**

Abstract: Invited Talk I -

Bio: William W. Cohen is a Principal Scientist at Google. He received his bachelor's degree in Computer Science from Duke University in 1984, and a PhD in Computer Science from Rutgers University in 1990. From 1990 to 2000 he worked at AT&T Bell Labs and later AT&T Labs-Research, and from April 2000 to May 2002 he worked at Whizbang Labs, a company specializing in extracting information from the web. From 2002 to 2018, he worked at Carnegie Mellon University in the Machine Learning Department, with a joint appointment in the Language Technology Institute, as an Associate Research Professor, a Research Professor, and a Professor. He is a past president of the International Machine Learning Society, and was General Chair for the 2008 International Machine Learning Conference, held July 6-9 at the University of Helsinki, in Finland; Program Co-Chair of the 2006 International Machine Learning Conference; and Co-Chair of the 1994 International Machine Learning Conference. He is a AAAI Fellow, and was a winner of the 2008 SIGMOD Test of Time Award for the most influential SIGMOD paper of 1998, and the 2014 SIGIR Test of Time Award for the most influential SIGIR paper of 2002-2004.

Keynote Talk: Invited 2

Ndapa Nakashole
University of California San Diego
2023-07-13 – Room: **Room 1**

Abstract: Invited Talk II -

Bio: Ndapa Nakashole is an Assistant Professor of Computer Science at the University of California, San Diego. Prior to this, she was a postdoctoral fellow in the Machine Learning department at Carnegie Mellon University. She obtained her PhD from the Max Planck Institute for Informatics, and Saarland University. She is a recipient of an NSF CAREER award, and an Otto Hahn Medal by the Max Planck Society for her dissertation.

Keynote Talk: Invited 3

Alan Ritter
Georgia Institute of Technology
2023-07-13 – Room: **Room 1**

Abstract: Invited Talk III -

Bio: Alan Ritter is an associate professor in the School of Interactive Computing at Georgia Tech. His research interests include natural language processing, with a focus on information extraction and data driven chatbots. He completed his Ph.D. at the University of Washington and was a postdoctoral fellow in the Machine Learning Department at Carnegie Mellon University. His research aims to solve challenging technical problems that can help machines learn to read vast quantities of text with minimal supervision. In a recent project, covered by WIRED, his group built a system that reads millions of tweets for mentions of new software vulnerabilities. Alan is the recipient of an NSF CAREER award and an Amazon Research Award.

Keynote Talk: Invited 4

Sameer Singh
University of California Irvine
2023-07-13 – Room: **Room 1**

Abstract: Invited Talk IV -

Bio: Dr. Sameer Singh is an Associate Professor of Computer Science at the University of California, Irvine (UCI). He is working primarily on the robustness and interpretability of machine learning algorithms and models that reason with text and structure for natural language processing. Sameer was a postdoctoral researcher at the University of Washington and received his Ph.D. from the University of Massachusetts, Amherst. He has received the NSF CAREER award, UCI Distinguished Early Career Faculty award, the Hellman Faculty Fellowship, and was selected as a DARPA Riser. His group has received funding from Allen Institute for AI, Amazon, NSF, DARPA, Adobe Research, Hasso Plattner Institute, NEC, Base 11, and FICO. Sameer has published extensively at machine learning and natural language processing venues and received conference paper awards at KDD 2016, ACL 2018, EMNLP 2019, AKBC 2020, ACL 2020, and NAACL 2022. (https://sameersingh.org/)

Table of Contents

Program

Thursday, July 13, 2023

08:30 - 08:40 *Welcome Message and Opening Remarks*

08:40 - 09:30 *Invited Talk I*

09:30 - 10:30 *Research Papers - Session I*

Text-To-KG Alignment: Comparing Current Methods on Classification Tasks
Sondre Wold, Lilja Øvrelid and Erik Velldal

Identifying Quantifiably Verifiable Statements from Text
Pegah Jandaghi and Jay Pujara

Toward Consistent and Informative Event-Event Temporal Relation Extraction
Xiaomeng Jin, Haoyang Wen, Xinya Du and Heng Ji

COFFEE: A Contrastive Oracle-Free Framework for Event Extraction
Meiru Zhang, Yixuan Su, Zaiqiao Meng, Zihao Fu and Nigel Collier

Knowledge-Augmented Language Model Prompting for Zero-Shot Knowledge Graph Question Answering
Jinheon Baek, Alham Aji and Amir Saffari

CoSiNES: Contrastive Siamese Network for Entity Standardization
Jiaqing Yuan, Michele Merler, Mihir Choudhury, Raju Pavuluri, Munindar Singh and Maja Vukovic

10:30 - 11:00 *Break*

11:00 - 12:00 *Invited Talk II*

12:00 - 13:00 *Lunch + Posters Session*

Text-To-KG Alignment: Comparing Current Methods on Classification Tasks
Sondre Wold, Lilja Øvrelid and Erik Velldal

Thursday, July 13, 2023 (continued)

Thursday, July 13, 2023 (continued)

INFOSYNC: Information Synchronization across Multilingual Semi-structured Tables
Siddharth Khincha, Chelsi Jain, Vivek Gupta, Tushar Kataria and Shuo Zhang

Aligning Instruction Tasks Unlocks Large Language Models as Zero-Shot Relation Extractors
Kai Zhang, Bernal Gutiérrez and Yu Su

13:00 - 13:50 *Invited Talk III*

13:50 - 14:40 *Research Papers - Session II*

ECOLA: Enhancing Temporal Knowledge Embeddings with Contextualized Language Representations
Zhen Han, Ruotong Liao, Jindong Gu, Yao Zhang, Zifeng Ding, Yujia Gu, Heinz Koeppl, Hinrich Schütze and Volker Tresp

Easy-to-Hard Learning for Information Extraction
Chang Gao, Wenxuan Zhang, Wai Lam and Lidong Bing

Silver Syntax Pre-training for Cross-Domain Relation Extraction
Elisa Bassignana, Filip GinterÚ, Sampo PyysaloÚ, Rob van der Goot and Barbara Plank

INFOSYNC: Information Synchronization across Multilingual Semi-structured Tables
Siddharth Khincha, Chelsi Jain, Vivek Gupta, Tushar Kataria and Shuo Zhang

Aligning Instruction Tasks Unlocks Large Language Models as Zero-Shot Relation Extractors
Kai Zhang, Bernal Gutiérrez and Yu Su

14:40 - 15:30 *Invited Talk IV*

15:30 - 16:00 *Break*

16:00 - 17:30 *Panel*

17:30 - 17:35 *Final Remarks*

Text-To-KG Alignment: Comparing Current Methods on Classification Tasks

Sondre Wold, Lilja Øvrelid, Erik Velldal
University of Oslo, Language Technology Group
{sondrewo, liljao, erikve}@ifi.uio.no

Abstract

In contrast to large text corpora, knowledge graphs (KG) provide dense and structured representations of factual information. This makes them attractive for systems that supplement or ground the knowledge found in pre-trained language models with an external knowledge source. This has especially been the case for classification tasks, where recent work has focused on creating pipeline models that retrieve information from KGs like ConceptNet as additional context. Many of these models consist of multiple components, and although they differ in the number and nature of these parts, they all have in common that for some given text query, they attempt to identify and retrieve a relevant subgraph from the KG. Due to the noise and idiosyncrasies often found in KGs, it is not known how current methods compare to a scenario where the aligned subgraph is completely relevant to the query. In this work, we try to bridge this knowledge gap by reviewing current approaches to text-to-KG alignment and evaluating them on two datasets where manually created graphs are available, providing insights into the effectiveness of current methods. We release our code for reproducibility.[1]

1 Introduction

There is a growing interest in systems that combine the implicit knowledge found in large pretrained language models (PLMs) with external knowledge. The majority of these systems use knowledge graphs (KG) like ConceptNet (Speer et al., 2017) or Freebase (Bollacker et al., 2008) and either inject information from the graph directly into the PLM (Peters et al., 2019; Chang et al., 2020; Wang et al., 2020; Lauscher et al., 2020; Kaur et al., 2022) or perform some type of joint reasoning between the PLM and the graph, for example by using a graph neural network on the graph and later intertwining the produced representations (Sun et al., 2022; Yasunaga et al., 2021; Zhang et al., 2022; Yasunaga et al., 2022). Beyond their competitive performance, these knowledge-enhanced systems are often upheld as more interpretable, as their reliance on structured information can be reverse-engineered in order to explain predictions or used to create reasoning paths.

One of the central components in these systems is the identification of the most relevant part of a KG for each natural language query. Given that most KGs are noisy and contain idiosyncratic phrasings, which leads to graph sparsity (Sun et al., 2022; Jung et al., 2022), it is non-trivial to align entities from text with nodes in the graph. Despite this, existing work often uses relatively simple methods and does not isolate and evaluate the effect of this component on the overall classification pipeline. Furthermore, due to the lack of datasets that contain manually selected relevant graphs, it is not known how well current methods perform relative to a potential upper bound where the graph provides a structured explanation as to why the sample under classification belongs to a class. Given that this problem applies to a range of typical NLP tasks, and subsequently can be found under a range of different names, such as grounding, etc., there is much to be gained from reviewing current approaches and assessing their effect in isolation.

In this paper, we address these issues by providing an overview of text-to-KG alignment methods. We also evaluate a sample of the current main approaches to text-to-KG alignment on two downstream NLP tasks, comparing them to manually created graphs that we use for estimating a potential upper bound. For evaluation, we use the tasks of binary stance prediction (Saha et al., 2021), transformed from a graph generation problem in order to get gold reference alignments, and a subset of the Choice of Plausible Alternatives (COPA) (Roemmele et al., 2011) that contain additional ex-

[1] https://github.com/SondreWold/graph_impact

Proceedings of the First Workshop on Matching From Unstructured and Structured Data (MATCHING 2023), pages 1–13
July 13, 2023 ©2023 Association for Computational Linguistics

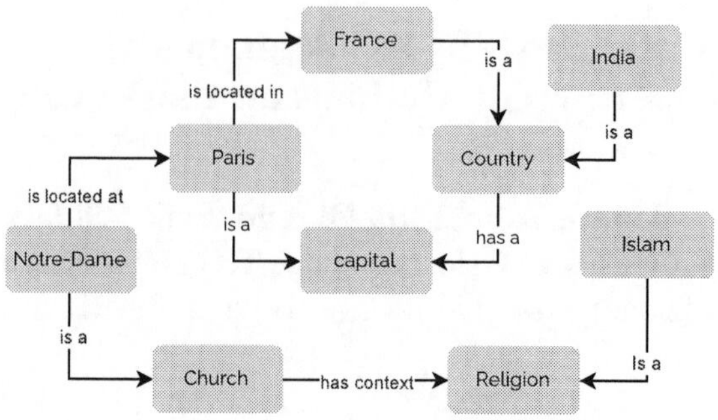

Figure 1: An example of a multi-relational knowledge graph.

planation graphs (Brassard et al., 2022). As the focus of this work is not how to best combine structured data with PLMs, but rather to report on how current text-to-KG alignment methods compare to manually created graphs, we use a rather simple integration technique to combine the graphs with a pre-trained language model. Through this work, we hope to motivate more research into methods that align unstructured and structured data sources for a range of tasks within NLP, not only for QA.

2 Background

Combining text with structured knowledge is a long-standing challenge in NLP. While earlier work focused more on the text-to-KG alignment itself, using rule-based systems and templates, recent work often approaches the problem as a part of a system intended for other NLP tasks than the alignment itself, such as question answering (Yasunaga et al., 2021), language modelling (Kaur et al., 2022) and text summarization (Feng et al., 2021).

As a consequence, approaches to what is essentially the same problem, namely to align some relevant subspace of a large KG with a piece of text, can be found under a range of terms, such as: *retrieval* (Feng et al., 2021; Kaur et al., 2022; Sun et al., 2022; Wang et al., 2020), *extraction* (Huang et al., 2021; Feng et al., 2020), *KG-to-text-alignment* (Agarwal et al., 2021), *linking* (Gao et al., 2022; Becker et al., 2021), *grounding* (Shu et al., 2022; Lin et al., 2019), and *mapping* (Yu et al., 2022). Although it is natural to use multiple of these terms to describe a specific technique, we argue that it would be beneficial to refer to the task itself under a common name and propose the term *text-to-KG alignment*. The following sections formalise the task and discuss current approaches found in the literature.

2.1 Task definition

The task of text-to-KG alignment involves two input elements: a piece of natural text and a KG. The KG is often a multi-relational graph, $G = (V, E)$, where V is a set of entity nodes and E is the set of edges connecting the nodes in V. The task is to align the text with a subset of the KG that is relevant to the text. What defines relevance is dependent on the specific use case. For example, given the question *Where is the most famous church in France located?* and the KG found in Figure 1, a well-executed text-to-KG alignment could, for example, link the spans *church* and *France* from the text to their corresponding entity nodes in the KG and return a subgraph that contains the minimal amount of nodes and edges required in order to guide any downstream system towards the correct behaviour.

2.2 Current approaches

Although the possibilities are many, most current approaches to text-to-KG alignment base themselves on some form of lexical overlap. As noted in Aglionby and Teufel (2022); Becker et al. (2021); Sun et al. (2022), the idiosyncratic phrasings often found in KGs make this problematic. One specific implementation based on lexical overlap is the one found in Lin et al. (2019), which has been later reused in a series of other works on QA without any major modifications (Feng et al., 2020; Yasunaga et al., 2021; Zhang et al., 2022; Yasunaga et al., 2022; Sun et al., 2022).

In the approach of Lin et al. (2019), a schema graph is constructed from each question-answer pair. The first step involves recognising concepts mentioned in the text that exists in the KG. Although they note that exact n-gram matches are not ideal, due to idiosyncratic phrasings and sparsity, they do little to improve on this naive approach besides lemmatisation and filtering of stop words,

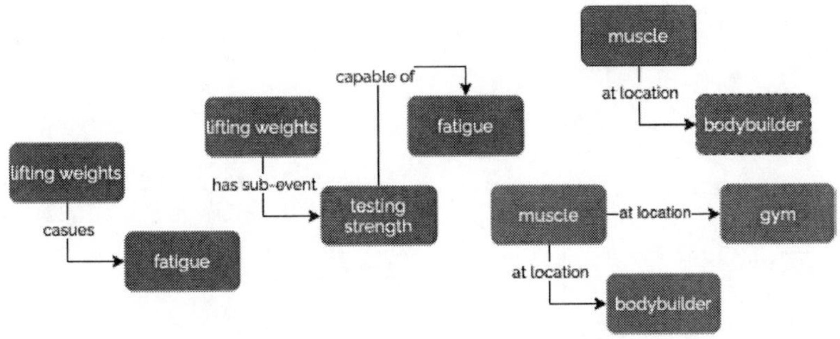

Figure 2: An example of the different graph construction approaches for COPA-SSE (Brassard et al., 2022). Here, the premise and answer options are: *P: The bodybuilder lifted weights*; *A1: The gym closed*; *A2: Her muscles became fatigued*, from left to right: Purple: Gold annotation, Brown: Approach 3, Green: Approach 2, and Blue: Approach 1.

leaving it for future work. The enhanced n-gram matching produces two sets of entities, one from the question and one from the answer, V_q and V_a. The graph itself is then constructed by adding the k-hop paths between the nodes in these two sets, with k often being 2 or 3. This returns a graph that contains a lot of noise in terms of irrelevant nodes found in the k-hop neighbourhoods of V_q and V_a and motivates some form of pruning applied to G_{sub} before it is used together with the PLM, such as node relevance scoring (Yasunaga et al., 2021), dynamic pruning via LM-to-KG attention (Kaur et al., 2022), and ranking using sentence representations of the question and answer pair and a linearized version of G_{sub} (Kaur et al., 2022).

Another approach based on lexical matching is from Becker et al. (2021), which is specifically developed for ConceptNet. Candidate phrases are first extracted from the text using a constituency parser, limited to noun, verb and adjective phrases. These are then lemmatized and filtered for articles, pronouns, conjunctions, interjections and punctuation. The same process is also applied to all the nodes in ConceptNet. This makes it possible to match the two modalities better, as both are normalised using the same pre-processing pipeline. Results on two QA dataset show that the proposed method is able to align more meaningful concepts and that the ratio between informative and uninformative concepts are superior to simple string matching. For the language modelling task, Kaur et al. (2022) uses a much simpler technique where a Named Entity Recognition model identifies named entity mentions in text and selects entities with the maximum overlap in the KG.

For the tasks of text summarisation and story ending generation, Feng et al. (2021) and Guan et al. (2019) use RNN-based architectures that read a text sequence word by word, and at each time step the current word is aligned to a triple from ConceptNet (We assume by lexical overlap). Each triple, and also its neighbours in the KG, is encoded using word embeddings and then combined with the context vector from the RNN using different attention style mechanisms.

As an alternative to these types of approaches based on some form of lexical matching for the alignment, Aglionby and Teufel (2022) experimented with embedding each entity in the KG using a PLM, and then for each question answer pair find the most similar concepts using euclidean distance. They conclude that this leads to graphs that are more specific to the question-answer pair, and that this helps performance in some cases. Wang et al. (2020) also experimented with using a PLM to generate the graphs instead of aligning them, relying on KGs such as ConceptNet as a fine-tuning dataset for the PLM instead of as a direct source during alignment. In a QA setting, the model is trained to connect entities from question-answer pairs with a multi-hop path. The generated paths can then be later used for knowledge-enhanced systems. This has the benefit of being able to use all the knowledge acquired during the PLMs pretraining, which might result in concepts that are not present in KGs.

3 KG and Datasets

This section explains the data used in our own experiments.

ConceptNet As our knowledge graph, we use *ConceptNet* (Speer et al., 2017) — a general-domain KG that contains 799,273 nodes and

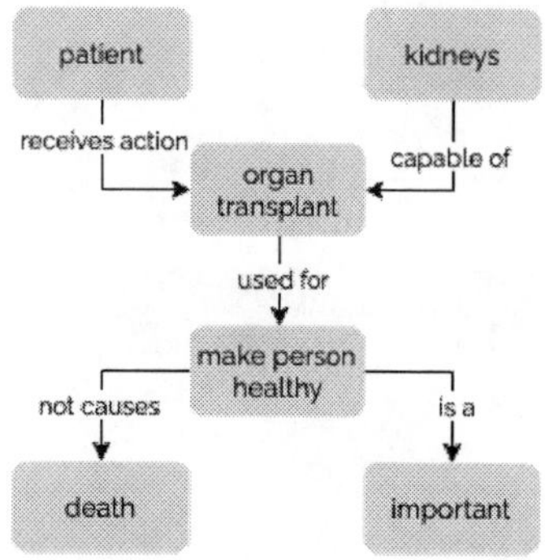

Figure 3: An example graph from ExplaGraphs (Saha et al., 2021) generated by a PLM for the belief argument pair: *Organ transplant is important*; *A patient with failed kidneys might not die if he gets organ donation.*

2, 487, 810 edges. The graph is structured as a collection of triples, each containing a head and tail entity connected via a relation from a pre-defined set of types.

ExplaGraphs ExplaGraphs (Saha et al., 2021) is originally a graph generation task for binary stance prediction. Given a belief and argument pair *(b,a)*, models should both classify whether the argument counters or supports the belief and construct a structured explanation as to why this is the correct label. An example of this can be seen in Figure 3.

The original dataset provides a train ($n = 2367$) and validation ($n = 397$) split, as well as a test set that is kept private for evaluation on a leaderboard. The node labels have been written by humans using free-form text, but the edge labels are limited to the set of relation types used in ConceptNet. We concatenate the train and validation split and partition the data into a new train, validation and test split with an 80–10–10 ratio.

COPA-SSE Introduced in Brassard et al. (2022), COPA-SSE adds semi-structured explanations created by human annotators to 1500 samples from Balanced COPA (Kavumba et al., 2019) — which is an extension to the original COPA dataset from Roemmele et al. (2011). In this task, given a scenario as a premise, models have to select the alternative that more plausibly stands in a causal relation with the premise. An example with a manually constructed explanation graph can be seen in Figure 4. As with ExplaGraphs, COPA-SSE uses free-form text for the head and tail entities of the triples and limits the relation types to the ones found in ConceptNet.

The dataset provides on average over six explanation graphs per sample. Five annotators have also rated the quality of each graph with respect to how well it captures the relationship between the premise and the correct answer choice. As we only need one graph per sample, we select the one with the highest average rating. As the official COPA-SSE set does not contain any training data, we keep the official development split as our training data and split the official test data by half for our in-house development and testing set.

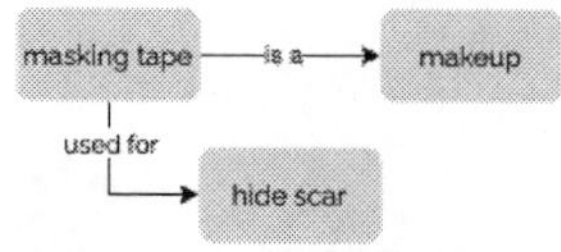

Figure 4: An example of a manually created graph from COPA-SSE (Brassard et al., 2022) for the premise and options: *P: The man felt ashamed of a scar on his face*; *A1: He hid the scar with makeup*; *A2: He explained the scar to strangers.*

4 Alignment approaches

As mentioned, the general procedure for grounding text to a graph is three-fold: we first have to identify entities mentioned in the text, then link them to entities in the graph, and lastly construct a graph object that is returned to the inference model as additional context to be used together with the original text. For QA the text aligned with the graph is typically a combination of the question and answer choices. As our two downstream tasks are not QA, and also different from each other, we have to rely on different pre-processing techniques than previous work. The following section presents the implementation of three different text-to-KG alignment approaches that we compare against manually created graphs. An illustration of the different approaches applied to the same text sample can be seen in Figure 2.

4.1 Approach 1: Basic String Matching

Our first approach establishes a simple baseline based on naive string matching. For ExplaGraphs, we first word-tokenize the belief and argument on whitespace, and then for each word we check whether or not it is a concept in ConceptNet by exact lexical overlap. This gives us two sets of entities: C_q and C_a. The graph is constructed by finding paths in ConceptNet between the concepts in C_q and C_a. For COPA-SSE, we do the same but create C_q from a concatenation of the premise and the first answer choice, and C_a from a concatenation of the premise and the second answer choice. We use Dijkstra's algorithm to find the paths (Dijkstra, 1959).[2] The reason to use this rather simple approach, also pointed out by Lin et al. (2019) and Aglionby and Teufel (2022), is that finding a minimal spanning graph that covers all the concepts from C_q and C_a, which seems like a more obvious choice, would be to solve the NP-complete "Steiner tree problem" (Garey and Johnson, 1977), and this would be too resource demanding given the size of ConceptNet.

As many of the retrieved paths are irrelevant to the original text, it is common to implement some sort of pruning. We follow Kaur et al. (2022) and linearize the `subject-relation-object` triples to normal text and then embed them into the same vector space as the original context using the SentenceTransformer (Reimers and Gurevych, 2019). We then calculate the cosine similarity between the linearized graphs and the original text context and select the one with the highest score.

4.2 Approach 2: Enhanced String Matching

Our second approach is based on the widely used method from Lin et al. (2019), found in the works of Feng et al. (2020); Yasunaga et al. (2021); Zhang et al. (2022); Yasunaga et al. (2022); Sun et al. (2022), but modified to our use case. We construct the set of entities C_q and C_a using n-gram matching enhanced with lemmatisation and filtering of stop words.[3] As in Approach 1, for ExplaGraphs, C_q is constructed from the belief, and C_a from the argument; for COPA-SSE, C_q is based on a concatenation of the premise and the first answer choice, while C_a is based on a concatenation of the premise and the second answer choice.

The graph is constructed by finding paths in ConceptNet from concepts in between C_q and C_a using the same method as in Approach 1. However, we limit the length of the paths to a variable k. In the aforementioned works, k is set as to retrieve either two or three-hop paths, essentially finding the 2-hop or 3-hop neighbourhoods of the identified concepts. For our experiments, we set $k = 3$.

As with Approach 1, many of the retrieved paths are irrelevant to the original text which warrants some sort of pruning strategy. In the aforementioned works, this is done by node relevance scoring. We follow Approach 1 and use sentence representations via linearization and cosine similarity in order to prune irrelevant paths from the graph.

4.3 Approach 3: Path Generator

Our third approach is based on a method where a generative LM is fine-tuned on the task of generating paths between concepts found in two sets. We use the implementation and already trained path generator (PG) from Wang et al. (2020) for this purpose. This model is a GPT-2 model (Radford et al., 2019) fine-tuned on generating paths between two nodes in ConceptNet. [4] One advantage of this method is that since GPT-2 already has unstructured knowledge encoded in its parameters from its original pre-training, it is able to generate paths between entities that might not exist in the original graph.

For both ExplaGraphs and COPA-SSE, we take the first and last entity identified by the entity linker from Approach 2 as the start and end points of the PG. As the model only returns one generated path, we do not perform any pruning. For the following example from COPA-SSE, *P: The man felt ashamed of a scar on his face*; *A1: He hid the scar with makeup*; *A2: He explained the scar to strangers.*, the PG constructs the following path: *masking tape used for hide scar, masking tape is a makeup*.

4.3.1 Start and end entities

We also experiment with the same setup, but with the first and last entity from the gold annotations as the start and end points for the PG. We do this to assess the importance of having nodes that are at least somewhat relevant to the original context as input to the PG. In our experiments, we refer to this sub-method as Approach 3-G.

4.4 Integration technique

As the focus of this work is not how to best combine structured data with PLMs, but rather to report on how current text-to-KG alignment methods compare to manually created graphs, we use a rather simple integration technique to combine the graphs with a pre-trained language model and use it uniformly for the different alignment approaches. We conjecture that the ranking of the different linking approaches with this technique would be similar to a more complex method for reasoning over the graph structures, for example using GNNs. By not

[2] Using the implementation from https://networkx.org

[3] We use the implementation from Yasunaga et al. (2021) to construct C_q and C_a

[4] See Wang et al. (2020) for details on the fine-tuning procedure.

relying on another deep learning model for the integration, we can better control the effect of the graph quality itself.

For each text and graph pair, we linearize the graph to text as in Kaur et al. (2022). For example, the graph in Figure 4 is transformed to the string *masking tape used for hide scar, masking tape is a makeup*. As linearization does not provide any natural way to capture the information provided by having directed edges, we transform all the graphs to undirected graphs before integrating them with the PLM [5]. For a different integration technique, such as GNNs, it would probably be reasonable to maintain information about the direction of edges.

For ExplaGraphs, which consists of belief and argument pairs, we feed the model with the following sequence: BELIEF [SEP] ARGUMENT [SEP] GRAPH [SEP], where [SEP] is a model-dependent separation token and the model classifies the sequence as either *support* or *counter*.

For COPA-SSE, which has two options for each premise, we use the following format: PREMISE + GRAPH [SEP] A1 [SEP] and PREMISE + GRAPH [SEP] A2 [SEP], where + just adds the linearized graph to the premise as a string and the model has to select the most likely sequence of the two.

5 Graph quality

The following section provides an analysis of the quality of the different approaches when used to align graphs for both ExplaGraphs and COPA-SSE.

Table 1 and Table 2 show the average number of triples per sample identified or created by the different approaches for the two datasets, as well as how many triples we count as containing some form of error ('Broken triples' in the table). The criterion for marking a triple as broken includes missing head or tail entities inside the triple, having more than one edge between the head and tail, and returning nothing from ConceptNet. It is, of course, natural that not all samples contain an entity that can be found in ConceptNet, and consequently, we decided to not discard the broken triples but rather to include them to showcase the expected performance in a realistic setting.

As can be seen from the tables, the approach based on the Path Generator (PG) from Wang et al. (2020) (Approach 3) returns fewer triples than the other approaches for both ExplaGraphs and COPA-SSE. When using the entities from Approach 2 as the start and end points, denoted by the abbreviation Approach 3, the number of triples containing some form of alignment error is over twenty percent. When using the gold annotation as the start and end point of the PG, abbreviated Approach 3-G, this goes down a bit but is still considerably higher than the approaches based on lexical overlap. Approach 2 is able to identify some well-formatted triple in all of the cases for both tasks, while Approach 1 fails to retrieve anything for five percent of the samples in COPA-SSE and two percent for ExplaGraphs.

In order to get some notion of semantic similarity between the different approaches and the original context they are meant to be a structural representation of, we calculate the cosine similarity between the context and a linearized (see Section 4.4 for details on this procedure) version of the graphs. The scores can be found in Table 3. Unsurprisingly, the similarity increases with the complexity of the approach. The basic string matching technique of Approach 1 creates the least similar graphs, followed by the tad more sophisticated Approach 2, while the generative approaches are able to create a bit more similar graphs despite having a low number of average triples per graph. All of the approaches are still far from the manually created graphs — which are also linearized using the same procedure as the others.

Approach	Avg. number of triples	Broken triples
Approach 1	2.90	0.05
Approach 2	2.90	0.00
Approach 3	1.39	0.20
Approach 3-G	1.64	0.12
Gold	2.12	0.00

Table 1: Statistics for the different approaches on the training set of COPA-SSE. The number of broken triples is reported as percentages.

Approach	Avg. number of triples	Broken triples
Approach 1	2.99	0.02
Approach 2	3.03	0.00
Approach 3	1.34	0.21
Approach 3-G	1.58	0.15
Gold	4.23	0.00

Table 2: Statistics for the different approaches on the training set of ExplaGraphs. The number of broken triples is reported as percentages.

[5] In practice, this is done by simply removing the underscore prepended to all reversed directions.

Approach	ExplaGraphs	COPA-SSE
Approach 1	0.39	0.32
Approach 2	0.45	0.42
Approach 3	0.48	0.45
Approach 3-G	0.55	0.46
Gold	0.75	0.57

Table 3: The different graphs and their average cosine similarity with the original text.

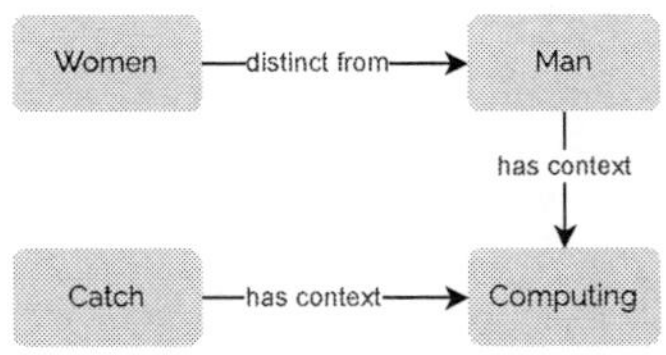

Figure 5: The graph aligned with ConceptNet for both the approaches based on lexical overlap. The original COPA-SSE context is *Premise: The women met for coffee Alt 1: The cafe reopened in a new location*; *Alt 2: They wanted to catch up with each other*

6 Experiments

We now present experiments where we compare the discussed approaches to text-to-KG alignment for ExplaGraphs and COPA-SSE. As our PLM, we use BERT (Devlin et al., 2019) for all experiments. We use the base version and conduct a hyperparameter grid search for both tasks. We do the same search both with and without any appended graphs as the former naturally makes it easier to overfit the data, especially since both ExplaGraphs and COPA-SSE are relatively small in size. The grid search settings can be found in Appendix A.2 and the final hyperparameters in Appendix A.3. We run all experiments over ten epochs with early stopping on validation loss with a patience value of five.

As few-sample fine-tuning with BERT is known to show instability (Zhang et al., 2021), we run all experiments with ten random seeds and report the mean accuracy scores together with standard deviations. We use the same random seeds for both tasks; they can be found in Appendix A.4.

We find that the experiments are highly susceptible to seed variation. Although we are able to match the performance of some previous work for the same PLM on some runs, this does not hold across seeds. Consequently, we also perform outlier detection and removal. Details on this procedure can be found in Appendix A.5.

Approach	ExplaGraphs	COPA-SSE
No graph	$69.67^{\pm 3.36}$	$67.05^{\pm 2.07}$
Approach 1	$66.46^{\pm 8.48}$	$51.20^{\pm 2.08}$
Approach 2	$70.03^{\pm 2.71}$	$53.33^{\pm 1.80}$
Approach 3	$73.55^{\pm 1.66}$	$56.20^{\pm 8.39}$
Approach 3-G	$70.57^{\pm 3.27}$	$85.86^{\pm 0.75}$
Gold	$80.28^{\pm 2.31}$	$96.60^{\pm 0.28}$

Table 4: Results of the different approaches on ExplaGraphs and COPA-SSE. Results are reported as average accuracy over ten runs together with standard deviations after outlier removal, if any.

7 Results

Table 4 shows the results on ExplaGraphs and COPA-SSE. For both datasets, we observe the following: Methods primarily based on lexical overlap provide no definitive improvement. The performance of Approach 1 (String matching) and Approach 2 (String matching with added lemmatisation and stop word filtering) is within the standard deviation of the experiments without any appended graph data, and might even impede the performance by making it harder to fit the data by introducing noise from the KG that is not relevant for the classification at hand.

For Approach 3, based on a generative model, we see that it too provides little benefit for ExplaGraphs, but that when it has access to the gold annotation entities as the start and end point of the paths, it performs significantly better than having access to no graphs at all for COPA-SSE.

For both tasks, having access to manually created graphs improves performance significantly.

8 Discussion

The most striking result is perhaps the performance of Approach 3-G on COPA-SSE. We hypothesise that this can be explained by the fact that annotators probably used exact spans from both the premise and the correct alternative from the text in their graphs, and consequently, they provide a strong signal as to why there is a relation between the premise and the correct answer choice and not the wrong one. This is easily picked up by the model. For ExplaGraphs, which is a text classification problem, this is not the case: the appended graph might provide some inductive bias, but it does not provide a direct link to the correct choice, as the task is to assign a label to the whole sequence, not to choose the most probable sequence out of two options. This conclusion is further supported

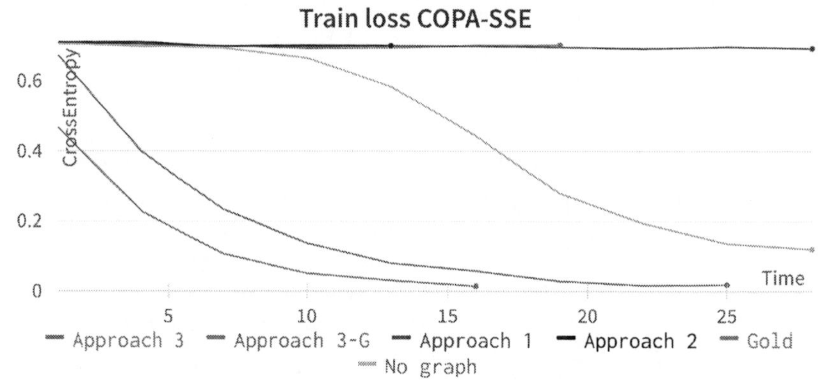

Figure 6: The train loss curves for the different approaches on COPA-SSE.

by the observation that appending the manually constructed graphs in their entirety has a much larger effect on COPA-SSE than ExplaGraphs.

Furthermore, for COPA-SSE, as pointed out in Table 1, the average triple length for the generative approaches is rather low, so the majority of the aligned graphs from Approach 3-G are actually from the manually written text, not generated by the model itself.

The key finding of our experiments is that having access to structured knowledge relevant to the sample at hand, here represented by the gold annotations, provides a significant increase in performance even with a simple injection technique and judging by today's standards, a small pre-trained language model. They also show that for datasets of low sample sizes, such as ExplaGraphs and COPA-SSE, the results are susceptible to noise. As the approaches based on lexical overlap are within the standard deviations of the experiments without any appended graphs, it is not possible to conclude that they add any useful information to the model. Based on Figure 6, we think it is fair to conclude that these methods based on lexical overlap only provide a signal that has no relation to the correct label. As to why the approaches based on lexical matching do not have any effect here but reportedly have an effect in previous work on QA, there is one major reason that has not been discussed so far: namely that both datasets require knowledge that is not represented in ConceptNet. As shown by Bauer and Bansal (2021), matching the task with the right KG is important. It is reasonable to question whether or not ConceptNet, which aims to represent commonsense and world knowledge, does indeed contain information useful for deciding whether or not an argument counters or supports a belief, in the case of ExplaGraphs, or if it can aid in the selection of the most likely follow-up scenario to a situation, in the case of COPA-SSE. In Figure 5, both the approaches based on lexical overlap (1 & 2) align the same exact graph with the text context, and judging from the result, it is pretty clear that the aligned graph has little to offer in terms of guiding the model towards the most likely follow-up.

9 Conclusion

In this work, we find that the process of identifying and retrieving the most relevant information in a knowledge graph is found under a range of different names in the literature and propose the term text-to-KG alignment. We systematise current approaches for text-to-KG alignment and evaluate a selection of them on two different tasks where manually created graphs are available, providing insights into how they compare to a scenario where the aligned graph is completely relevant to the text. Our experiments show that having access to such a graph could help performance significantly, and that current approaches based on lexical overlap are unsuccessful under our experimental setup, but that a generative approach using a PLM to generate a graph based on manually written text as start and end entities adds a significant increase in performance for multiple-choice type tasks, such as COPA-SSE. For the approaches based on lexical overlap, we hypothesise that the lack of performance increase can be attributed to the choice of knowledge graph, in our case ConceptNet, which might not contain any information useful for solving the two tasks.

Limitations

While there is a lot of work on creating and making available large pre-trained language models for a range of languages, there is to our knowledge not that many knowledge graphs for other languages than English — especially general knowledge ones, like ConceptNet. This is a major limitation, as it restricts research to one single language and the structured representation of knowledge found in the culture associated with that specific group of language users. Creating commonsense KGs from unstructured text is a costly process that requires financial resources for annotation as well as available corpora to extract the graph from.

Ethics Statement

We do not foresee that combining knowledge graphs with pre-trained language models in the way done here, add to any of the existing ethical challenges associated with language models. However, this rests on the assumption that the knowledge graph does not contain any harmful information that might inject or amplify unwanted behaviour in the language model.

References

Oshin Agarwal, Heming Ge, Siamak Shakeri, and Rami Al-Rfou. 2021. Knowledge graph based synthetic corpus generation for knowledge-enhanced language model pre-training. In *Proceedings of the 2021 Conference of the North American Chapter of the Association for Computational Linguistics: Human Language Technologies*, pages 3554–3565, Online. Association for Computational Linguistics.

Guy Aglionby and Simone Teufel. 2022. Identifying relevant common sense information in knowledge graphs. In *Proceedings of the First Workshop on Commonsense Representation and Reasoning (CSRR 2022)*, pages 1–7, Dublin, Ireland. Association for Computational Linguistics.

Lisa Bauer and Mohit Bansal. 2021. Identify, align, and integrate: Matching knowledge graphs to commonsense reasoning tasks. In *Proceedings of the 16th Conference of the European Chapter of the Association for Computational Linguistics: Main Volume*, pages 2259–2272, Online. Association for Computational Linguistics.

Maria Becker, Katharina Korfhage, and Anette Frank. 2021. COCO-EX: A tool for linking concepts from texts to ConceptNet. In *Proceedings of the 16th Conference of the European Chapter of the Association for Computational Linguistics: System Demonstrations*, pages 119–126, Online. Association for Computational Linguistics.

Kurt Bollacker, Colin Evans, Praveen Paritosh, Tim Sturge, and Jamie Taylor. 2008. Freebase: a collaboratively created graph database for structuring human knowledge. In *Proceedings of the 2008 ACM SIGMOD international conference on Management of data*, pages 1247–1250.

Ana Brassard, Benjamin Heinzerling, Pride Kavumba, and Kentaro Inui. 2022. COPA-SSE: Semi-structured explanations for commonsense reasoning. In *Proceedings of the Thirteenth Language Resources and Evaluation Conference*, pages 3994–4000, Marseille, France. European Language Resources Association.

Ting-Yun Chang, Yang Liu, Karthik Gopalakrishnan, Behnam Hedayatnia, Pei Zhou, and Dilek Hakkani-Tur. 2020. Incorporating commonsense knowledge graph in pretrained models for social commonsense tasks. In *Proceedings of Deep Learning Inside Out (DeeLIO): The First Workshop on Knowledge Extraction and Integration for Deep Learning Architectures*, pages 74–79, Online. Association for Computational Linguistics.

Jacob Devlin, Ming-Wei Chang, Kenton Lee, and Kristina Toutanova. 2019. BERT: Pre-training of deep bidirectional transformers for language understanding. In *Proceedings of the 2019 Conference of the North American Chapter of the Association for Computational Linguistics: Human Language Technologies, Volume 1 (Long and Short Papers)*, pages 4171–4186, Minneapolis, Minnesota. Association for Computational Linguistics.

Edsger Wybe Dijkstra. 1959. A note on two problems in connexion with graphs. *Numerische Mathematik*, 1:269–271.

Xiachong Feng, Xiaocheng Feng, and Bing Qin. 2021. Incorporating commonsense knowledge into abstractive dialogue summarization via heterogeneous graph networks. In *Chinese Computational Linguistics: 20th China National Conference, CCL 2021, Hohhot, China, August 13–15, 2021, Proceedings*, pages 127–142. Springer.

Yanlin Feng, Xinyue Chen, Bill Yuchen Lin, Peifeng Wang, Jun Yan, and Xiang Ren. 2020. Scalable multi-hop relational reasoning for knowledge-aware question answering. In *Proceedings of the 2020 Conference on Empirical Methods in Natural Language Processing (EMNLP)*, pages 1295–1309, Online. Association for Computational Linguistics.

Silin Gao, Jena D. Hwang, Saya Kanno, Hiromi Wakaki, Yuki Mitsufuji, and Antoine Bosselut. 2022. ComFact: A benchmark for linking contextual commonsense knowledge. In *Findings of the Association for Computational Linguistics: EMNLP 2022*, pages 1656–1675, Abu Dhabi, United Arab Emirates. Association for Computational Linguistics.

Michael R Garey and David S. Johnson. 1977. The rectilinear steiner tree problem is np-complete. *SIAM Journal on Applied Mathematics*, 32(4):826–834.

Jian Guan, Yansen Wang, and Minlie Huang. 2019. Story ending generation with incremental encoding and commonsense knowledge. *Proceedings of the AAAI Conference on Artificial Intelligence*, 33(01):6473–6480.

Canming Huang, Weinan He, and Yongmei Liu. 2021. Improving unsupervised commonsense reasoning using knowledge-enabled natural language inference. In *Findings of the Association for Computational Linguistics: EMNLP 2021*, pages 4875–4885, Punta Cana, Dominican Republic. Association for Computational Linguistics.

Yong-Ho Jung, Jun-Hyung Park, Joon-Young Choi, Mingyu Lee, Junho Kim, Kang-Min Kim, and SangKeun Lee. 2022. Learning from missing relations: Contrastive learning with commonsense knowledge graphs for commonsense inference. In *Findings of the Association for Computational Linguistics: ACL 2022*, pages 1514–1523, Dublin, Ireland. Association for Computational Linguistics.

Jivat Kaur, Sumit Bhatia, Milan Aggarwal, Rachit Bansal, and Balaji Krishnamurthy. 2022. LM-CORE: Language models with contextually relevant external knowledge. In *Findings of the Association for Computational Linguistics: NAACL 2022*, pages 750–769, Seattle, United States. Association for Computational Linguistics.

Pride Kavumba, Naoya Inoue, Benjamin Heinzerling, Keshav Singh, Paul Reisert, and Kentaro Inui. 2019. When choosing plausible alternatives, clever hans can be clever. In *Proceedings of the First Workshop on Commonsense Inference in Natural Language Processing*, pages 33–42, Hong Kong, China. Association for Computational Linguistics.

Anne Lauscher, Olga Majewska, Leonardo F. R. Ribeiro, Iryna Gurevych, Nikolai Rozanov, and Goran Glavaš. 2020. Common sense or world knowledge? investigating adapter-based knowledge injection into pretrained transformers. In *Proceedings of Deep Learning Inside Out (DeeLIO): The First Workshop on Knowledge Extraction and Integration for Deep Learning Architectures*, pages 43–49, Online. Association for Computational Linguistics.

Bill Yuchen Lin, Xinyue Chen, Jamin Chen, and Xiang Ren. 2019. KagNet: Knowledge-aware graph networks for commonsense reasoning. In *Proceedings of the 2019 Conference on Empirical Methods in Natural Language Processing and the 9th International Joint Conference on Natural Language Processing (EMNLP-IJCNLP)*, pages 2829–2839, Hong Kong, China. Association for Computational Linguistics.

Matthew E. Peters, Mark Neumann, Robert Logan, Roy Schwartz, Vidur Joshi, Sameer Singh, and Noah A. Smith. 2019. Knowledge enhanced contextual word representations. In *Proceedings of the 2019 Conference on Empirical Methods in Natural Language Processing and the 9th International Joint Conference on Natural Language Processing (EMNLP-IJCNLP)*, pages 43–54, Hong Kong, China. Association for Computational Linguistics.

Alec Radford, Jeffrey Wu, Rewon Child, David Luan, Dario Amodei, Ilya Sutskever, et al. 2019. Language models are unsupervised multitask learners. *OpenAI blog*, 1(8):9.

Nils Reimers and Iryna Gurevych. 2019. Sentence-BERT: Sentence embeddings using Siamese BERT-networks. In *Proceedings of the 2019 Conference on Empirical Methods in Natural Language Processing and the 9th International Joint Conference on Natural Language Processing (EMNLP-IJCNLP)*, pages 3982–3992, Hong Kong, China. Association for Computational Linguistics.

Melissa Roemmele, Cosmin Adrian Bejan, and Andrew S Gordon. 2011. Choice of plausible alternatives: An evaluation of commonsense causal reasoning. In *AAAI spring symposium: logical formalizations of commonsense reasoning*, pages 90–95.

Swarnadeep Saha, Prateek Yadav, Lisa Bauer, and Mohit Bansal. 2021. ExplaGraphs: An explanation graph generation task for structured commonsense reasoning. In *Proceedings of the 2021 Conference on Empirical Methods in Natural Language Processing*, pages 7716–7740, Online and Punta Cana, Dominican Republic. Association for Computational Linguistics.

Yiheng Shu, Zhiwei Yu, Yuhan Li, Börje Karlsson, Tingting Ma, Yuzhong Qu, and Chin-Yew Lin. 2022. TIARA: Multi-grained retrieval for robust question answering over large knowledge base. In *Proceedings of the 2022 Conference on Empirical Methods in Natural Language Processing*, pages 8108–8121, Abu Dhabi, United Arab Emirates. Association for Computational Linguistics.

Robyn Speer, Joshua Chin, and Catherine Havasi. 2017. Conceptnet 5.5: An open multilingual graph of general knowledge. In *Thirty-first AAAI conference on artificial intelligence*.

Yueqing Sun, Qi Shi, Le Qi, and Yu Zhang. 2022. JointLK: Joint reasoning with language models and knowledge graphs for commonsense question answering. In *Proceedings of the 2022 Conference of the North American Chapter of the Association for Computational Linguistics: Human Language Technologies*, pages 5049–5060, Seattle, United States. Association for Computational Linguistics.

Peifeng Wang, Nanyun Peng, Filip Ilievski, Pedro Szekely, and Xiang Ren. 2020. Connecting the dots: A knowledgeable path generator for commonsense question answering. In *Findings of the Association for Computational Linguistics: EMNLP 2020*, pages 4129–4140, Online. Association for Computational Linguistics.

Michihiro Yasunaga, Antoine Bosselut, Hongyu Ren, Xikun Zhang, Christopher D Manning, Percy Liang, and Jure Leskovec. 2022. Deep bidirectional language-knowledge graph pretraining. In *Advances in Neural Information Processing Systems*.

Michihiro Yasunaga, Hongyu Ren, Antoine Bosselut, Percy Liang, and Jure Leskovec. 2021. QA-GNN: Reasoning with language models and knowledge graphs for question answering. In *Proceedings of the 2021 Conference of the North American Chapter of the Association for Computational Linguistics: Human Language Technologies*, pages 535–546, Online. Association for Computational Linguistics.

Donghan Yu, Chenguang Zhu, Yuwei Fang, Wenhao Yu, Shuohang Wang, Yichong Xu, Xiang Ren, Yiming Yang, and Michael Zeng. 2022. KG-FiD: Infusing knowledge graph in fusion-in-decoder for open-domain question answering. In *Proceedings of the 60th Annual Meeting of the Association for Computational Linguistics (Volume 1: Long Papers)*, pages 4961–4974, Dublin, Ireland. Association for Computational Linguistics.

Tianyi Zhang, Felix Wu, Arzoo Katiyar, Kilian Q Weinberger, and Yoav Artzi. 2021. Revisiting few-sample BERT fine-tuning. In *International Conference on Learning Representations*.

Xikun Zhang, Antoine Bosselut, Michihiro Yasunaga, Hongyu Ren, Percy Liang, Christopher D Manning, and Jure Leskovec. 2022. GreaseLM: Graph REASoning enhanced language models. In *International Conference on Learning Representations*.

A Appendix A

A.1 SentenceTransformer

We use the model with id ALL-MPNET-BASE-V2 to prune the different paths and to calculate similarity.

A.2 Grid search

Based on the following values, we do a grid search checking every possible combination.

Hyperparameter	Value
lr	$4*10^{-5}, 3*10^{-5}$ $5*10^{-5}, 6*10^{-6}$ $4*10^{-6}, 1*10^{-6}$
Weight decay	0.01 | 0.1
Batch size	4 | 8 | 16
Dropout	0.2 | 0.3

Table 5: The values used for the grid search

A.3 Hyperparameters

Based on the grid search, we select the following hyperparameters:

Hyperparameter	With graphs	w/o graphs
Learning rate	$3*10^{-5}$	$4*10^{-5}$
Dropout	0.3	0.3
Weight decay	0.01	0.1
Batch size	16	8

Table 6: The hyperparameters used for ExplaGraphs

Hyperparameter	With graphs	w/o graphs
Learning rate	$4*10^{-5}$	$4*10^{-5}$
Dropout	0.2	0.3
Weight decay	0.01	0.1
Batch size	8	16

Table 7: The hyperparameters used for COPA-SSE

A.4 Seeds

Seeds used for both tasks during fine-tuning: $[9, 119, 7230, 4180, 6050, 257, 981, 1088, 416, 88]$

A.5 Outliers

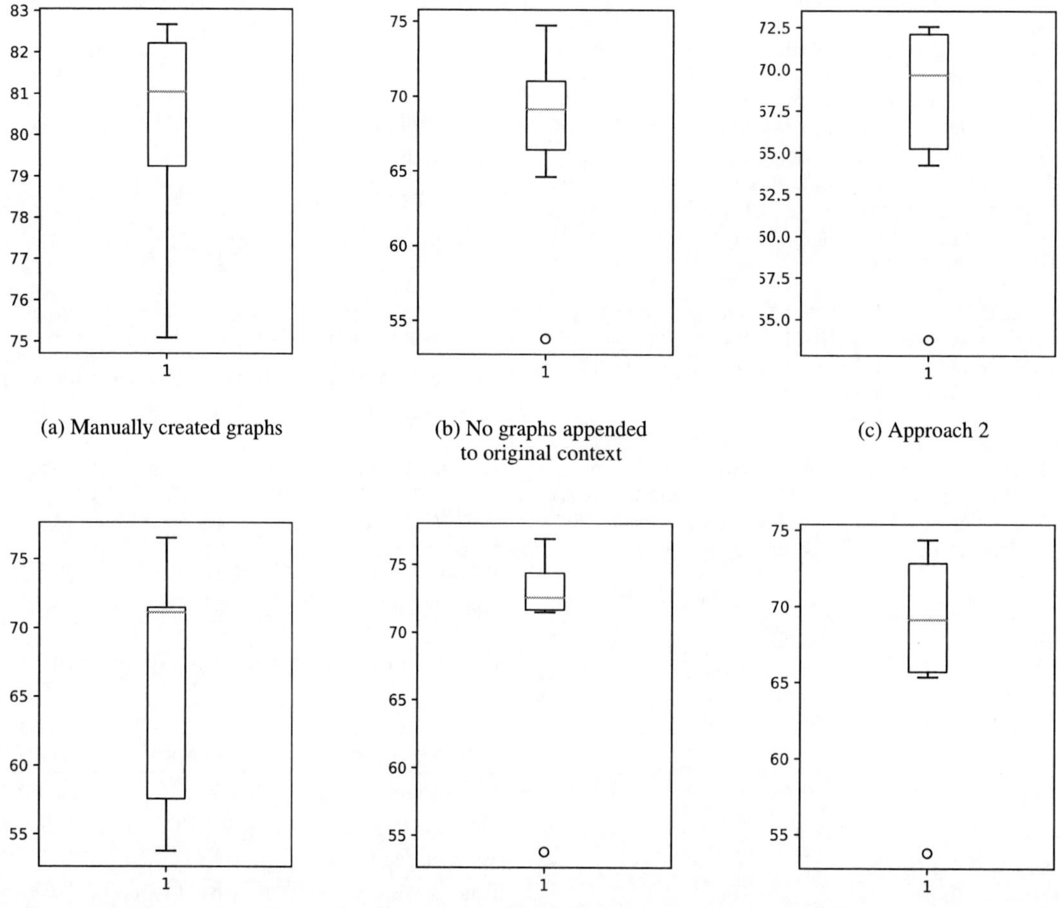

(a) Manually created graphs

(b) No graphs appended to original context

(c) Approach 2

(d) Approach 1

(e) Approach 3

(f) Approach 3-G

Figure 7: Outliers from the different runs for all graph configurations for ExplaGraphs. Circular dots mark outliers that were removed, if any.

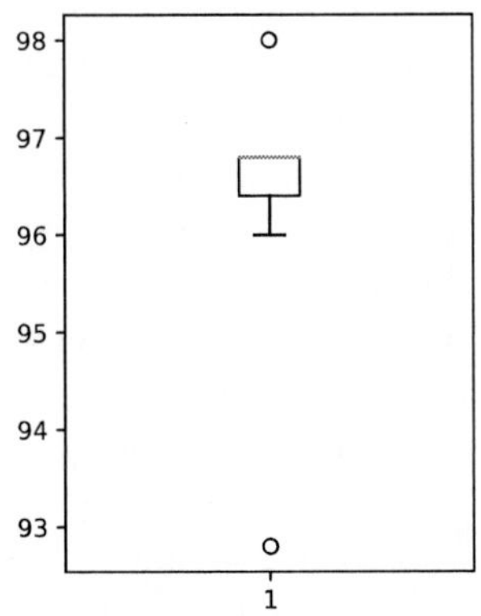

(a) Manually created graphs

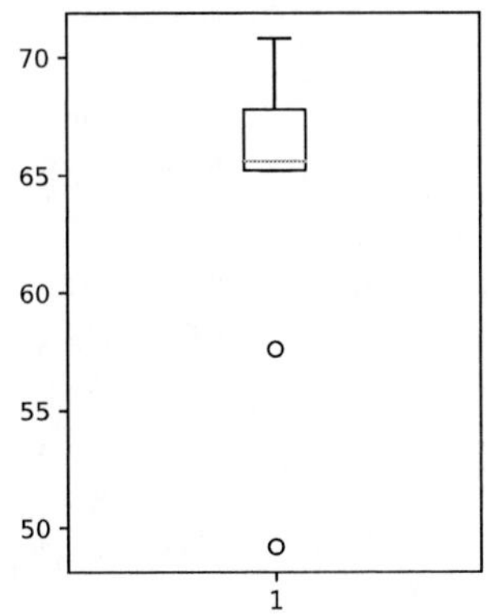

(b) No graphs appended to original context

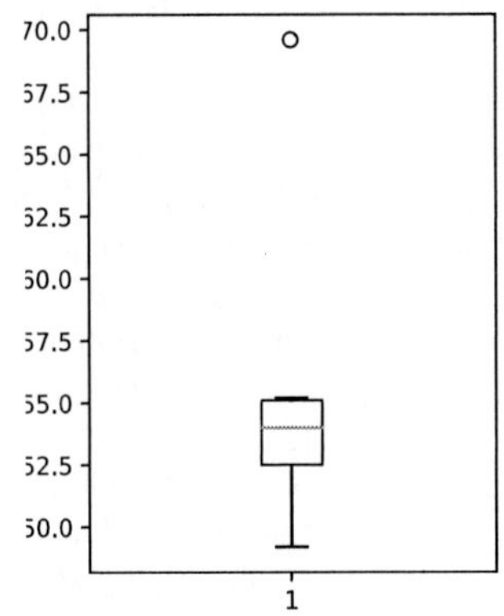

(c) Approach 2

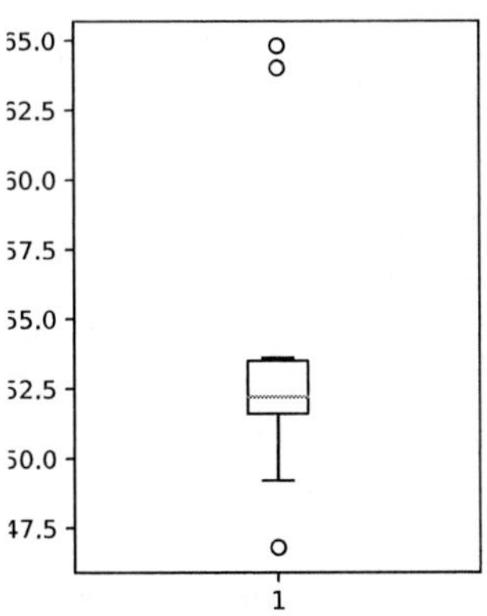

(d) Approach 1

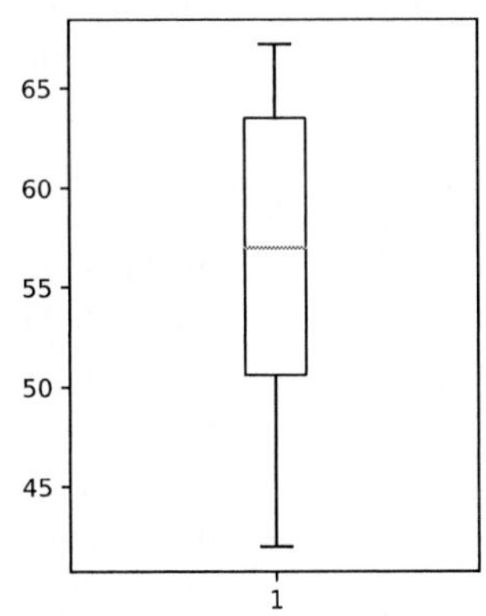

(e) Approach 3

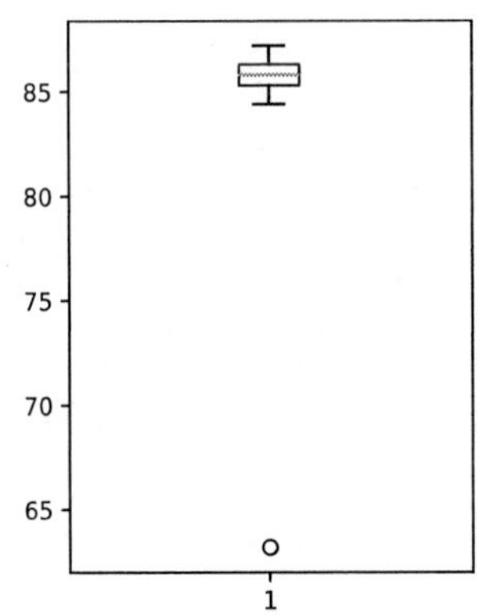

(f) Approach 3-G

Figure 8: Outliers from the different runs for all graph configurations for COPA-SSE. Circular dots mark outliers that were removed, if any.

Identifying Quantifiably Verifiable Statements from Text

Pegah Jandaghi
University of Southern California
jandaghi@usc.edu

Jay Pujara
Information Sciences Institute
jpujara@isi.edu

Abstract

Humans often describe complex quantitative data using trend-based patterns. Trend-based patterns can be interpreted as higher order functions and relations over numerical data such as extreme values, rates of change, or cyclical repetition. One application where trends abound are descriptions of numerical tabular data. Therefore, the alignment of numerical tables and textual description of trends enables easier interpretations of tables. Most existing approaches can align quantities in text with tabular data but are unable to detect and align trend-based patterns about data. In this paper, we introduce the initial steps for aligning trend-based patterns about the data, i.e. the detection of textual description of trends and the alignment of trends with a relevant table. We introduce the problem of identifying *quantifiably verifiable statements (QVS)* in the text and aligning them with tables and datasets. We define the structure of these statements and implement a structured based detection. In our experiments, we demonstrate our method can detect and align these statements from several domains and compare favorably with traditional sequence labeling methods.

1 Introduction

There is a wealth of information locked in the numerical tables, spanning different domains and real world applications (e.g., financial reports). Since numerical tables can contain dense, high-dimensional quantitative data, they are often accompanied by textual descriptions that support easy interpretation. In many cases, these textual interpretations are used without inspecting the raw data in the numerical table. [1]

When humans generate textual descriptions of numerical data, they rarely refer to the individual quantitative points, but frequently use trend-based patterns in their statements. Trend-based patterns in numerical data are description of functions and patterns over one or more dataset points in the numerical dataset. In other words, trend-based patterns are created by quantitative analysis over numerical data. The ability to identify these statements and their underlying data source is a prerequisite for many tasks such as fact-checking, natural language understanding in specific domains (e.g stock market), question answering and etc.

To date, many existing works (Ciampaglia et al., 2015; Shi and Weninger, 2016; Pan et al., 2018) have focused on the extraction of subject, predicate, object triples from text. Triple representations readily align with factual data stored as triples in knowledge graphs. However, in a trend-based statement, the supporting data is generally a derived measure on dimensionally-aligned data (such as time series) which cannot readily be validated with triple-based data. Another major limitation of current extraction and alignment methods(Ibrahim et al., 2019; Madaan et al., 2016; Roy et al., 2015) is that they are limited to the statements with first-order trends and are unable to detect and match the second-order descriptions over quantities. In this work, we focus on statements containing higher order trends about numerical data. These higher order trends are created by quantitative analysis over data. Hence, their detection and alignment requires linguistic, symbolic and quantitative reasoning.

In this paper, we introduce a pipeline, for identification and alignment of quantifiably verifiable statement i.e., statements that contain trend-based patterns about data. In the first step of our pipeline, the quantifiably verifiable statements are identified. Then they are aligned with the relevant evidence from a pre-collected dataset.

We define a quantifiably verifiable statement (QVS) as a textual span that expresses a numerical relationship in a dataset and can be objectively validated using an authoritative data set. For example, the statement "US gas prices rose in

[1]NON-ARCHIVAL submission

Proceedings of the First Workshop on Matching From Unstructured and Structured Data (MATCHING 2023), pages 14–22
July 13, 2023

2018." describes a change in value (rise) and can be objectively validated using a dataset of commodity pricing information collected by the World Bank. In the effort to align these statements, the detection component converts these statements into an *indicator* and a *trend* structure, formally defined in the next section. Intuitively, indicators allow a system to identify a specific dataset as reference dataset that is described the claim, while the trend expresses a particular data relationship that can be computationally checked on the data. The next step after identifying QVS is the alignment. The alignment step aims to find the relevant information that can be used in verification of the statement. In this paper, we presume the relevant information appears as datasets from which the QVS can be generated without any external source of information or reasoning step. For example, the statement " House prices continued their record-setting growth into May," can be generated using the US house price index dataset. As the initial step for finding the relevant information, the alignment component finds candidate datasets from a pool of pre-created datasets. The candidate selection is based on finding the datasets which are semantically similar to the indicator of the statement. e.g the indicator "Mortgage rate" is more likely to be related to the table "US house price" rather than "Cigarette sales". Our contributions are:

- We define the class of quantifiably verifiable facts and their structure
- We implement a method that detects and aligns quantifiably verifiable statement with a relevant dataset
- We create the first dataset containing real world news from public sources with parallel relevant tables.

2 Problem Definition

In this section, we formally define the problem of identification and alignment of quantifiably verifiable statements(QVS). Let T be a textual corpus consisting of assertions $A \in T$ where each assertion is a natural language statement that can be represented as a sequence of tokens. A quantifiably verifiable assertion makes a claim about a value or set of values in a single or multiple datasets. In this paper, we focus on a subset of verifiable assertions that make a claim about a single dataset. We assume all such claims can be represented by a function $f(A, D_A)$, that, given a claim (A) and a dataset (D_A) as input, designates the claim as true ($\top$) or false ($\bot$). Let V be the set of all claims in verifiable assertions. Formally, for each $A \in V$ if $\exists D_A, f_A$ s.t. $f_A(A, D_A) \in \{\top, \bot\}$ where f_A is a function that can verify A by analyzing the values of D_A. Table 1 contains examples of QVS. In the following subsections we define the substasks of QVS identification and alignment.

2.1 Identification of QVS

A QVS is structured as a sentence which contains an indicator i and a trend t linked to that indicator. Trend and Indicator are each a sequence of tokens. An *indicator* is defined as a concept that can be quantitatively measured either directly or using a commonly agreed upon proxy and its value can vary in time. Therefore, there exists a corresponding time series for each indicator. Indicators are either expressed in text as noun phrases, e.g., "Africa's GDP", "the price of crude oil in Nigeria", or they are expressed in multiple noun phrases in a statement, e.g "sales for durable goods" in the sentence 'Sales increased for durable goods in US'. In this paper, we limit the domain of indicators to the single noun phrases. Indicators provide a reference of the dataset which the statement is describing. More specifically for a claim A, an indicator can be used when looking for D_A i.e reference dataset. In other words, indicators are text spans in the statement referring to a dataset (D_A). They are either name of a currently available dataset or a potential dataset. *Trends* are sequences of words in the sentences and can have several different forms, ranging from a statement about a specific data point or points ("San Francisco's temperatures in January were an outlier"), a pattern spanning several values ("overnight rainfall will increase"), a reference to an aggregate measure ("low temperatures for Sunday"), a comparison against another dataset("compared to last year's snowfall") or a recurring pattern. Table 1 contains sample statements for each trend form. This definition of trends includes higher order descriptions i.e they do not directly express the quantities in dataset and are describing a function over data points. e.g in the statement "The world's population continues to grow" the trend is referring to the continuous increase in the value and does not mention the exact value of the world's population. For assured alignment of these statements to numerical data, the method should be able to detect the increasing patterns in this dataset. In other words, alignment of these statements requires more in-depth reasoning over data which we call functional reasoning. In considering verifiable assertions, we define a quantifiably verifiable assertion (trend-indicator verifiable assertion) to be a subset $V_{ti} \in V$ where each assertion $A \in V_{ti}$ can be expressed in the form of $\langle t, i \rangle$. For example, the statement "The Netherlands trade surplus narrowed to EUR 4.05 billion" will be expressed as $\langle$The Netherlands trade surplus, narrowed to EUR 4.05 billion$\rangle$. The challenges in identification of QVS include:

Variability: A trend-based pattern can be described in numerous ways. For example the phrases "the sharp upward trend began" and "demands has been rising since" are both describing the same increasing pattern in the data. Therefore, there is a high linguistic variability on QVS.

Domain Dependency: Trend-based patterns are interpreted differently depending on their domains i.e the terminology used to describe a trend-based pattern varies between domains . For example, the cyclic pattern is interpreted as "measles annual wave" in the epidemiology domain while it is interpreted as "cycles of glacial advance and retreat" in the environment domain.

2.2 Alignment of quantifiably verifiable statements to datasets

With the extracted statement $A = \langle t, i \rangle$, we now define the task of finding the relevant dataset D_A. In this work, D_A is a time series stored in a table. Let D be the set of all time series indicators. The alignment of A is the task of finding $D_A \in D$ such that the values in D_A are necessary and sufficient for the verification of A and every $A' = \langle t', i \rangle$ which has the same indicator as A. For example the quantifiably verifiable statement "In 2012, non-metro child poverty increased to 26.7", expressed as $\langle$ non-metro child poverty, increased to 26.7$\rangle$ is aligned with a dataset called "child poverty rate in non metropolitan areas". The alignment problem is similar to the entity linking problem (Shen et al., 2015) and has similar challenges i.e name variation and ambiguity. Name variation addresses the challenge that dataset may be referred to with different names in texts e.g "Senior citizen Population" and "The Population 65 Years and Older" are referring to the same indicator. The ambiguity addresses the challenge that the indicator in the sentence might be referring to more than a single dataset and in order to align it to the dataset correctly more information is required. e.g the indicator "growth" in the statement "Many developing countries, like India and China are experiencing robust growth" can be referring to "economic growth in China" or "Chinas growth in production" or etc. In addition to the mentioned challenges, indicators can be highly correlated or be subset of each others which causes the ambiguity in the alignment e.g the indicator "Midwest gasoline price" is the subset of "US gasoline price". Another challenge is the appearance of operations over indicators. e.g "average sea temparature", "Total operating expenses".

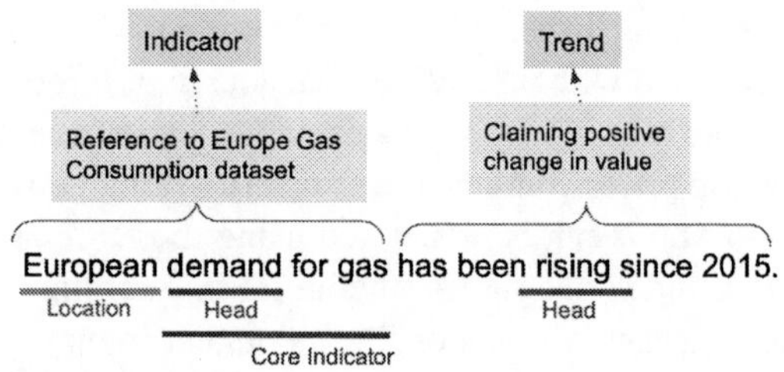

Figure 1: An example of a QVS identified by trend and indicator.

3 Method

In this section, we describe the process of identification and alignment of QVS. Given a set of documents as input, the identification method determines if they are QVS based on their structure. It also provides the trend and indicator representation $\langle t, i \rangle$ of the detected statements which will be used in the alignment method. The alignment method finds D_A for a given quantifiably verifiable statement $A = \langle t, i \rangle$ by using the indicator structure. Ideally the alignment method is provided with a list of all of the datasets (i.e. time series indicators in tables) and finds the dataset (time series) which the statement is making claim about. The dataset alignment is based on the detected i in the statement. For example in the statement "European gas demand has been rising", where "European gas demand" is identified as the indicator by detection component, the alignment selects the "Europe gas consumption" as the output. We describe the method for each task in the following subsections.

3.1 Identification of QVS

A QVS is structured as a sentence containing an indicator i and a trend t linked to that indicator where

Trend Type	Representative Words	Statement
Value at an instant	recorded, been	The official poverty rate in 2019 was 10.5 percent
Statistical function	minimum, average	Volatility peaked at 52% on Tuesday in Brent
Changes over interval	drop, fall	TSLA stock has plummeted 15% in the past three months
Second order effect	accelerated, rebound	South Africa Private Credit Growth Accelerates
Comparison	higher, relative	Prices are up 5.2 percent from the same quarter last year
Recurrent pattern	cycle, seasonality	The sun exhibits a slight brightening and dimming on 11-year cycle

Table 1: Sample quantifiably verifiable statements

trend and indicator are each a sequence of tokens in that statement. Our method is a pipeline, containing a module to detect candidate sequences for trends followed by a module that detects candidate indicator sequences.

We describe each module in the following subsections:

3.1.1 Trend Candidate Detection

As defined previously, a trend expresses a particular data relationship in the text and can have several different forms. The sequence of tokens in a trend are structured to have a head term. Head term is often a trend independent of the context. The trend candidate detection module identifies the keywords in the sentence that are highly likely to be a trend head. e.g., in the statement "About 4 million children did not have any health insurance coverage in 2018, an increase of 425k from the previous year." the detection module selects *increase* as a trend candidate. Our approach for trend detection is based on the similarity between the trends i.e., the words that appear as trends in statements are likely to have high semantic or context similarity. For example in the statements "Egg prices are skyrocketing" and "TSLA stock has plummeted 15 percent", "skyrocket" and "plummet" have high semantic similarity. Given the prior knowledge that "plummet" is a trend in that statement, we can infer that "skyrocket" is likely a trend as well. With the similarity assumption, we created a trend lexicon and a binary classifier to determine whether a word is a trend candidate. We explain each of these components in the following subsections.

Trend Lexicon Now we describe how we collected a set of keywords that are frequently used to express trends. We collected a corpus of 76 web articles from different domains, including financial and economic reports, environmental science articles, and health and medical writing. Across these different domains, we identified six general classes of trends that were used in time series trend analysis tools (Lloyd et al., 2014; Streibel et al., 2013) which are: values at an instant, statistical functions over a series, changes over an interval, recurrent patterns, second-order effects, and comparisons to baselines or other data. Table 1 contains examples from these classes of trends. To ensure having adequate samples from every trend class, for each trend class, we manually curated a sample set of statements containing a trend from that class i.e., a sample statement set for statistical functions. Then, for each trend sequence in the sample sets, we specified a representative word as trend keyword. e.g., for the statistical function trend type with the sample statements "Inflation Rate in the United States averaged 3.27 percent", "The year 1969 marked a peak in population growth", the words "average", "peak" where selected as representative words for this trend type. These words are representative for trend classes and are used as the initial lexicon. This lexicon contains 60 trend keywords a subset of them is in Table 1. The words which are highly similar to this lexicon are potential trend candidates since words that appear as trends tend to have high semantic or contextual similarity.

Trend Candidate Classifier Given an input document and a set of lexicon, this component classifies the tokens of the document as trend candidates or not based on their similarity to the trend lexicon. As mentioned previously, the trend lexicon contains representative words from all trend types and high similarity of a word with members of this set is an indicator of potential trend. Contextualized word embedding (ELMo) (Peters et al., 2018) have been shown to capture semantic and context of the words. ELMo embeddings capture both the context dependent and context independent features of words. By using ELMo internal states, we can asses the similarity of the words at different levels. Therefore, we used ELMo embeddings to assess the syntactic, semantic and contextual similarity of the words in our task i.e we assumed that trends from a same trend type have close ELMo representation. More specifically, we assumed that any trend candidate will have similar ELMo representation with a member in the collected lexicon. With this assumption, we created a binary probabilistic classifier (logistic regression) to decide whether a word is a trend candidate based on its similarity to the members in the lexicon. We created a feature vector for each input token in the input document by computing the similarity of the token with elements in the trend lexicon. i.e each entry in the similarity vector of a token w, is a semantic similarity score of w and a member from the lexicon. The similarity score is the cosine similarity between ELMO embeddings of the tokens. We use the created similarity vector of each token as the feature vector of that token for the classifier. To reduce the effort of labeling data and creating a training set for this classifier, we used bootstrapping (Yarowsky, 1995) in the training process. The process started with a subset of labeled trends randomly selected from economic news articles[2]. We expanded the initial labeled data iteratively. In each iteration, a set of unlabeled words were sampled and a human annotator labeled them as trend and non-trend. The samples were selected by uncertainty sampling to improve the classifier recall. With uncertainty sampling, we selected a subset of unlabeled tokens that the classifier was not confident about their label i.e the probability of being trend and not trend were close. Then, the new annotated samples were added to the training data. At each iteration, after adding the new labeled samples, we retrained the classifier and evaluated its performance on a development set. We continued the process of expanding the labeled set and retraining until the classifier achieved high accuracy on the development set.

3.2 Indicator Candidates Detection

We defined indicators as text spans in the statement that refer to a dataset. An indicators is a name of an existing dataset, a proxy to an existing dataset or a measurable concept that we can create a dataset by collecting its values over time. In this paper, we are interested in detecting indicators that trends are making claim about. Therefore, our method should capture the dependency between trend and indicators while detecting QVS. To incorporate the dependency of indicators to the trends, our indicator detection utilizes the notion of triggers. (Lin et al., 2020) introduced "entity triggers" as group of tokens in a sentence explaining why humans recognize named entities. Similar to the named entity triggers, we consider trends as triggers for indicators i.e. explanations for why human recognize indicators in the sentences. The indicator detection module training phase includes the trends in the QVS labeled as explanation.

[2]https://data.world/crowdflower/us-economic-performance

3.3 Dataset Alignment

In this component, with the identified $A = \langle t, i \rangle$ and a set of dataset indicators D, our method finds the most relevant indicator $D_A \in D$ such that the values in D make it possible to verify A. In other words, A is a valid assertion created by reasoning over values in D_A. The alignment component utilizes the structure of the detected indicator i. For each indicator, we have defined a structure consisting of a *core indicator*, *head term*, and *dimensions*. The core indicator is defined as a subtree of the phrase dependency tree that is both necessary and sufficient to identify the corresponding dataset. Specifically, this corresponds to the smallest subtree that is conceptually meaningful and can be measured and adding additional contextual phrases will not affect the identity of measured quantity. The root of the core indicator subtree is identified as the head term and corresponds to the general concept class of the indicator. Finally, the dimensions specify the particular subset of the core indicator measurements that are relevant. As a concrete example, for "the price of crude oil in Nigeria", the core indicator is "price of crude oil," the head term is "price" and the dimension is "Nigeria" (location of measurements). Figure 1 shows a sample indicator with its components. To find an aligned dataset with i, i is decomposed to dimensions using spaCy(Honnibal et al., 2020) name entity recognizer. The decomposition reduces the task of indicator alignment to core indicator alignment i.e our goal is find elements in D with similar core indicator to is core indicator. We used SentenceTransformer(Reimers and Gurevych, 2019) for computing the semantic similarity between different core indicators. Using semantic similarity enables us to overcome dataset name variation e.g "new loans" indicator in "Since 1988, Sub Saharan Africa is getting very little in terms of new loans" is considered similar to "Foreign Direct Investment"

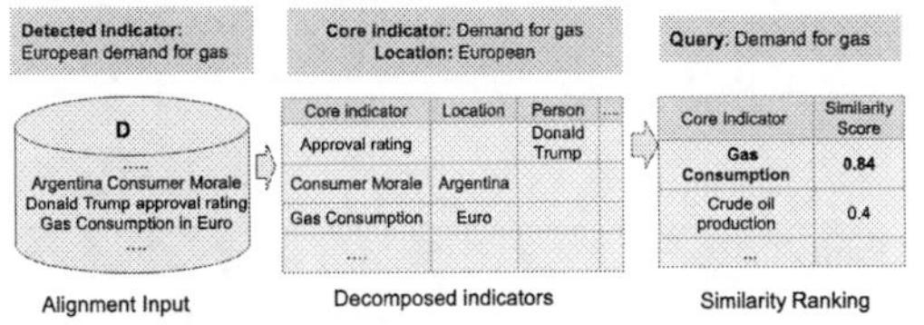

Figure 2: Steps in dataset alignment

dataset despite the textual difference. Our method selects the element with the most similar core indicator to i as the candidate for aligned indicator. In the presence of dimensions (e.g. location) in the detected indicator i, we further use the dimensions for more accurate alignment. More specifically, we select all indicators from D which have the same core indicator as i, then we select the indicator with same dimensions from this indicator pool as the aligned indicator. We also use temporal information in the statement to guarantee the existence of the trend in the aligned indicator values i.e., We extract temporal information about the detected trend t from the statement and check availability of values in the detected time span in the aligned indicator. Our method finally outputs the indicator from D which has the closest core indicator to i core indicator and its other dimensions matches those dimensions of i. Figure 2 shows the alignment process for an example indicator.

4 Experiments

We designed and conducted experiments to show the effectiveness of QVS detection and alignment.

4.1 Detection Experiment

In this experiment, we evaluated the performance of QVS detection. Our detection method relies on extracting trend and indicators from the statements i.e it assigns a tag from $\{trend, indicator, none\}$ to every token in the statement and classifies a sentence as quantifiably verifiable if $trend$ and $indicator$ tags appear in the statement. We compare the detection method with sequence tagging and claim detection methods as baselines:

ClaimBuster(Hassan et al., 2017) is an automated Fact-checking system that assigns a checkworthiness score to claims. Since a QVS is a valid claim about a dataset, any claim detection method should identify it. We used ClaimBuster as a baseline, ran claim detection and selected the claims with scores higher than 0.5 as QVS.

LSTM(Lample et al., 2016) has shown great performance for sequence tagging tasks e.g. Named Entity Recognition. We used LSTM with ELMo embeddings of the tokens as inputs. We trained the model using the data we used for training trend candidate detection and classified a QVS if both $trend$ and $indicator$ tags appeared in the statement.

For this experiment, we created 3 dataset, manually labeled them using brat (Stenetorp et al., 2011) annotation tool. The datasets are:

TE: We collected 100 articles from Trading Economic[3] containing news about economic indicators. There are 375 sentences from which 341 are QVS. The content of these articles follow the same structure but vary in terminology.

WSJ: We believed that articles published in wall street journal frequently contain QVS. We collected 100 articles from this source and sampled a statements from each article. The final dataset contains 45 QVS. The articles in this dataset have similar context however the statements demonstrate a high variability in terms of trends descriptions.

Covid: We sampled 1000 news headlines [4] during the coronavirus pandemic in 2020. Our sample consists of 1159 sentences from which 152 are QVS. These articles are from different domains and sources, making this dataset challenging for the detection task.

Table 2 shows the results of this experiment. As expected, ClaimBuster has a high recall and low precision since it detects a wide range of claims. We also observe that our methods achieves the highest accuracy in all datasets and outperforms LSTM model. For the TE dataset, since the majority of the articles are QVS, the recall is the important criteria. Though our method does not have the highest F-1 scores, the recall of our method is as high as ClaimBuster. Which indicates our method ability to overcome context dependency challenge in the TE and detect QVS. For the WSJ and Covid dataset, our method outperforms in terms of F-1 i.e. it achieves higher recall and precision.

4.2 Indicator Alignment Experiment

In this experiment, we evaluated the performance of dataset alignment. We created 3 dataset:

TE: This dataset contains a list of 234 indicators from Trading Economics as D. For a subset of 40 of these indicators, we collected sentences about that indicator from TE and ran the alignment for

[3]https://tradingeconomics.com

[4]https://www.kaggle.com/sagunsh/coronavirus-news-headline

Dataset	TE			WSJ			Covid		
Method	Pr	Re	F-1	Pr	Re	F-1	Pr	Re	F-1
LSTM	.81	.89.	.84	.57	.33	.41	.12	.72	.21
ClaimBuster	.91	.99	**.99**	.45	.95	.61	.19	.94	.32
Our method	.92	.99	.95	.71	.89	**.79**	.5	.57	**.53**

Table 2: Results of experiment 1: quantifiably verifiable statements detection

Method	Our method		String matching		GloVe matching	
Dataset	Pr	Re@3	Pr	Re@3	Pr	Re@3
Gov	**.96**	.98	.78	.88	.51	.67
TE	**.66**	.76	.43	.56	.17	.23
Covid	.91	.93	**.93**	.94	.4	.48

Table 3: Results for experiment 2: dataset alignment. The Pr columns shows the precision and Re@3 is the recall at 3.

the detected indicator in those statements. The indicators in TE dataset are classified to tables based on their topic which includes: Government, Labour, Markets and etc. This classification alludes that each topic include semantically similar indicators. For example the indicators "Corporate tax rate" and "Sales tax rate" are under the "Tax rate" topic.

Gov: We extracted 52 tables and sentences about an indicator in those tables from US government domains. We extracted indicators in those tables which resulted in 52 reference indicators. In this dataset, name variation is low i.e the majority of the indicators appear exactly as they are in the table

Covid: We sampled 234 news headlines about Covid. The sample statements were about Covid infection, death and recovered indicators. We used the indicator list from the TE and Gov as the reference set and evaluated the accuracy of aligning the Covid related indicators. Although the number of indicators in the headlines are limited, the ambiguity is high in this dataset. For example, the statement "UK coronavirus toll passes 19,000" could be aligned with the "covid confirmed cases" and "covid death cases".

We compare our alignment method with baseline methods: string matching and GloVe(Pennington et al., 2014) similarity. For each method, we choose the closest dataset indicator as the aligned dataset. We report the precision of the aligned dataset. For a more thorough evaluation, we also selected the top 3 matched datasets from each method, and reported whether the correct dataset is withing those choices (Recall@3). The results of the experiment are in Table 3. As shown in the table, the baseline methods have good performance in the Gov dataset. This is due to the low ambiguity and name variation in this dataset. The GloVe matchings poor performance in the TE and Covid dataset is rooted in the prevalence of domain specific words(OOV) in these datasets. However our method is robust in those cases. The string matching method has its lowest perforamnce in the TE dataset since the matching fails to achieve high performance in the datasets with high name variation. We observe that for the TE dataset, the difference of Recall@3 and precision are higher compared to the other datasets. This is caused by the presence of indicators which are semantically similar. Overall we observe that our method achieves a reasonable accuracy in all datasets. While it has a slightly lower accuracy in covid dataset where the indicators in the statements are similar to the reference set, it outperforms other methods in more challenging datasets.

4.3 Conclusion and Future Work

We introduced a novel problem of identifying QVS in text and aligning them with tables. We designed a system that extracts and aligns QVS using natural language processing toolkits and semantic features. In our ongoing work, we are working to create more specific alignment of QVS and tables i.e. finding the underlying datapoints and the relation between them. We hope to extend the application of our method and assemble an end-to-end solution for verification of QVS that includes identifying indicators in documents, finding relevant datapoints for verification, and trend analysis systems to compare assertions with data.

4.4 Related Work

The problem of finding alignment between text and tables has been studied for the non-numerical tables (Bhagavatula et al., 2015). (Chen et al., 2021; Cheng et al., 2021) created datasets containing text and numerical tables aligned with them which are used for question answering with quatitative reasoning. The general problem of validating facts in textual data has largely been studied from the perspective of verifying specific triplified knowledge with an explicit set of relationships (Ciampaglia et al., 2015; Shi and Weninger, 2016; Pan et al., 2018). There have been recent studies on verifying statement about tabular and semi-structured data (Wenhu Chen and Wang, 2020; Schlichtkrull et al., 2021; Gupta et al., 2020). These approaches are can decide whether a statement is entailed from tables. There have been several studies on identifying check-worthy claims in text recently (Hassan et al., 2017, 2015; Jaradat et al., 2018). These approaches assign a check-worthy score to each sentence in a document. However, they lack a formal definition for check-worthy claims and do not support quantifiably verifying these claims. The approach in (Konstantinovskiy et al., 2018) has a very general definition for check-worthy claims and it is not possible to check the verifiability of most of them using any data set. (Thorne and Vlachos, 2017) checks the veracity of claims containing temporal numerical information associated with named entities. Information extraction approaches for relations have been intensely studied in both open-world (Etzioni et al., 2008) and ontology-based settings (Wimalasuriya and Dou, 2010). A subfield of extraction approaches that is closely related to our task is that of identifying cause-effect relationships in text (Asghar, 2016). In this subfield, common approaches include bootstrapping from a known set of keywords (Marcu and Echihabi, 2002), using NLP feature sets and semantic features (Rink and Harabagiu, 2010), analysis of graph relationships (Rink et al., 2010) and more recently, neural-network based approaches (de Silva et al., 2017). Identifying and summarizing trends in natural language, the inverse of the problem we tackle, has been notably studied in approaches such as the Automated Statistician (Lloyd et al., 2014; Hwang et al., 2016) and subsequent papers. A relevant research area is the quantification of cognitive expectations for specific increase and decrease trends using crowdsourced studies (Sharp et al., 2018).

References

Nabiha Asghar. 2016. Automatic extraction of causal relations from natural language texts: a comprehensive survey. *arXiv preprint arXiv:1605.07895*.

Chandra Bhagavatula, Thanapon Noraset, and Doug Downey. 2015. Tabel: Entity linking in web tables. In *SEMWEB*.

Zhiyu Chen, Wenhu Chen, Charese Smiley, Sameena Shah, Iana Borova, Dylan Langdon, Reema Moussa, Matthew I. Beane, Ting-Hao Kenneth Huang, Bryan R. Routledge, and William Yang Wang. 2021. Finqa: A dataset of numerical reasoning over financial data. *ArXiv*, abs/2109.00122.

Zhoujun Cheng, Haoyu Dong, Zhiruo Wang, Ran Jia, Jiaqi Guo, Yan Gao, Shi Han, Jian-Guang Lou, and Dongmei Zhang. 2021. Hitab: A hierarchical table dataset for question answering and natural language generation.

Giovanni Luca Ciampaglia, Prashant Shiralkar, Luis M Rocha, Johan Bollen, Filippo Menczer, and Alessandro Flammini. 2015. Computational fact checking from knowledge networks. *PloS one*, 10(6):e0128193.

Tharini N de Silva, Xiao Zhibo, Zhao Rui, and Mao Kezhi. 2017. Causal relation identification using convolutional neural networks and knowledge based features. *World Academy of Science, Engineering and Technology, International Journal of Computer, Electrical, Automation, Control and Information Engineering*, 11(6):697–702.

Oren Etzioni, Michele Banko, Stephen Soderland, and Daniel S Weld. 2008. Open information extraction from the web. *Communications of the ACM*, 51(12):68–74.

Vivek Gupta, Maitrey Mehta, Pegah Nokhiz, and Vivek Srikumar. 2020. INFOTABS: Inference on tables as semi-structured data. In *Proceedings of the 58th Annual Meeting of the Association for Computational Linguistics*, pages 2309–2324, Online. Association for Computational Linguistics.

Naeemul Hassan, Chengkai Li, and Mark Tremayne. 2015. Detecting check-worthy factual claims in presidential debates. *Proceedings of the 24th ACM International Conference on Information and Knowledge Management (CIKM)*, pages 1835–1838.

Naeemul Hassan, Anil Nayak, Vikas Sable, Chengkai Li, Mark Tremayne, Gensheng Zhang, Fatma Arslan, Josue Caraballo, Damian Jimenez, Siddhant Gawsane, Shohedul Hasan, Minumol Joseph, and Aaditya Kulkarni. 2017. Claimbuster: the first-ever end-to-end fact-checking system. *Proceedings of the VLDB Endowment*, 10:1945–1948.

Matthew Honnibal, Ines Montani, Sofie Van Landeghem, and Adriane Boyd. 2020. spaCy: Industrial-strength Natural Language Processing in Python.

Yunseong Hwang, Anh Tong, and Jaesik Choi. 2016. Automatic construction of nonparametric relational regression models for multiple time series. In *International Conference on Machine Learning*, pages 3030–3039.

Yusra Ibrahim, Mirek Riedewald, Gerhard Weikum, and Demetrios Zeinalipour-Yazti. 2019. Bridging quantities in tables and text. In *2019 IEEE 35th International Conference on Data Engineering (ICDE)*, pages 1010–1021.

Israa Jaradat, Pepa Gencheva, Alberto Barrón-Cedeño, Lluís Màrquez, and Preslav Nakov. 2018. Claimrank: Detecting check-worthy claims in arabic and english. pages 26–30.

Lev Konstantinovskiy, Oliver Price, Mevan Babakar, and Arkaitz Zubiaga. 2018. Towards automated factchecking: Developing an annotation schema and benchmark for consistent automated claim detection.

Guillaume Lample, Miguel Ballesteros, Sandeep Subramanian, Kazuya Kawakami, and Chris Dyer. 2016. Neural architectures for named entity recognition. In *NAACL*.

Bill Yuchen Lin, Dong-Ho Lee, Ming Shen, Ryan Moreno, Xiao Huang, Prashant Shiralkar, and Xiang Ren. 2020. Triggerner: Learning with entity triggers as explanations for named entity recognition.

James Robert Lloyd, David K Duvenaud, Roger B Grosse, Joshua B Tenenbaum, and Zoubin Ghahramani. 2014. Automatic construction and natural-language description of nonparametric regression models. In *AAAI*, pages 1242–1250.

Aman Madaan, Ashish Mittal, Mausam, Ganesh Ramakrishnan, and Sunita Sarawagi. 2016. Numerical relation extraction with minimal supervision. In *AAAI*.

Daniel Marcu and Abdessamad Echihabi. 2002. An unsupervised approach to recognizing discourse relations. In *Proceedings of the 40th Annual Meeting on Association for Computational Linguistics*, pages 368–375. Association for Computational Linguistics.

Jeff Z Pan, Siyana Pavlova, Chenxi Li, Ningxi Li, Yangmei Li, and Jinshuo Liu. 2018. Content based fake news detection using knowledge graphs. In *International Semantic Web Conference*, pages 669–683. Springer.

Jeffrey Pennington, Richard Socher, and Christopher D. Manning. 2014. Glove: Global vectors for word representation. In *Empirical Methods in Natural Language Processing (EMNLP)*, pages 1532–1543.

Matthew E. Peters, Mark Neumann, Mohit Iyyer, Matt Gardner, Christopher Clark, Kenton Lee, and Luke Zettlemoyer. 2018. Deep contextualized word representations. In *Proc. of NAACL*.

Nils Reimers and Iryna Gurevych. 2019. Sentence-bert: Sentence embeddings using siamese bert-networks. In *Proceedings of the 2019 Conference on Empirical Methods in Natural Language Processing*. Association for Computational Linguistics.

Bryan Rink, Cosmin Adrian Bejan, and Sanda M Harabagiu. 2010. Learning textual graph patterns to detect causal event relations. In *FLAIRS Conference*.

Bryan Rink and Sanda Harabagiu. 2010. Utd: Classifying semantic relations by combining lexical and semantic resources. In *Proceedings of the 5th International Workshop on Semantic Evaluation*, pages 256–259. Association for Computational Linguistics.

Subhro Roy, Tim Vieira, and Dan Roth. 2015. Reasoning about quantities in natural language. *Transactions of the Association for Computational Linguistics*, 3:1–13.

Michael Sejr Schlichtkrull, Vladimir Karpukhin, Barlas Oguz, Mike Lewis, Wen-tau Yih, and Sebastian Riedel. 2021. Joint verification and reranking for open fact checking over tables. *Proceedings of the 59th Annual Meeting of the Association for Computational Linguistics and the 11th International Joint Conference on Natural Language Processing (Volume 1: Long Papers)*.

Rebecca Sharp, Mithun Paul, Ajay Nagesh, Dane Bell, and Mihai Surdeanu. 2018. Grounding gradable adjectives through crowdsourcing. In *Proceedings of the Eleventh International Conference on Language Resources and Evaluation (LREC-2018)*.

Wei Shen, Jianyong Wang, and Jiawei Han. 2015. Entity linking with a knowledge base: Issues, techniques, and solutions. *IEEE Transactions on Knowledge and Data Engineering*, 27:443–460.

Baoxu Shi and Tim Weninger. 2016. Discriminative predicate path mining for fact checking in knowledge graphs. *Knowledge-Based Systems*, 104:123–133.

Pontus Stenetorp, Goran Topić, Sampo Pyysalo, Tomoko Ohta, Jin-Dong Kim, and Jun'ichi Tsujii. 2011. Bionlp shared task 2011: Supporting resources. In *Proceedings of BioNLP Shared Task 2011 Workshop*, pages 112–120, Portland, Oregon, USA. Association for Computational Linguistics.

Olga Streibel, Lars Wissler, Robert Tolksdorf, and Danilo Montesi. 2013. Trend template: Mining trends with a semi-formal trend model. volume 1088.

James Thorne and Andreas Vlachos. 2017. An extensible framework for verification of numerical claims.

Jianshu Chen Yunkai Zhang Hong Wang Shiyang Li Xiyou Zhou Wenhu Chen, Hongmin Wang and William Yang Wang. 2020. Tabfact : A large-scale dataset for table-based fact verification. In *International Conference on Learning Representations (ICLR)*, Addis Ababa, Ethiopia.

Daya C Wimalasuriya and Dejing Dou. 2010. Ontology-based information extraction: An introduction and a survey of current approaches.

David Yarowsky. 1995. Unsupervised word sense disambiguation rivaling supervised methods. In *ACL*.

Toward Consistent and Informative Event-Event Temporal Relation Extraction

Xiaomeng Jin
University of Illinois Urbana-Champaign
xjin17@illinois.edu

Haoyang Wen
Carnegie Mellon University
hwen3@cs.cmu.edu

Xinya Du
University of Texas at Dallas
xinya.du@utdallas.edu

Heng Ji
University of Illinois Urbana-Champaign
hengji@illinois.edu

Abstract

Event-event temporal relation extraction aims to extract the temporal order between a pair of event mentions, which is usually used to construct temporal event graphs. However, event graphs generated by existing methods are usually *globally inconsistent* (event graphs containing cycles), *semantically irrelevant* (two unrelated events having temporal links), and *context unaware* (neglecting neighborhood information of an event node). In this paper, we propose a novel event-event temporal relation extraction method to address these limitations. Our model combines a pretrained language model and a graph neural network to output event embeddings, which captures the contextual information of event graphs. Moreover, to achieve global consistency and semantic relevance, (1) event temporal order should be in accordance with the norm of their embeddings, and (2) two events have temporal relation only if their embeddings are close enough. Experimental results on a real-world event dataset demonstrate that our method achieves state-of-the-art performance and generates high-quality event graphs.

1 Introduction

Event-event temporal relation extraction aims to extract the temporal order between a pair of event mentions in natural language text (i.e., an event is BEFORE or AFTER another event), which is essential for constructing temporal event graphs. Event-event temporal relation extraction enables researchers to understand the dynamics of complex events, and benefits a variety of downstream tasks, including event graph construction (Li et al., 2018), future event prediction (Li et al., 2021; Du et al., 2022; Wang et al., 2022; Jin et al., 2022), question answering (Souza Costa et al., 2020; Wang et al., 2021), and summarization (Glavaš and Šnajder, 2014).

Researchers have proposed many methods (Dligach et al., 2017; Han et al., 2020; Wen and Ji, 2021) to tackle this challenging task. Previous work usually formulates the problem as a pairwise classification task (Dligach et al., 2017; Han et al., 2020; Wen and Ji, 2021). However, they have three major issues when applied to constructing the temporal event graph:

(1) *Global inconsistency*. Local pairwise classification is likely to introduce conflicting predictions when constructing temporal event graphs. Figure 1a shows an example of conflicting local predictions, where yellow links (e.g., DIE $\rightarrow$ INJURE) conflict with blue links (e.g., DETONATE $\rightarrow$ INJURE). Although previous work can address conflicts through inference methods such as Integer Linear Programming (Bramsen et al., 2006; Han et al., 2019), resolving this issue directly in temporal relation extraction models yet receives limited attention. (2) *Semantic irrelevance*. Existing methods output a predicted temporal relation for any two given atom events, regardless of their semantic relevance. For example, as shown in Figure 1b, given two events MEDICAL INTERVENTION and SENTENCE, existing models will predict that there is a temporal link from MEDICAL INTERVENTION to SENTENCE. Though it is very likely that MEDICAL INTERVENTION happens before SENTENCE in a real bombing event, those two events have no direct semantic relation, which makes the predicted temporal link semantically irrelevant.

(3) *Context unawareness*. Events with sharing arguments are usually closely related in a temporal event graph, which provides valuable information about the nature of a particular event (Vo and Bagheri, 2019). As shown in Figure 1c, CRIMINAL (rather than VICTIM) is shared by SENTENCE event and DIE event, so it is not likely that the MOURN event follows the DIE (yellow link). However, existing work considers information from candidate event pairs only, while ignoring those rich connections among other related events.

In this paper, we propose a new event-event tem-

Proceedings of the First Workshop on Matching From Unstructured and Structured Data (MATCHING 2023), pages 23–32
July 13, 2023 ©2023 Association for Computational Linguistics

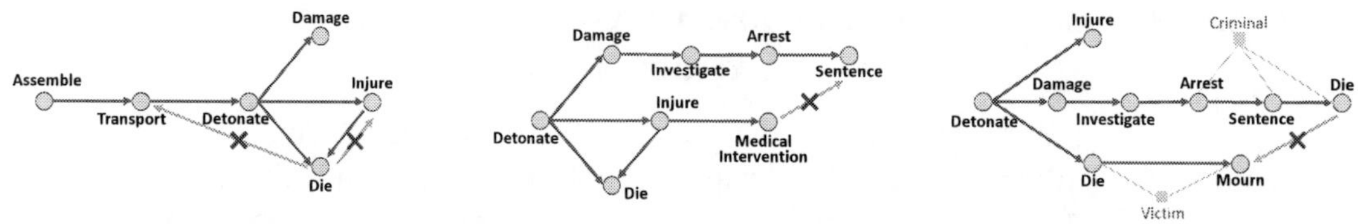

(a) Global inconsistency (b) Semantic irrelevance (c) Context unawareness

Figure 1: Limitations of existing event-event temporal relation extraction methods. Yellow links are incorrect predictions, but existing methods are prone to making such mistakes. (a) Global inconsistency. The yellow links will introduce cycles to the event graph and make the event graph globally inconsistent. (b) Semantic irrelevance. The yellow link is semantically irrelevant because its two endpoint events have no direct relevance. (c) Context unawareness. The yellow link is incorrect because its DIE event shares an argument with the SENTENCE event (rather than the MOURN event), indicating that this DIE event is associated with criminal rather than victim.

poral relation extraction approach that addresses the above limitations of existing methods. The goal of our approach is to learn event representations that are *globally consistent*, *semantically relevant*, and *context-aware*. As shown in Figure 2, given an input document as well as the entity mentions, we first use off-the-shelf information extraction tools (Du et al., 2022) to extract arguments of events. We then use a pretrained language model (PLM, Devlin et al., 2018) to encode events/arguments and get their PLM-based embeddings. To allow events to be aware of their contextual information, we construct an initial event graph consisting of events/arguments as nodes and event-argument links as edges, then use a graph neural network (GNN, Scarselli et al., 2008) to aggregate neighborhood information for each node iteratively and get their GNN-based embeddings. The PLM-based and GNN-based embeddings are combined together as the final embeddings of events.

Moreover, to ensure that the learned event embeddings are globally consistent and semantically relevant, we hypothesize that the event embedding space should be geometrically meaningful, in which event embeddings satisfy the following two rules: (1) The temporal order of events is in accordance with the norm of event embeddings. Specifically, if event A happens before event B, then the embedding norm of event A should be smaller than that of event B. (2) There exists a temporal link between two events if and only if their embeddings are close enough to each other in the event embedding space. Specifically, if events A and B are connected by a temporal edge (either A happens before B or after B), then the distance between A's and B's embedding should be smaller than a predefined threshold, and vice versa. The first rule ensures that the constructed event graph is globally consistent, and the second rule ensures that there will be a temporal link between two events only if they are semantically relevant. We implement these two rules in our model by minimizing a corresponding margin-based loss w.r.t the model parameters, thus the whole model can be trained in an end-to-end fashion.

We conduct experiments on the Event Story Line dataset (Caselli and Vossen, 2017). The experimental results demonstrate that our proposed method achieves state-of-the-art performance on event-event temporal relation extraction. We also show that compared with baseline methods, event graphs generated by our method are globally consistent and semantically relevant.

In summary, our contributions are as follows:

- We review the literature on event-event temporal relation extraction thoroughly, and observe that a well-behaved event temporal relation extraction method should be *globally consistent*, *semantically relevant*, and *context aware*.
- Methodologically, we use graph neural networks to process event graphs and learn event representations, which enables the model to learn event embeddings that are *context aware*. Moreover, we use the distance between event embeddings as the criterion for judging the existence of event temporal edges, and use the norm of event embeddings as the criterion for determining the direction of event temporal edges, which enables our model to be *globally consistent* and *semantically relevant*.
- We conduct extensive experiments on event-event temporal relation extraction task, and the results demonstrate that our proposed method achieves substantial improvements over state-of-the-art baseline methods.

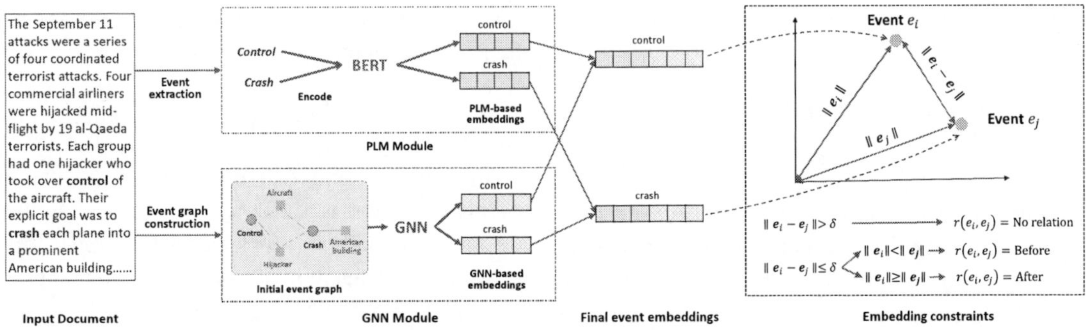

Figure 2: The architecture of our model. Given an input document, our model uses a pretrained language model (PLM) to encode event mentions and get their PLM-based embeddings, and uses a graph neural network (GNN) to aggregate contextual information on the initial event graph and get their GNN-based embeddings. The PLM-based and GNN-based embeddings are combined together as the final embeddings of events. To achieve global consistency and semantic relevance, we hypothesize that the event embedding space is geometrically meaningful by imposing two constraints on event embeddings. See Section 3.3 for details.

2 Problem Formulation

The event-event temporal relation extraction problem is formulated as follows. Given a document, we use $\{e_1, e_2, \cdots\}$ to denote the set of event mentions, and $\{a_1, a_2, \cdots\}$ to denote the set of argument mentions. An event node e_i and an argument a_j are connected by a link if a_j is an argument of e_i. The event mentions are obtained from the gold standard annotations for the dataset. The arguments and event-argument links can be obtained by applying off-the-shelf information extraction (IE) tools (Luan et al., 2019; Wen et al., 2021) to the input document. We also assume they are given as our input.

Our task is to predict the temporal relation between a pair of events (e_i, e_j), which can be BEFORE, AFTER, or NO RELATION. The predicted results can then be used to construct a temporal event graph, in which each node represents an event, and each directed edge $e_i \rightarrow e_j$ represents a temporal relation indicating that event e_i happens before event e_j (or equivalently, event e_j happens after event e_i). If the relation type between e_i and e_j is predicted as NO RELATION, then there is no edge between the two event nodes in the temporal event graph. Our goal is to propose a *globally consistent* and *semantically relevant* event-event temporal relation extraction method, so that the generated temporal event graph is *valid* (no conflict), *concise* (only related events can be connected), and *meaningful* (temporal links should be aware of the meaning of event nodes).

3 Our Approach

The overall framework of our proposed approach is shown in Figure 2. In this section, we will introduce each part of the framework in detail.

3.1 PLM Module

Pretrained language models (PLMs) are usually trained on a large corpus and thus is able to encode words as vector representations while preserving their semantics. Following most existing methods, we feed an input document into a PLM[1] first to obtain an initial vector representation for each token in the document. Specifically, for a document with a sequence of tokens $\{w_1, w_2, \cdots\}$, we first sum the token, segment, and positional embeddings for each token to compute its initial input representation $\{\boldsymbol{h}_1^0, \boldsymbol{h}_2^0, \cdots\}$, and then compute an output representation for each PLM layer l:

$$\{\boldsymbol{h}_1^l, \cdots\} = \text{PLM-Layer}(\{\boldsymbol{h}_1^{l-1}, \cdots\}) \quad (1)$$

for $l = 1, \cdots, L$, where PLM-Layer$(\cdot)$ is a single PLM encoder layer, whose parameters are initialized using a pretrained model, and L is the number of PLM layers. We suggest readers to refer to Devlin et al. (2018) for technical details of these layers.

The representation of event mention e_i output by the last PLM layer is denoted as $\boldsymbol{h}_i^L$. If an event mention consists of multiple tokens, we simply average the embeddings of all tokens in this event mention. Finally, we use an MLP with two hidden

[1] In our case, we use BERT (Devlin et al., 2018).

layers to compute the final PLM-based representation of event e_i:

$$h_{e_i}^{\text{PLM}} = \text{MLP}(h_i^L). \quad (2)$$

3.2 GNN Module

Note that in a temporal event graph, an event is usually closely related to its contextual events, which share common argument entities with the given event. Contextual events provide valuable information about the nature of a particular event and help improve the performance of temporal link prediction. As shown in Figure 1c, The contextual events of the right DIE (i.e., SENTENCE, ARREST) and the contextual events of the left DIE (i.e., MOURN) indicate that they are associated with criminal and victim, respectively, so the right DIE event should not be followed by a MOURN event.

To let our model be aware of contextual event information, we first construct an initial event graph where nodes represent event mentions and argument mentions extracted from the given input document, and edges represent event-argument links. Then we use Graph Neural Networks (GNNs, Kipf and Welling, 2017) to perform message passing on the initial event graph and learn event representations. Specifically, for an initial event graph G, we use s_i^k to denote the representation of node $i \in G$ at iteration k (which can be either an event or an entity). Then the node representation is updated by aggregating its neighborhood information:

$$s_i^k = \sigma\Big(\mathbf{W}^k \sum\nolimits_{j \in \mathcal{N}(i) \cup \{i\}} \alpha_{ij} s_j^{k-1}\Big) \quad (3)$$

for $k = 1, \cdots, K$, where K is the number of GNN layers.

For each node i, $\mathcal{N}(\cdot)$ denotes the set of its neighbors [2]. $\alpha_{ij} = 1/\sqrt{|\mathcal{N}(i)| \cdot |\mathcal{N}(j)|}$ is the weight coefficient. s_i^0 is initialized as the embedding of event mention e_i (i.e., $s_i^0 = h_i^L$), which is provided by PLM in Section 3.1.

The output of the GNN's last layer is taken as the final GNN-based representation of event e_i:

$$s_{e_i}^{\text{GNN}} = s_i^K. \quad (4)$$

3.3 Globally Consistent and Semantically Relevant Event Representation

After obtaining the PLM-based and GNN-based event representations, we concatenate these two types of embeddings for each event and get the final event embedding:

$$e_i = \text{CONCAT}\left(h_{e_i}^{\text{PLM}}, s_{e_i}^{\text{GNN}}\right). \quad (5)$$

To predict the temporal relation between a pair of events, a straightforward way is to train a classifier on their embeddings, for example, an MLP that takes the concatenation of two event embeddings as input and outputs labels of BEFORE, AFTER, or NO RELATION. However, the trained classifier is not guaranteed to be globally consistent (no cycle in event graphs) and semantically relevant (temporal links only exist between events that are closely related), which makes the predicted temporal event links invalid and irrelevant.

To address these issues, we hypothesize that the event embedding space should be geometrically meaningful, and event embeddings should satisfy the following two constraints:

- *The temporal order of events is in accordance with the norm* [3] *of event embeddings.* Specifically, if there is a temporal link from event e_i to event e_j, then the length of event e_i's embedding should be smaller than the length of event e_j's, embedding:

  $$e_i \to e_j \Rightarrow \|\mathbf{e}_i\| < \|\mathbf{e}_j\|. \quad (6)$$

  It is clear to see that event graphs will be cycle-free under the above constraint. Otherwise, assume that there is cycle $e_i \to e_j \to \cdots \to e_i$, then according to Eq. (6), we have $\|\mathbf{e}_i\| < \|\mathbf{e}_j\| < \cdots < \|\mathbf{e}_i\|$, which is impossible.
- *There exists a temporal relation between two events if and only if their embeddings are close enough in the event embedding space*, since we assume that a temporal relation is meaningful only if the two events are semantically related. Specifically, if events e_i and e_j are connected by a temporal edge (e_i happens either before or after e_j), then the distance between e_i's and e_j's embeddings should be less than a threshold δ that is a pre-defined real positive number, and vice versa:

  $$e_i \to e_j \vee e_j \to e_i \Leftrightarrow \|\mathbf{e}_i - \mathbf{e}_j\| < \delta. \quad (7)$$

  Under the constraint in Eq. (7), two events can be connected by a temporal link only if their

[2] To alleviate the sparsity issue of event graphs, all edges in event graphs are treated undirected when counting neighbors.

[3] We use L2 norm in this paper.

embeddings are close to each other, which discourages the model from predicting a temporal link for two events that are distant in the timeline. In this way, our model will learn to output a "minimal" temporal event graph that preserves its essential chronological structure.

3.4 Model Training and Inference

Training. Each training document consists of a set of event temporal links used for training the model. According to the ground-truth label of an event temporal link, the loss function is designed as follows:

- If $r(e_i, e_j) = \text{BEFORE}$, i.e., event e_i happens before event e_j, then the loss term for event pair (e_i, e_j) is

$$L_{ij}^{\text{BEFORE}} = \left[\|\boldsymbol{e}_i\| - \|\boldsymbol{e}_j\|\right]^+ + \left[\|\boldsymbol{e}_i - \boldsymbol{e}_j\| - \delta\right]^+,$$

where the function $[\cdot]^+ = \max(\cdot, 0)$. The first term encourages the embedding length of e_i to be smaller than e_j, and the second term encourages the distance between e_i's and e_j's embedding to be less than δ.

- Similarly, if $r(e_i, e_j) = \text{AFTER}$, i.e., event e_i happens after event e_j, then the loss term for event pair (e_i, e_j) is

$$L_{ij}^{\text{AFTER}} = \left[\|\boldsymbol{e}_j\| - \|\boldsymbol{e}_i\|\right]^+ + \left[\|\boldsymbol{e}_j - \boldsymbol{e}_i\| - \delta\right]^+.$$

- Otherwise, if $r(e_i, e_j) = \text{NO RELATION}$, i.e., there is no explicit temporal ordering between e_i and e_j, then the loss term for event pair (e_i, e_j) is

$$L_{ij}^{\text{NO-REL}} = \left[\delta - \|\boldsymbol{e}_i - \boldsymbol{e}_j\|\right]^+,$$

which encourages the distance between e_i's and e_j's embedding to be larger than δ.

The total loss function of our model is therefore as follows:

$$L = \sum_{D \in \mathcal{D}} \sum_{(e_i, e_j) \in D} \Big(\mathbb{1}[r(e_i, e_j) = \text{BEFORE}] L_{ij}^{\text{BEFORE}} + \mathbb{1}[r(e_i, e_j) = \text{AFTER}] L_{ij}^{\text{AFTER}} + \mathbb{1}[r(e_i, e_j) = \text{NO RELATION}] L_{ij}^{\text{NO-REL}} \Big),$$

where $\mathcal{D}$ is the training dataset, and $D \in \mathcal{D}$ is a training document. The whole model can thus be trained by minimizing the above total loss using gradient-based optimization methods.

# train/val/test documents	206 / 26 / 26
# avg events / document	12.6
# avg arguments / document	30.1
# avg relations / document	21.4

Table 1: Statistics of the Event StoryLine Corpus.

Inference. In the inference stage, to predict the temporal relation between two events e_i and e_j, we first calculate the event embeddings of e_i and e_j using the PLM module and GNN module in our model, then output the label of (e_i, e_j) according to the following criteria:

$$r(e_i, e_j) = \begin{cases} \text{BEFORE, if } \|\boldsymbol{e}_i - \boldsymbol{e}_j\| < \delta \wedge \|\boldsymbol{e}_i\| < \|\boldsymbol{e}_j\|, \\ \text{AFTER, if } \|\boldsymbol{e}_i - \boldsymbol{e}_j\| < \delta \wedge \|\boldsymbol{e}_i\| \geq \|\boldsymbol{e}_j\|, \\ \text{NO RELATION, if } \|\boldsymbol{e}_i - \boldsymbol{e}_j\| \geq \delta. \end{cases}$$

4 Experiments

4.1 Datasets

We conduct experiments on Event StoryLine Corpus (Caselli and Vossen, 2017), which contains 258 documents on 22 calamity topics.[4] It consists of human-annotated event temporal links: RISING_ACTION, which means the former event happens earlier than and implicitly enables the later event, or FALLING_ACTION, which means the former event happens later than and is the outcome/effect of the later event. We map RISING_ACTION to BEFORE and FALLING_ACTION to AFTER in our method.

The statistics of the dataset are summarized in Table 1. We split the documents into train, validation, and test sets. There are also entity annotations in each document including location and person. We use these entity mentions as argument nodes in the initial event graph construction.

4.2 Baseline Methods

We compare our method with the following event-event temporal relation extraction methods:

- **BERT+MLP.** Given two events e_i and e_j, we use BERT base model to encode each event and get their embeddings $\boldsymbol{h}_{e_i}^{\text{BERT}}$ and $\boldsymbol{h}_{e_j}^{\text{BERT}}$. Then the temporal relation between e_i and e_j is computed by $r(e_i, e_j) = \text{MLP}(\text{CONCAT}(\boldsymbol{h}_{e_i}^{\text{BERT}}, \boldsymbol{h}_{e_j}^{\text{BERT}}))$.

[4]We do not conduct experiments on another popular dataset MATRES (Ning et al., 2018) because a large portion of the annotated temporal edges in MATRES are redundant and semantically irrelevant.

Methods	Accuracy			Consistency	
	Precision	Recall	F_1	SCR	CCR
BERT+MLP	0.617 ± 0.013	0.655 ± 0.017	0.633 ± 0.016	0.214 ± 0.020	0.130 ± 0.018
GNN+MLP	0.629 ± 0.010	0.663 ± 0.014	0.644 ± 0.011	0.286 ± 0.014	0.170 ± 0.016
Wen and Ji (2021)	$\mathbf{0.692} \pm 0.017$	0.618 ± 0.022	0.652 ± 0.019	0.754 ± 0.026	0.481 ± 0.028
Our method	0.633 ± 0.014	$\mathbf{0.719} \pm 0.019$	$\mathbf{0.673} \pm 0.016$	$\mathbf{1.000} \pm 0.000$	$\mathbf{0.626} \pm 0.020$
Ablations					
- w/o GNN	0.699 ± 0.018	0.613 ± 0.015	0.651 ± 0.017	1.000 ± 0.000	0.592 ± 0.024
- w/o PLM	0.505 ± 0.023	0.684 ± 0.016	0.585 ± 0.020	1.000 ± 0.000	0.513 ± 0.017

Table 2: The results of ternary classification (BEFORE, AFTER, or NO RELATION). The best results are highlighted in bold. SCR and CCR mean "Simple Consistency Rate" and "Correct Consistency Rate", respectively.

Methods	Accuracy			Consistency	
	Precision	Recall	F_1	SCR	CCR
BERT+MLP	0.020 ± 0.015	0.662 ± 0.012	0.038 ± 0.014	0.246 ± 0.013	0.127 ± 0.011
GNN+MLP	0.018 ± 0.012	$\mathbf{0.683} \pm 0.018$	0.035 ± 0.016	0.352 ± 0.010	0.137 ± 0.016
Liu et al. (2021)	0.419	0.625	0.501	-	-
Our method	$\mathbf{0.596} \pm 0.016$	0.632 ± 0.009	$\mathbf{0.618} \pm 0.013$	$\mathbf{1.000} \pm 0.000$	$\mathbf{0.470} \pm 0.017$
Ablations					
- w/o GNN	0.552 ± 0.017	0.572 ± 0.022	0.565 ± 0.019	1.000 ± 0.000	0.431 ± 0.013
- w/o PLM	0.571 ± 0.019	0.585 ± 0.024	0.580 ± 0.022	1.000 ± 0.000	0.368 ± 0.014

Table 3: The results of binary classification (HAVE RELATION or NO RELATION).

- **GNN+MLP.** This is similar to BERT+MLP, except that we use GNN to encode each event and get their embeddings. Specifically, the temporal relation between e_i and e_j is computed by $r(e_i, e_j) = \mathrm{MLP}(\mathrm{CONCAT}(\boldsymbol{h}_{e_i}^{\mathrm{GNN}}, \boldsymbol{h}_{e_j}^{\mathrm{GNN}}))$.
- **Wen and Ji (2021)** propose a joint model for event-event temporal relation classification. It is the state-of-the-art event-event temporal relation extraction approach, which adopts a stack-propagation framework to incorporate relative event time prediction for temporal relation classification.
- **Liu et al. (2021)** propose an event causality identification model. It is an event-event causal relation identification model that uses a mechanism called event mention masking generalization. Note that this model performs a causality existence prediction on Event StoryLine Corpus. To make a fair comparison with this baseline, we modify our model output to binary classification. Specifically, the relation between two events i and j is decided by the distance between two event embeddings $\boldsymbol{e}_i$ and $\boldsymbol{e}_j$: If $\|\boldsymbol{e}_i - \boldsymbol{e}_j\| < \delta$, then $r(e_i, e_j) = \text{HAVE RELATION}$, otherwise $r(e_i, e_j) = \text{NO RELATION}$.

In addition, to examine the effectiveness of using GNN to learn contextual information, we conduct ablation study and design the following reduced version of our model:

- Our method without GNN module, which uses the PLM-based embedding as the event embedding. Instead of Eq. (5), the final embedding of event e_i is $\boldsymbol{e}_i = \boldsymbol{h}_{e_i}^{\mathrm{PLM}}$.
- Our method without PLM module, which uses the GNN-based embedding as the event embedding, i.e., the final embedding of event e_i is $\boldsymbol{e}_i = \boldsymbol{h}_{e_i}^{\mathrm{GNN}}$.

4.3 Experimental Setup

Dataset preprocessing. Our model predicts the relation between events, which is a classification task. The ground truth annotation only includes the relation type BEFORE and AFTER, without NO RELATION. To compare with baselines, we randomly select negative samples from all event pairs that are not in the annotation set, and label them as NO RELATION. The number of negative samples is one half of annotated event pairs for each document to ensure that labels are balanced. To compare with Liu's method (Liu et al., 2021), we merge the BEFORE and AFTER labels to HAVE RELATION, and treat all negative pairs as NO RELATION.

To construct the initial input graph, we first include event nodes which represent event mentions in the ground truth annotations. In addition, there are also annotations of person and location spans in the ground truth annotations. We add the annotations as argument nodes in the initial input graph.

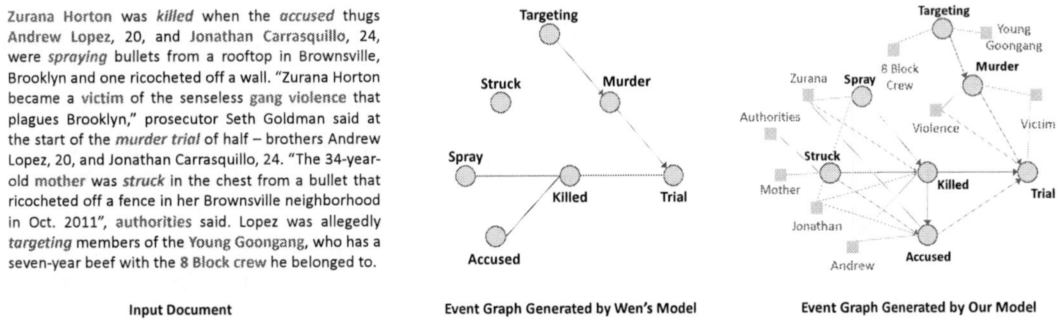

Figure 3: Case study on the quality of generated temporal event graphs. Given the input document, the event graph generated by Wen's model (Wen and Ji, 2021) is drawn in the middle, in which more than one half of edges are inconsistent (highlighted in red). Moreover, it fails to identify the edge STRUCK → KILLED since it does not consider argument information. In contrast, our model predicts all edges precisely and consistently.

We connect an event node and an argument node as an event-argument relation if they belong to the same sentence or consecutive sentences.

Evaluation metrics. We use the following metrics to evaluate our model and baseline methods:

- **Accuracy**. We use $Precision$, $Recall$, and F_1 score to evaluate performance of our model and baseline methods. We report our averaged test performance on 5 random seeds.
- **Consistency**. Note that whether a temporal relation extraction model satisfies global consistency greatly affects its practical reliability. To investigate the global consistency of our model as well as baselines, we exchange the two events in an input event pair, and feed the reversed event pair into the model and obtain the prediction. For a pair of events (e_i, e_j), the consistent prediction of its reversed pair should be

$$r(e_j, e_i) = \begin{cases} \text{BEFORE}, \text{ if } r(e_i, e_j) = \text{AFTER}, \\ \text{AFTER}, \text{ if } r(e_i, e_j) = \text{BEFORE}, \\ \text{NO-REL}, \text{ if } r(e_i, e_j) = \text{NO-REL}. \end{cases}$$

We count the number of event pairs in the test set whose reversed pair has the consistent prediction with the original pair, and define the Simple Consistency Rate (SCR) as

$$\text{SCR} = \frac{\text{\# consistent event pairs}}{\text{\# all event pairs}}.$$

Note that SCR does not consider the model's prediction accuracy. Therefore, we define the Correct Consistency Rate (CCR) as

$$\text{CCR} = \frac{\text{\# consistent and correct event pairs}}{\text{\# all event pairs}}.$$

Hyperparameter Settings. For the GNN module, we use a three-layer GCN as the encoder, whose dimensions of hidden layers are 256, 128, and 16, respectively. For the PLM module, we use BERT base model uncased (Devlin et al., 2018) and the dimensions of the MLP hidden layers in Eq. (2) are 128 and 16, respectively. The learning rate is 10^{-5}, the number of training epochs is 200, and δ is set to 16.

4.4 Results and Analysis

Comparison with baseline methods. The results of ternary and binary classification are reported in Tables 2 and 3, respectively. It is clear that our method achieves substantial gains over all baseline methods in both classification tasks. Specifically, the F1 score of our method surpass the the best baseline method by 2.1% and 11.2% in ternary and binary classification, respectively. This demonstrates that utilizing contextual information of event graphs and preserving the global consistency as well as semantic relevance are essential to improving the performance of event temporal relation extraction.

It is also worth noticing that the Simple Consistency Rate of all baseline methods are significantly lower than our method. Moreover, the Correct Consistency Rate is much lower than the Simple Consistency Rate. This is because these models do not take into account the global consistency during training and thus causing conflicts in prediction results. In contrast, our method is theoretically guaranteed to be globally consistent.

Ablation study. The results of the ablation study are shown in Tables 2 and 3. We observe a substantial performance degradation after removing the GNN module or PLM module from our model. The result demonstrates that both GNN module and PLM module are essential to learning high-quality event representations, since PLM provides general sense of events while GNN explicitly utilizes contextual information in event graphs.

Case study. The example temporal event graphs generated by Wen's model (Wen and Ji, 2021) and our model are drawn in Figure 3. The input document is shown on the left of Figure 3, where texts in blue are event mentions and texts in orange are the annotated named entities (arguments). The graph in the middle is the temporal event graph predicted by Wen's model. We use blue links to denote consistent temporal edges and red links to denote inconsistent temporal edges according to the prediction of Wen's model. We observe that the prediction of Wen's model has inconsistency problem since more than one half of the predicted temporal links are inconsistent. Specifically, the prediction of r(SPRAY, KILLED) is BEFORE whereas the prediction of r(KILLED, SPRAY) is NO RELATION. This is because Wen's model does not consider the consistency issue, thus causes conflicts in its generated temporal event graph. In addition, Wen's model fails to identify the relation between STRUCK and KILLED.

The graph on the right is predicted by our model. The additional green rectangles are arguments. As opposed to the middle graph, all the predictions by our model are correct and consistent. An important reason is that our model takes the contextual information of event graphs into account. For example, there are three named entities connecting STRUCK and KILLED (i.e., JONATHAN, ANDREW, and ZURANA), which provides valuable information to identify the temporal relation between them.

5 Related Work

Event-event temporal relation extraction can be viewed as a classification task that predicts the relation type between two event mentions. In general, existing event-event temporal relation extraction methods can be classified into two categories: traditional rule-based methods and neural network based methods.

The traditional rule-based methods apply linguistic rules to the features extracted from documents to predict the relation between a given event pair. For example, Laokulrat et al. (2013) propose a system that uses a rule-based approach as baseline to determine temporal links and a machine learning classifier to filter out baseline candidates. Chambers et al. (2014) design a sieve-based architecture CAEVO that applies a sequence of temporal relation classifiers to label event-event temporal relations. This supports a combination of both rule-based and machine learned classifiers. However, these rule-based methods require substantial manual design of rules, which greatly limits their usage in practice. Moreover, rules are usually not comprehensive enough to capture the complex event-event temporal relations.

Another line of related work focuses on the neural network based methods, which extracts event-event temporal relations via deep neural networks and pre-trained language models. For example, Wang et al. (2020) introduce a joint constrained learning framework that incorporates contextual features encoded with pre-trained language models and external knowledge from commonsense knowledge bases. Wen and Ji (2021) adopt a stack-propagation framework to combine relative time prediction and event-event temporal relation classification. However, they do not consider global consistency and semantic relevance of the generated event graphs.

6 Conclusion and Future Work

In this paper, we propose a *globally consistent*, *semantically relevant*, and *context aware* event-event relation extraction framework, which addresses the limitations of existing methods. Our model uses a pretrained language model module and graph neural network module to jointly represent event graphs. In addition, we make the event embedding space geometrically meaningful by imposing two constraints on event embeddings: event temporal order should be in accordance with event embedding norm, and event temporal relations should only exist between events whose embeddings are close enough. Experiments demonstrate that our method significantly outperforms baselines by generating accurate and globally consistent temporal event graphs.

In the future, we aim to incorporate external background knowledge and commonsense knowledge into our framework. We also plan to make use of the generated temporal event graphs in downstream tasks, such as future event prediction and question answering.

Limitations

In the current design setting, our proposed model is only able to classify temporal relations between event pairs into one of three classes: BEFORE, AFTER, and NO RELATION. Our model should be more practically useful if we can extend it to predict more relation types in addition to temporal relations, such as PARENT-CHILD and CAUSE-CAUSED_BY relations. We believe that our model is able to make such extension without too much modification.

In addition, as mentioned in the previous section, our model does not make use of any external knowledge, e.g., commonsense knowledge of event temporal relations. Our framework should be more powerful to deal with domain-specific articles if utilizing such knowledge in the framework.

Ethical Considerations

We acknowledge that our work is aligned with the *ACL Code of the Ethics* (Gotterbarn et al., 2018) and will not raise ethical concerns. We do not use sensitive datasets/models that may cause any potential issues. The design, implementation, and evaluation of our proposed method are robust and secure.

References

Philip Bramsen, Pawan Deshpande, Yoong Keok Lee, and Regina Barzilay. 2006. Inducing temporal graphs. In *Proceedings of the 2006 Conference on Empirical Methods in Natural Language Processing*, pages 189–198. Citeseer.

Tommaso Caselli and Piek Vossen. 2017. The event storyline corpus: A new benchmark for causal and temporal relation extraction. In *Proceedings of the Events and Stories in the News Workshop*, pages 77–86.

Nathanael Chambers, Taylor Cassidy, Bill McDowell, and Steven Bethard. 2014. Dense event ordering with a multi-pass architecture. *Transactions of the Association for Computational Linguistics*, 2:273–284.

Jacob Devlin, Ming-Wei Chang, Kenton Lee, and Kristina Toutanova. 2018. Bert: Pre-training of deep bidirectional transformers for language understanding. *arXiv preprint arXiv:1810.04805*.

Dmitriy Dligach, Timothy Miller, Chen Lin, Steven Bethard, and Guergana Savova. 2017. Neural temporal relation extraction. In *Proceedings of the 15th Conference of the European Chapter of the Association for Computational Linguistics: Volume 2, Short Papers*, pages 746–751.

Xinya Du, Zixuan Zhang, Sha Li, Pengfei Yu, Hongwei Wang, Tuan Manh Lai, Xudong Lin, Ziqi Wang, Iris Liu, Ben Zhou, et al. 2022. Resin-11: Schema-guided event prediction for 11 newsworthy scenarios. In *Proc. 2022 Annual Conference of the North American Chapter of the Association for Computational Linguistics (NAACL2022) System Demonstration Track*.

Goran Glavaš and Jan Šnajder. 2014. Event graphs for information retrieval and multi-document summarization. *Expert systems with applications*, 41(15):6904–6916.

DW Gotterbarn, Bo Brinkman, Catherine Flick, Michael S Kirkpatrick, Keith Miller, Kate Vazansky, and Marty J Wolf. 2018. Acm code of ethics and professional conduct.

Rujun Han, Qiang Ning, and Nanyun Peng. 2019. Joint event and temporal relation extraction with shared representations and structured prediction. In *Proceedings of the 2019 Conference on Empirical Methods in Natural Language Processing and the 9th International Joint Conference on Natural Language Processing, EMNLP-IJCNLP 2019, Hong Kong, China, November 3-7, 2019*, pages 434–444. Association for Computational Linguistics.

Rujun Han, Yichao Zhou, and Nanyun Peng. 2020. Domain knowledge empowered structured neural net for end-to-end event temporal relation extraction. In *Proceedings of the 2020 Conference on Empirical Methods in Natural Language Processing (EMNLP)*, pages 5717–5729.

Xiaomeng Jin, Manling Li, and Heng Ji. 2022. Event schema induction with double graph autoencoders. In *Proceedings of the 2022 Conference of the North American Chapter of the Association for Computational Linguistics: Human Language Technologies*, pages 2013–2025.

Thomas N. Kipf and Max Welling. 2017. Semi-supervised classification with graph convolutional networks. In *5th International Conference on Learning Representations, ICLR 2017, Toulon, France, April 24-26, 2017, Conference Track Proceedings*. OpenReview.net.

Natsuda Laokulrat, Makoto Miwa, Yoshimasa Tsuruoka, and Takashi Chikayama. 2013. Uttime: Temporal relation classification using deep syntactic features. In *Second Joint Conference on Lexical and Computational Semantics (* SEM), Volume 2: Proceedings of the Seventh International Workshop on Semantic Evaluation (SemEval 2013)*, pages 88–92.

Manling Li, Sha Li, Zhenhailong Wang, Lifu Huang, Kyunghyun Cho, Heng Ji, Jiawei Han, and Clare Voss. 2021. Future is not one-dimensional: Graph modeling based complex event schema induction for event prediction. *arXiv preprint arXiv:2104.06344*.

Zhongyang Li, Xiao Ding, and Ting Liu. 2018. Constructing narrative event evolutionary graph for script event prediction. *arXiv preprint arXiv:1805.05081*.

Jian Liu, Yubo Chen, and Jun Zhao. 2021. Knowledge enhanced event causality identification with mention masking generalizations. In *Proceedings of the Twenty-Ninth International Conference on International Joint Conferences on Artificial Intelligence*, pages 3608–3614.

Yi Luan, Dave Wadden, Luheng He, Amy Shah, Mari Ostendorf, and Hannaneh Hajishirzi. 2019. A general framework for information extraction using dynamic span graphs. *arXiv preprint arXiv:1904.03296*.

Qiang Ning, Hao Wu, and Dan Roth. 2018. A multi-axis annotation scheme for event temporal relations. *arXiv preprint arXiv:1804.07828*.

Franco Scarselli, Marco Gori, Ah Chung Tsoi, Markus Hagenbuchner, and Gabriele Monfardini. 2008. The graph neural network model. *IEEE transactions on neural networks*, 20(1):61–80.

Tarcísio Souza Costa, Simon Gottschalk, and Elena Demidova. 2020. Event-qa: A dataset for event-centric question answering over knowledge graphs. In *Proceedings of the 29th ACM International Conference on Information & Knowledge Management*, pages 3157–3164.

Duc-Thuan Vo and Ebrahim Bagheri. 2019. Extracting temporal event relations based on event networks. In *European Conference on Information Retrieval*, pages 844–851. Springer.

Haoyu Wang, Muhao Chen, Hongming Zhang, and Dan Roth. 2020. Joint constrained learning for event-event relation extraction. *arXiv preprint arXiv:2010.06727*.

Hongwei Wang, Zixuan Zhang, Sha Li, Jiawei Han, Yizhou Sun, Hanghang Tong, Joseph P. Olive, and Heng Ji. 2022. Schema-guided event graph completion. In *arXiv*.

Jiexin Wang, Adam Jatowt, Michael Färber, and Masatoshi Yoshikawa. 2021. Improving question answering for event-focused questions in temporal collections of news articles. *Information Retrieval Journal*, 24(1):29–54.

Haoyang Wen and Heng Ji. 2021. Utilizing relative event time to enhance event-event temporal relation extraction. In *Proceedings of the 2021 Conference on Empirical Methods in Natural Language Processing*, pages 10431–10437.

Haoyang Wen, Ying Lin, Tuan Lai, Xiaoman Pan, Sha Li, Xudong Lin, Ben Zhou, Manling Li, Haoyu Wang, Hongming Zhang, et al. 2021. Resin: A dockerized schema-guided cross-document cross-lingual cross-media information extraction and event tracking system. In *Proceedings of the 2021 Conference of the North American Chapter of the Association for Computational Linguistics: Human Language Technologies: Demonstrations*, pages 133–143.

COFFEE: A Contrastive Oracle-Free Framework for Event Extraction

Meiru Zhang♠ **Yixuan Su**♠ **Zaiqiao Meng**♠◇
Zihao Fu♠ **Nigel Collier**♠
♠Language Technology Lab, University of Cambridge
◇School of Computing Science, University of Glasgow
♠{mz468, ys484, zf268, nhc30}@cam.ac.uk
◇zaiqiao.meng@glasgow.ac.uk

Abstract

Event extraction is a complex task that involves extracting events from unstructured text. Prior classification-based methods require comprehensive entity annotations for joint training, while newer generation-based methods rely on heuristic templates containing oracle information such as event type, which is often unavailable in real-world scenarios. In this study, we consider a more realistic task setting, namely the Oracle-Free Event Extraction (OFEE) task, where only the input context is given, without any oracle information including event type, event ontology, or trigger word. To address this task, we propose a new framework, COFFEE. This framework extracts events solely based on the document context, without referring to any oracle information. In particular, COFFEE introduces a contrastive selection model to refine the generated triggers and handle multi-event instances. Our proposed COFFEE outperforms state-of-the-art approaches in the oracle-free setting of the event extraction task, as evaluated on two public variants of the ACE05 benchmark. The code used in our study has been made publicly available[1].

1 Introduction

The event extraction task aims to identify events and their arguments from the given textual input context (Nguyen et al., 2016; Wadden et al., 2019; Yang et al., 2019). Conventionally, this task can be decomposed into four sub-tasks (Nguyen et al., 2016): (i) detecting the trigger word that most directly describes the event; (ii) event type classification for defining its event-specific attributes; (iii) argument identification and (iv) argument classification that maps the argument entities to the corresponding role attributes based on the structure of each event type, namely event schema. For instance, Figure 1 shows the input context of an event extraction example that contains two events:

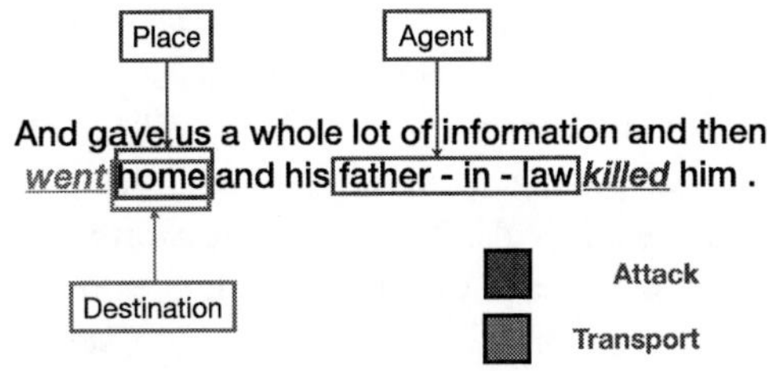

Figure 1: An event extraction example with two events: **Transport** and **Attack**. In the 'Transport' event, '*went*' is the trigger word, and 'home' is the 'Destination' argument. In the 'Attack' event, '*killed*' is the trigger word while 'father-in-law' and 'home' are the 'Agent' and 'Place' arguments, respectively.

a 'Transport' event triggered by the trigger word 'went' and an 'Attack' event triggered by the trigger word 'killed', where 'Transport' and 'Attack' are two event types.

Many prior studies formulate the event extraction task as a token-level classification problem, which extracts event triggers and arguments using sequence tagging models based on tailor-designed neural networks (Nguyen et al., 2016; Liu et al., 2018; Li et al., 2019; Yang et al., 2019; Wadden et al., 2019; Huang et al., 2020; Lin et al., 2020; Nguyen et al., 2021). However, such methods cannot leverage rich label semantics since the target outputs (e.g., event triggers and arguments) are fixed tagging labels. Recently, with advances in generative pre-trained language models, several generation-based approaches (Hsu et al., 2022; Huang et al., 2022; Li et al., 2021; Zhang et al., 2021) have been applied to solve this problem. These approaches transform the event extraction task into a conditional generation task. By utilizing the autoregressive generation nature of generative pre-trained language models (e.g., BART-Gen (Li et al., 2021), DEGREE (Hsu et al., 2022)) and some manual prompts, it becomes possible to harness the semantics of labels and conduct both entity extraction and classification in an autoregressive manner simultaneously.

[1]https://github.com/meiru-cam/COFFEE

Proceedings of the First Workshop on Matching From Unstructured and Structured Data (MATCHING 2023), pages 33–44
July 13, 2023 ©2023 Association for Computational Linguistics

While impressive results are reported, we identify two major limitations of the current generation-based event extraction methods. Firstly, most of these methods rely on heuristic templates and extensive human knowledge engineering. According to the experiments conducted by Hsu et al. (2022), a slight change in the template might lead to significant performance changes, thus raising the issue of using sub-optimal templates. Secondly, most of these generation-based approaches still require certain oracle information, such as event type and event schema, which necessitate extensive manual annotations. For example, the DEGREE model's inference process, as demonstrated by Hsu et al. (2022), requires manually designed event-specific templates for each example and iterates over all event types. On the other hand, Text2Event (Lu et al., 2021) also constrains the generation with manually designed templates, which require event schema to be given. However, obtaining this oracle information, such as event type and schema, is unrealistic for a real-world inference system to achieve automatically. Hence, this paper aims to address the Oracle-Free Event Extraction (OFEE) task where only the input context is given.

In this study, we propose a novel Contrastive Oracle-Free Framework for Event Extraction (COFFEE), which addresses the event extraction task without using any oracle information. Our COFFEE consists of two parts, a generator that performs the extraction of events and a selector that aims to refine the generated results. The generator of our COFFEE generates both the candidate triggers and event arguments, where the shared generator allows for cross-task knowledge sharing between these sub-tasks. The selector of our COFFEE learns to re-rank and select the candidate triggers to obtain more accurate trigger predictions, which is inspired by (Su et al., 2021). One challenge of the sentence-level event extraction is that a sentence may contain more than one event record (Si et al., 2022; Subburathinam et al., 2019) (e.g., the example in Figure 1), and event specific templates can help the model to identify and extract events in a targeted manner. Prior approaches tackling this challenge have necessitated either multi-label tagging (Ramponi et al., 2020; Lin et al., 2020), event-specific templates (Hsu et al., 2022), or multi-turn question answering techniques (Du and Cardie, 2020; Li et al., 2020). In contrast, our proposed model can concurrently generate and select multiple event candidates, encompassing both the event trigger and its associated type, thereby effectively addressing the aforementioned challenge.

The contribution of this work is as follows:

- We highlight the challenge of the current event extraction task setting and introduce the oracle-free setting of this task that requires the model to produce the structural event without using oracle information beyond the context.
- We propose COFFEE, a novel Contrastive Oracle-Free Framework for Event Extraction which use a generator and a selector to generatively obtain structural event information from context without using any oracle information.
- We conduct experiments on two variants of the ACE05 benchmark under the oracle-free setting to evaluate our COFFEE. The results demonstrate that the template-based baselines heavily rely on the additional oracle information, whereas our COFFEE exhibits superior empirical performance over these baselines in the absence of an oracle.

2 Task Definition

Conventionally, the event extraction task entails the following terminologies (Nguyen et al., 2016; Liu et al., 2020; Paolini et al., 2021).

- *Input Context*: The input sentence or sentences that contain one or more events.
- *Trigger Word*: The main word that most clearly expresses the occurrence of an event (e.g., words 'went' and 'killed' in Figure 1).
- *Event Type*: The event type that defines the semantic structure of a specific event (e.g., events 'Transport' and 'Attack' in Figure 1).
- *Event Argument*: Event arguments identify the entities involved in events and their roles based on their relationships with the event triggers. An entity can be an object, place or person that participates in the event. For example, 'home' is an entity that serves as both the 'Place' argument of the 'Transport' event and the 'Destination' argument of the 'Attack' event in Figure 1.

Given the input context $\mathbf{c}$, which is a sequence of tokens $[c_1, \cdots, c_n]$, the conventional event extraction task aims to identify the trigger words, classify the events triggered by these words and extract the arguments in each of the events with their

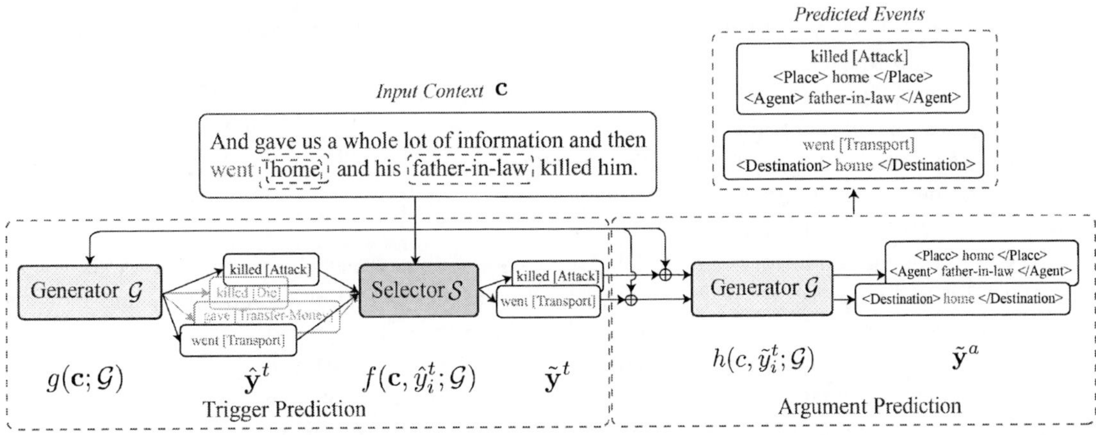

Figure 2: Overview of our proposed COFFEE framework. We train $\mathcal{G}$ to generate trigger candidates $\hat{\mathbf{y}}^t$ that contain trigger word and event type first. These trigger candidates then used to train $\mathcal{S}$ to select the final trigger predictions $\tilde{\mathbf{y}}^t$. In the argument prediction stage, the trained generator is re-used to generate arguments $\tilde{\mathbf{y}}^a$ based on $\tilde{\mathbf{y}}^t$ selected by $\mathcal{S}$. Only the input context $\mathbf{c}$ is required to predict events.

corresponding roles (Nguyen et al., 2016; Chen et al., 2015). Assume that an input sentence context $\mathbf{c}$ contains $|e|$ different events, then its ground truth triggers $\mathbf{y}^t$ can be represented as $[y_1^t, \cdots, y_{|e|}^t]$, where y_i^t denotes the i-th trigger word and event type of the given context sentence. For each event, there is a list of ground truth arguments, denoted by $\mathbf{y}^a$, which is a list of $\langle$*role, argument*$\rangle$ pairs, i.e., $\mathbf{y}^a = [\langle r_1, a_1\rangle, \cdots, \langle r_m, a_m\rangle]$, where a_j is the j-th entity participating in the event and r_j is the corresponding role type for that entity.

For this conventional event extraction task, the current state-of-the-art generation-based approaches rely on manual templates, which require trigger words or event types to be given, to simplify this task (Hsu et al., 2022; Lu et al., 2021). However, in a realistic scenario, although argument roles are event-specific, gold trigger words or event type information may not be readily available during event argument extraction We focus on the Oracle-Free Event Extraction (OFEE) task, which presents a more practical scenario by only providing the input context during inference. The goal of OFEE is to infer event triggers and arguments without relying on pre-defined event specific templates, making it more challenging to solve due to the absence of external guidance or oracle information.

3 Methodology

As mentioned in the task definition, our goal is to extract event frames without using any templates. This adds complexity to the generation model, particularly when dealing with contexts containing multiple events, such as the example given in Figure 1. To address the challenging OFEE task, we propose a novel contrastive framework called COFFEE, which comprises two primary components: a generator $\mathcal{G}$, responsible for generating event frames present in the provided context, and a selector $\mathcal{S}$, which re-ranks and selects the triggers generated by $\mathcal{G}$. In our proposed COFFEE framework, $\mathcal{G}$ is fine-tuned using ground truth triggers and arguments (i.e. $\mathbf{y}^t$ and $\mathbf{y}^a$) to generate candidate triggers $\hat{\mathbf{y}}^t$ and arguments $\tilde{\mathbf{y}}^a$ (see §3.1). At the inference stage, $\mathcal{S}$ is fine-tuned to refine and select final trigger predictions $\tilde{\mathbf{y}}^t$ based on the generated candidate triggers $\hat{\mathbf{y}}^t$ and gold triggers $\mathbf{y}$ on the training set (see §3.2). The final trigger predictions are forwarded to $\mathcal{G}$ for argument prediction (see §3.1). We next present the details of COFFEE's components, i.e. the generator and the selector.

3.1 Generator

The generator is fine-tuned on both trigger prediction and argument prediction simultaneously by training on the pairs of instances with different prefixes 'TriggerEvent: ' and 'Argument: ' (see §4.4). In order to take the context as input and generate structured event frames, the generator $\mathcal{G}$ of COFFEE is employed using an encoder-decoder transformer model, such as BART, T5 and mT5 (Lewis et al., 2020; Raffel et al., 2020; Xue et al., 2021). We resort T5 (Raffel et al., 2020) as the base model and encode only '[and]' and '[none]' as additional special tokens based on experimental results.

During the inference stage, we apply beam search (Jelinek, 1976) to generate candidate triggers $\hat{\mathbf{y}}^t$ and output the beam score of these triggers. Given the context $\mathbf{c}$, the generator outputs the top-l triggers with the highest beam scores, denoted by $\hat{\mathbf{y}}^t = g(\mathbf{c}; \mathcal{G})$, where $\hat{\mathbf{y}}^t$ is a list of triggers $[\hat{y}_1^t, \cdots, \hat{y}_l^t]$, with beam scores $[b_1, \cdots, b_l]$, and $\hat{y}_i^t$ represents a generated candidate trigger in the context $\mathbf{c}$. After obtaining the list of candidate triggers, we use a contrastive-learning based selector $\mathcal{S}$ (see §3.2 for details) to further re-rank the generated candidates using $f(\mathbf{c}, \hat{\mathbf{y}}^t; \mathcal{S})$ and select the final set of trigger predictions $\tilde{\mathbf{y}}^t$. The predicted trigger words are then concatenated to the context iteratively, and the generator performs argument prediction on each event using $h(\mathbf{c}, \tilde{y}_i^t; \mathcal{G})$. Specifically, given the input $[c_1, \cdots, c_n, \tilde{y}_i^t]$, G generates $\tilde{\mathbf{y}}^a = [\langle \tilde{r}_1, \tilde{a}_1 \rangle, \cdots, \langle \tilde{r}_m, \tilde{a}_m \rangle]$ for a predicted trigger $\tilde{y}_i^t$.

3.2 Selector

In our approach, we employ contrastive learning to re-rank the candidate triggers $\hat{\mathbf{y}}^t$. Contrastive learning (Chen et al., 2020) is a technique that aims to learn meaningful representations by maximizing the similarity between positive pairs while minimizing the similarity between negative pairs. In the context of our problem, we define the ground truth triggers $\mathbf{y}^t$ for context $\mathbf{c}$ as the positive anchors, while the negative samples are the other incorrect candidates generated, i.e., $\hat{y}_j^t \notin \mathbf{y}^t$.

To apply contrastive learning for re-ranking, we first encode the context and candidate triggers using a shared encoder. Specifically, given a list of candidate triggers $\hat{\mathbf{y}}^t$, for each $\hat{y}_i^t \in \hat{\mathbf{y}}^t$ we concatenate it to the context and use $\mathcal{S}$ to map the concatenated text $[\mathbf{c} : \hat{y}_i^t]$ into a real-valued ranking score by preforming linear projection $f(\mathbf{c}, \hat{y}_i^t; \mathcal{S})$. In this study, we employ RoBERTa (Liu et al., 2019) as the backbone selector model to encode the text input, and $\mathcal{S}$ predicts the ranking score for each of the candidate triggers in $\hat{\mathbf{y}}^t$ through optimizing over a contrastive objective $\mathcal{L}_{\mathcal{S}}$, which encourages $\mathcal{S}$ to predict higher scores for true trigger candidates and lower scores for false trigger candidates.

Formally, given a context $\mathbf{c}$ and the generated candidate triggers $\hat{\mathbf{y}}^t$, $\mathcal{S}$ is fine-tuned to optimize:

$$\mathcal{L}_{\mathcal{S}} = \sum_{i=1}^{|e|} \sum_{j=1}^{k} \max\{0, \rho - f(\mathbf{c}, y_i^t; \mathcal{S}) + f(\mathbf{c}, \hat{y}_j^t; \mathcal{S})\}, \quad (1)$$

where $\hat{y}_j^t \notin \mathbf{y}^t$, $\rho \in [-1, 1]$ is a pre-defined margin and k represents the number of negatives sampled from $\hat{\mathbf{y}}^t$. By taking into account the implicit correlation between the context and generated candidates, $\mathcal{S}$ captures the semantic relevance between context and correct trigger candidates, thus enhancing trigger extraction and positively impacting the performance of argument extraction.

		ACE05-E		ACE05-E+	
	# sent	# triggers	# args	# triggers	# args
train	17172	4202	4859	4419	6607
val	923	450	605	468	759
test	832	403	576	424	689

Table 1: The statistics of our used datasets.

Since the number of events in the context is unknown, we use a threshold to automatically control the number of events predicted. Let α represent the weight parameter and θ represent the threshold parameter in our model. These hyperparameters are used for combining the beam score b_i with the ranking score s_i and filtering out the false candidate triggers, respectively. We determine the threshold θ and the weight α on the development set, which is exclusively utilized for hyperparameter tuning, to ensure an unbiased evaluation on the test set. The final set of trigger predictions is defined as $\tilde{\mathbf{y}}^t = \{\tilde{y}_1^t, \cdots, \tilde{y}_{|\tilde{\mathbf{y}}^t|}^t\}$, which satisfies that $\forall \tilde{y}_i^t$,

$$\alpha \cdot \sigma(f(\mathbf{c}, \tilde{y}_i^t; \mathcal{S})) + (1 - \alpha) \cdot \sigma(b_i) > \theta, \quad (2)$$

where σ denotes the softmax function.

4 Experiments

4.1 Dataset

In this work, we evaluate our COFFEE based on a public event extraction benchmark ACE05 (Walker and Consortium, 2005), which consists of 599 English documents, 33 event types, and 22 argument roles. Building upon previous works (Wadden et al., 2019; Lin et al., 2020) that split and preprocess this dataset, we use two variants for the event extraction dataset, namely **ACE05-E** and **ACE05-E+**. Detailed split and statistics of the two datasets can be found in Table 1.

4.2 Evaluation Metrics

The evaluation of trigger identification, event type classification, argument identification, and argument role classification tasks utilizes the F1-score metric, consistent with the previous studies (Zhang et al., 2019; Wadden et al., 2019). A correct trigger classification prediction requires accurate trigger word and event type prediction, i.e., $\tilde{y}_i^t = y_i^t$. Correct argument identification necessitates accurate classification of the event type and argument entity, while a correct argument role classification demands accurate identification of the argument and role type prediction. Specifically, a predicted event type $\tilde{t}_e$, argument $\tilde{a}$, and role type $\tilde{r}$ are considered correct if $(\tilde{a}, \tilde{r}, \tilde{t}_e) = (a, r, t_e)$.

4.3 Baselines

To validate the effectiveness of our proposed method, we compared our COFFEE with five state-of-the-art baselines:

- **OneIE** (Lin et al., 2020) is a joint neural model that simultaneously extracts entities and relations using a dynamic relation graph.
- **Text2Event** (Lu et al., 2021) is a sequence-to-structure controlled generation model with constrained decoding for event extraction. It focuses on the structured generation that uses event schema to form event records.
- **BART-Gen** (Li et al., 2021) is designed for document-level event extraction that can deal with the long-distance dependence issue and co-reference problem. Constrained generation is applied for argument extraction that requires event-specific templates.
- **DEGREE** (Hsu et al., 2022) is a generative event extraction approach that highly relies on the designed template.
- **TANL** (Paolini et al., 2021) is a model that extracts event triggers and arguments by so called augmented translation that embeds target outputs into the context sentence.

4.4 Implementation

We preprocess the data by separating original samples into event samples and inserting placeholders for target entities. The instances are processed with distinct prefixes for subtasks: 'TriggerEvent: ' and 'Arguments: '. Figure 3 shows a data preprocessing example. Details pertaining to our pipeline training and inference process, including specifics about the two-stage fine-tuning, such as the learning rate and batch size, as well as the beam search strategy employed during inference, are elaborated in Appendix A.1.

5 Results

5.1 OFEE performance

As described in Section 4.3, Text2Event, BART-Gen and DEGREE utilize different oracle information. To compare the performance of our COFFEE framework with these methods under the OFEE setting, we implemented the following adaptations to these baseline approaches:

Input:
"*TriggerEvent:* And gave ... then went home ... killed him .",
"*Arguments:* And gave ... then went home ... killed him . <*Trigger*> killed",
"*TriggerEvent:* And gave ... then went home ... killed him .",
"*Arguments:* And gave ... then went home ... killed him. < *Trigger*> went",

Target:
"killed [Life_Die]",
"<*Agent*> father - in - law </*Agent*> . . . <*Place*> home </ *Place* >",
"went [Movement_Transport]",
"<*Artifact*> [None] </*Artifact*> . . . <*Place*> [None] </*Place*>",

Figure 3: Example of input and target for the model.

- Text2Event (Lu et al., 2021) relies on a complex constrained decoding mechanism that depends on the event schema. For the oracle-free setting, we utilized the default decoding of the T5 model to generate results.
- BART-Gen (Li et al., 2021) adopts a constrained generation mechanism, which necessitates the use of templates. We removed the template and the constrained decoding, thereby enabling the model to function. The trigger extraction performance of BART-Gen is not reported in our study due to an implementation error stemming from different preprocessing methods, which prevented us from applying this approach to the ACE-05E+ dataset. Consequently, we depended on the ground truth triggers for argument extraction in this instance.
- The DEGREE (Hsu et al., 2022) model is designed to generate 'invalid' instances during both the training and inference phases, wherein event-specific knowledge is combined with context even if no such event is mentioned in the context. We eliminated these event-specific templates, leaving only the context sentence as input.

As presented in Table 2, we report F1 scores of the compared methods over four sub-tasks described in 4.1, namely trigger identification, trigger classification, argument identification, and argument classification. We observe the following:

- Firstly, it is crucial to highlight that the oracle-free setting poses a more challenging scenario. When all oracle information is removed, generation-based baselines relying on templates exhibit a varying degree of performance decline on both datasets ($\downarrow$ 0.5% to 37.42% in argument classification). Although DEGREE is effective with the oracle information, it struggles to filter

	Model	ACE-05E				ACE-05E+			
		Trig I	Trig C	Arg I	Arg C	Trig I	Trig C	Arg I	Arg C
	OneIE	76.83	73.05	57.26	54.31	77.31	74.01	56.66	54.29
	Text2Event♮	73.93	69.06	51.59	49.52	73.40	68.99	52.64	50.39
	BARTGen♮	74.36	71.13	55.22	53.71	-	-	66.62	64.28
	DEGREE♮◇♭	74.57	70.96	56.03	53.41	74.90	70.30	55.74	53.61
Oracle Free	Text2Event	73.49	68.60	51.24	49.32	72.73	68.30	52.48	50.35
Oracle Free	BARTGen	70.96	66.59	48.47	46.36	-	-	51.43	47.49
Oracle Free	DEGREE	43.64	2.18†	28.54	25.99	54.32	2.26†	30.09	28.79
Oracle Free	TANL	**81.10**	**77.09**	55.28	52.16	**80.28**	**76.03**	54.56	52.57
Oracle Free	**COFFEE**	<u>79.61</u>	<u>75.73</u>	**59.88**	**55.43**	<u>78.28</u>	<u>74.70</u>	<u>56.87</u>	<u>54.11</u>
Oracle Free	+*TANL*	**81.10**	**77.09**	<u>58.74</u>	<u>55.24</u>	**80.28**	**76.03**	**59.78**	**57.06**

Table 2: Performance comparison of COFFEE and SOTA generation-based approaches. † The trigger classification F1 of DEGREE is nearly zero because the model cannot exclude the negative samples constructed without a template.♮, ◇, and ♭ denote the model that requires a manually designed template, example keywords, and event description, respectively. The highest results are in **bold** and the second highest results are <u>underlined</u>.

out the 'invalid' events in the oracle-free setting, resulting in an almost zero (2.18%) trigger classification F1. This indicates that the information leaked in the template significantly contributes to the performance of DEGREE.

- Our proposed COFFEE outperforms the classification-based approach OneIE and the generation-based approaches Text2Event, BARTGen, and DEGREE in both the presence and absence of oracle information across **all four metrics**. This demonstrates that our COFFEE can effectively leverage the input context to extract event frames.
- In comparison to TANL, our COFFEE achieves similar results in trigger extraction, with a difference of only 1.36%. One possible explanation is that the threshold-based method results in a smaller recall value due to more false positives. However, our model possesses robust argument extraction capabilities and attained superior performance in argument extraction with these extracted triggers (↑ 3.33% and ↑ 2.46% on ACE-05E and ACE05E+, respectively). These findings corroborate the effectiveness of the shared generator on trigger and argument prediction.

5.2 Ablation study

We conducted an ablation study on the threshold and weight parameters to demonstrate the effectiveness of our selector $\mathcal{S}$ and the influence of these parameters on the COFFEE performance.

Figure 4 illustrates the effect of the threshold parameter on COFFEE. The threshold determines the minimum score a candidate must achieve to be selected. Increasing the threshold results in fewer candidates being selected but with higher accuracy. Conversely, an overly high threshold could filter out some of the correct candidates, decreasing performance. The optimal threshold value is 0.2, which achieves the best performance on all four subtasks.

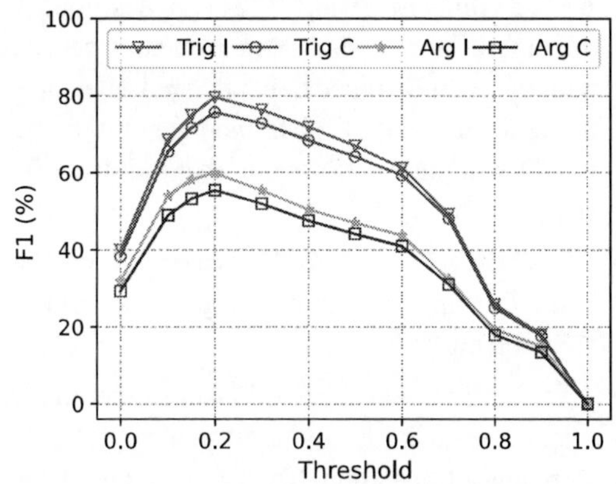

Figure 4: Effect of threshold in COFFEE framework.

In addition, Figure 5 demonstrates the influence of the weight parameter on COFFEE. The weight represents the ratio of combining the ranking score and generation score. When the weight is set to 0, only the generation score is considered, while a weight of 1 means that only the ranking score is considered. As depicted in Figure 5, the best extraction performance is achieved with a fixed threshold and an optimal weight value of $\alpha = 0.4$. The initial improvement in the F1 score with increasing weight suggests that the ranking score can effectively refine the results of the beam search.

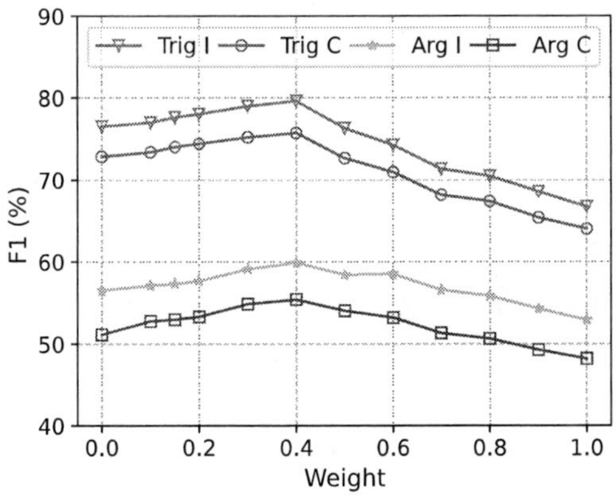

Figure 5: The influence of the weight α on performance.

However, the ranking scores exhibit significant variations, leading to a corresponding fluctuation in softmax probability as the weight increases. As the final probability becomes increasingly reliant on the ranker probability, fewer candidates are selected at the same threshold, resulting in a decline in performance.

5.3 Qualitative Case Analysis

In order to demonstrate the ability of our model to select event candidates, we analyze the results of two instances selected from the test set. For comparison, we select COFFEE without ranking and TANL, given its high performance. As shown in Table 3, our proposed model successfully extracts the missing events not detected by the baselines. The re-ranking mechanism enables the model to select more accurate candidates.

In particular, only COFFEE successfully predicts all the events within the context. In Example 1, both TANL and COFFEE without ranking fail to extract **E1**, triggered by 'pay', suggesting that the baselines may have difficulty identifying complex event triggers. In this case, there is not a specific amount of money to be paid, but a mention of cost. In Example 2, TANL fails to extract **E2**, which is triggered by 'becoming', and COFFEE without ranking fails to extract **E1**, highlighting the inability of the baselines to identify events and their corresponding arguments consistently. In contrast, our COFFEE successfully identifies the events and extracts the target arguments, demonstrating its superior performance.

Comparing COFFEE with and without ranking, we can conclude that re-ranking in the selector is crucial. In both examples, COFFEE fails to detect all events without re-ranking. Even though both candidates are the correct targets, the beam scores differ more than expected, which leads to incorrect ranking. The re-ranking can increase the probability of the second candidate and thus allowing it to be selected under the chosen threshold.

These examples demonstrate the improvements in event extraction offered our selector S, which allows the framework to re-rank and select the correct triggers for multi-event instances, outperforming the baselines and establishing our model as a more effective and reliable solution for OFEE tasks.

6 Related Work

6.1 Event Extraction

Early event extraction research primarily relied on rule-based methods involving hand-written patterns to identify event triggers and arguments in text (Li et al., 2013, 2015). Supervised machine learning techniques became popular, with various feature-based classification models employed (Hsi et al., 2016). However, these methods faced limitations due to manual feature engineering and the need for large annotated datasets. Researchers then turned to deep learning approaches, utilizing convolutional neural networks (CNNs) (Chen et al., 2015; Nguyen and Grishman, 2015; Björne and Salakoski, 2018; Yang et al., 2019), recurrent neural networks (RNNs) (Nguyen et al., 2016), and Tree-LSTM (Li et al., 2019) for event extraction, which automatically learned relevant features and improved performance.

The introduction of pre-trained language models revolutionized event extraction. Fine-tuning these models achieved state-of-the-art performance across various benchmarks (Lin et al., 2020; Ramponi et al., 2020; Wadden et al., 2019; Yang et al., 2021). These models captured deep contextual information and benefited from knowledge transfer, enhancing performance with limited annotated data. Some studies framed event extraction as a multi-turn question answering task (Du and Cardie, 2020; Li et al., 2020; Liu et al., 2020; Zhou et al., 2021), while others approached it as a sequence-to-sequence generation task (Hsu et al., 2022; Lu et al., 2021; Li et al., 2021). Although effective, these methods heavily relied on manually designed prompts and templates, except for Text2Event (Paolini et al., 2021), which depended solely on context information. In contrast, our work focuses on oracle-free event extraction and addresses the task via generation without tem-

	Example 1	
Context	Kommersant business daily joined in , declaring in a furious front - page headline : " The United States is demanding that Russia , France and Germany pay for the Iraqi war .	
Reference	**E1**: pay [Transfer-Money]	**Args**: [Giver] Germany
	E2: war [Attack]	**Args**: [Place] Iraqi
TANL + COFFEE	**E1**:	**Args**:
	E2: war [Attack]	**Args**: [Place] Iraq
COFFEE w/o Ranker	**E1**:	**Args**:
	E2: war [Attack]	**Args**: [Place] Iraq
COFFEE	**E1**: pay [Transfer-Money]	**Args**: [Giver] Germany
	E2: war [Attack]	**Args**: [Place] Iraq

	Example 2	
Context	Welch specifically is seeking performance evaluations , correspondence between his estranged wife and partners while she worked at the law firm 's office in London , and documents related to her prospects of becoming a partner .	
Reference	**E1**: correspondence [Phone-Write]	**Args**: [Entity] partners; [Place] office
	E2: becoming [Start-Position]	**Args**: [Entity] firm
TANL + COFFEE	**E1**: correspondence [Phone-Write]	**Args**: [Entity] partners; [Place] office
	E2:	**Args**:
COFFEE w/o Ranker	**E1**:	**Args**:
	E2: becoming [Start-Position]	**Args**:
COFFEE	**E1**: correspondence [Phone-Write]	**Args**: [Entity] partners; [Place] office
	E2: becoming [Start-Position]	**Args**:

Table 3: Event extraction examples from the test set using COFFEE, COFFEE without ranking and TANL+COFFEE. The triggers and arguments missed by the baselines but captured by COFFEE are highlighted. It is evident that COFFEE is generally more effective in detecting the events.

plates. The most recent studies have focused on event detection or event argument extraction separately (Zhang et al., 2022; Huang et al., 2022; Ma et al., 2022), which is not directly comparable to our study as we consider the complete event extraction process.

6.2 Post-Generation Ranking

Post-generation re-ranking is usually applied in two-stage systems, that is, generation and re-ranking, to re-score the output from the first stage by training an additional re-ranking module. This technique has been widely used in neural translation and summarization. For example, Ng et al. (2019); Yee et al. (2019) re-score and select the best hypotheses using Noisy Channel Modeling to improve translation quality. Zhong et al. (2020) formulate the summarization as text matching and re-ranks the summary candidates based on similarity score. Liu and Liu (2021) introduce an additional scoring model with contrastive training to predict the score of generated summaries. Both methods utilize a margin-based ranking loss that initializes candidates with orders. For the event trigger selection, we assume that the beam score is not a reliable indicator and consequently treat the candidates equally. Su et al. (2021) use a contrastive re-ranking module with hinge loss to select prototypes for a table-to-text generation. To the best of our knowledge, our work is the first to focus on enhancing the oracle-free generation-based event extraction models using re-ranking.

7 Conclusion

In this work, we study a more realistic setting of the event extraction task, namely the oracle-free event extraction, where no additional information beyond the context is required for event inference. To address this task, we propose a generation-based event extraction framework called COFFEE. Our COFFEE introduces a contrastive selector to improve trigger extraction performance by re-ranking and automatically determining the number of triggers to be selected in a given context. Additionally, we investigate the dependence of current generation-based models on extra knowledge, such as designed event-specific templates, event trigger keywords, and event descriptions. Our results show that this reliance on templates and human-designed trigger sets is unnecessary, and a pure oracle-free model applied directly can perform very well on general event extraction. In the future, we plan to extend sentence-level event extraction to document-level and explore zero-shot settings to handle the emergence of unseen events.

8 Limitations

Despite its promising results, our study has limitations. Our model primarily works with English text, limiting its applicability to other languages. Its focus on sentence-level extraction doesn't consider document context, which could be investigated in future research. The employed training dataset is relatively small, potentially not encompassing all possible event types, thus affecting the model's performance and generalizability. Additionally, our two-stage inference framework, while enhanced by a ranking module, is prone to error propagation. If a trigger isn't identified in the first stage, its associated arguments cannot be extracted. Future work should address these issues for improved performance and broader applicability.

9 Ethics Statement

In preparing and submitting this research paper, we affirm that our work adheres to the highest ethical standards and is devoid of any ethical issues. The study presented in the manuscript was conducted in a manner that respects the principles of academic integrity, transparency, and fairness.

References

Jari Björne and Tapio Salakoski. 2018. Biomedical event extraction using convolutional neural networks and dependency parsing. In *Proceedings of the BioNLP 2018 workshop*, pages 98–108, Melbourne, Australia. Association for Computational Linguistics.

Ting Chen, Simon Kornblith, Mohammad Norouzi, and Geoffrey E. Hinton. 2020. A simple framework for contrastive learning of visual representations. In *Proceedings of the 37th International Conference on Machine Learning, ICML 2020, 13-18 July 2020, Virtual Event*, volume 119 of *Proceedings of Machine Learning Research*, pages 1597–1607. PMLR.

Yubo Chen, Liheng Xu, Kang Liu, Daojian Zeng, and Jun Zhao. 2015. Event extraction via dynamic multi-pooling convolutional neural networks. In *Proceedings of the 53rd Annual Meeting of the Association for Computational Linguistics and the 7th International Joint Conference on Natural Language Processing (Volume 1: Long Papers)*, pages 167–176, Beijing, China. Association for Computational Linguistics.

Xinya Du and Claire Cardie. 2020. Event extraction by answering (almost) natural questions. In *Proceedings of the 2020 Conference on Empirical Methods in Natural Language Processing (EMNLP)*, pages 671–683, Online. Association for Computational Linguistics.

Andrew Hsi, Yiming Yang, Jaime Carbonell, and Ruochen Xu. 2016. Leveraging multilingual training for limited resource event extraction. In *Proceedings of COLING 2016, the 26th International Conference on Computational Linguistics: Technical Papers*, pages 1201–1210, Osaka, Japan. The COLING 2016 Organizing Committee.

I-Hung Hsu, Kuan-Hao Huang, Elizabeth Boschee, Scott Miller, Prem Natarajan, Kai-Wei Chang, and Nanyun Peng. 2022. DEGREE: A data-efficient generation-based event extraction model. In *Proceedings of the 2022 Conference of the North American Chapter of the Association for Computational Linguistics: Human Language Technologies*, pages 1890–1908, Seattle, United States. Association for Computational Linguistics.

Kuan-Hao Huang, I-Hung Hsu, Prem Natarajan, Kai-Wei Chang, and Nanyun Peng. 2022. Multilingual generative language models for zero-shot cross-lingual event argument extraction. In *Proceedings of the 60th Annual Meeting of the Association for Computational Linguistics (Volume 1: Long Papers)*, pages 4633–4646, Dublin, Ireland. Association for Computational Linguistics.

Kung-Hsiang Huang, Mu Yang, and Nanyun Peng. 2020. Biomedical event extraction with hierarchical knowledge graphs. In *Findings of the Association for Computational Linguistics: EMNLP 2020*, pages 1277–1285, Online. Association for Computational Linguistics.

Frederick Jelinek. 1976. Continuous speech recognition by statistical methods. *Proceedings of the IEEE*, 64(4):532–556.

Mike Lewis, Yinhan Liu, Naman Goyal, Marjan Ghazvininejad, Abdelrahman Mohamed, Omer Levy, Veselin Stoyanov, and Luke Zettlemoyer. 2020. BART: Denoising sequence-to-sequence pre-training for natural language generation, translation, and comprehension. In *Proceedings of the 58th Annual Meeting of the Association for Computational Linguistics*, pages 7871–7880, Online. Association for Computational Linguistics.

Diya Li, Lifu Huang, Heng Ji, and Jiawei Han. 2019. Biomedical event extraction based on knowledge-driven tree-LSTM. In *Proceedings of the 2019 Conference of the North American Chapter of the Association for Computational Linguistics: Human Language Technologies, Volume 1 (Long and Short Papers)*, pages 1421–1430, Minneapolis, Minnesota. Association for Computational Linguistics.

Fayuan Li, Weihua Peng, Yuguang Chen, Quan Wang, Lu Pan, Yajuan Lyu, and Yong Zhu. 2020. Event extraction as multi-turn question answering. In *Findings of the Association for Computational Linguistics: EMNLP 2020*, pages 829–838, Online. Association for Computational Linguistics.

Qi Li, Heng Ji, and Liang Huang. 2013. Joint event extraction via structured prediction with global features. In *Proceedings of the 51st Annual Meeting of the Association for Computational Linguistics (Volume 1: Long Papers)*, pages 73–82, Sofia, Bulgaria. Association for Computational Linguistics.

Sha Li, Heng Ji, and Jiawei Han. 2021. Document-level event argument extraction by conditional generation. In *Proceedings of the 2021 Conference of the North American Chapter of the Association for Computational Linguistics: Human Language Technologies*, pages 894–908, Online. Association for Computational Linguistics.

Xiang Li, Thien Huu Nguyen, Kai Cao, and Ralph Grishman. 2015. Improving event detection with Abstract Meaning Representation. In *Proceedings of the First Workshop on Computing News Storylines*, pages 11–15, Beijing, China. Association for Computational Linguistics.

Ying Lin, Heng Ji, Fei Huang, and Lingfei Wu. 2020. A joint neural model for information extraction with global features. In *Proceedings of the 58th Annual Meeting of the Association for Computational Linguistics*, pages 7999–8009, Online. Association for Computational Linguistics.

Jian Liu, Yubo Chen, Kang Liu, Wei Bi, and Xiaojiang Liu. 2020. Event extraction as machine reading comprehension. In *Proceedings of the 2020 Conference on Empirical Methods in Natural Language Processing (EMNLP)*, pages 1641–1651, Online. Association for Computational Linguistics.

Jian Liu, Yubo Chen, Kang Liu, and Jun Zhao. 2018. Event detection via gated multilingual attention mechanism. In *Proceedings of the Thirty-Second AAAI Conference on Artificial Intelligence, (AAAI-18), the 30th innovative Applications of Artificial Intelligence (IAAI-18), and the 8th AAAI Symposium on Educational Advances in Artificial Intelligence (EAAI-18), New Orleans, Louisiana, USA, February 2-7, 2018*, pages 4865–4872. AAAI Press.

Yinhan Liu, Myle Ott, Naman Goyal, Jingfei Du, Mandar Joshi, Danqi Chen, Omer Levy, Mike Lewis, Luke Zettlemoyer, and Veselin Stoyanov. 2019. Roberta: A robustly optimized bert pretraining approach. *ArXiv preprint*, abs/1907.11692.

Yixin Liu and Pengfei Liu. 2021. SimCLS: A simple framework for contrastive learning of abstractive summarization. In *Proceedings of the 59th Annual Meeting of the Association for Computational Linguistics and the 11th International Joint Conference on Natural Language Processing (Volume 2: Short Papers)*, pages 1065–1072, Online. Association for Computational Linguistics.

Ilya Loshchilov and Frank Hutter. 2017. Fixing weight decay regularization in adam. *CoRR*, abs/1711.05101.

Yaojie Lu, Hongyu Lin, Jin Xu, Xianpei Han, Jialong Tang, Annan Li, Le Sun, Meng Liao, and Shaoyi Chen. 2021. Text2Event: Controllable sequence-to-structure generation for end-to-end event extraction. In *Proceedings of the 59th Annual Meeting of the Association for Computational Linguistics and the 11th International Joint Conference on Natural Language Processing (Volume 1: Long Papers)*, pages 2795–2806, Online. Association for Computational Linguistics.

Yubo Ma, Zehao Wang, Yixin Cao, Mukai Li, Meiqi Chen, Kun Wang, and Jing Shao. 2022. Prompt for extraction? PAIE: Prompting argument interaction for event argument extraction. In *Proceedings of the 60th Annual Meeting of the Association for Computational Linguistics (Volume 1: Long Papers)*, pages 6759–6774, Dublin, Ireland. Association for Computational Linguistics.

Nathan Ng, Kyra Yee, Alexei Baevski, Myle Ott, Michael Auli, and Sergey Edunov. 2019. Facebook FAIR's WMT19 news translation task submission. In *Proceedings of the Fourth Conference on Machine Translation (Volume 2: Shared Task Papers, Day 1)*, pages 314–319, Florence, Italy. Association for Computational Linguistics.

Minh Van Nguyen, Viet Dac Lai, and Thien Huu Nguyen. 2021. Cross-task instance representation interactions and label dependencies for joint information extraction with graph convolutional networks. In *Proceedings of the 2021 Conference of the North American Chapter of the Association for Computational Linguistics: Human Language Technologies*, pages 27–38, Online. Association for Computational Linguistics.

Thien Huu Nguyen, Kyunghyun Cho, and Ralph Grishman. 2016. Joint event extraction via recurrent neural networks. In *Proceedings of the 2016 Conference of the North American Chapter of the Association for Computational Linguistics: Human Language Technologies*, pages 300–309, San Diego, California. Association for Computational Linguistics.

Thien Huu Nguyen and Ralph Grishman. 2015. Event detection and domain adaptation with convolutional neural networks. In *Proceedings of the 53rd Annual Meeting of the Association for Computational Linguistics and the 7th International Joint Conference on Natural Language Processing (Volume 2: Short Papers)*, pages 365–371, Beijing, China. Association for Computational Linguistics.

Giovanni Paolini, Ben Athiwaratkun, Jason Krone, Jie Ma, Alessandro Achille, Rishita Anubhai, Cícero Nogueira dos Santos, Bing Xiang, and Stefano Soatto. 2021. Structured prediction as translation between augmented natural languages. In *9th International Conference on Learning Representations, ICLR 2021, Virtual Event, Austria, May 3-7, 2021*. OpenReview.net.

Colin Raffel, Noam Shazeer, Adam Roberts, Katherine Lee, Sharan Narang, Michael Matena, Yanqi Zhou, Wei Li, Peter J Liu, et al. 2020. Exploring the limits of transfer learning with a unified text-to-text transformer. *J. Mach. Learn. Res.*, 21(140):1–67.

Alan Ramponi, Rob van der Goot, Rosario Lombardo, and Barbara Plank. 2020. Biomedical event extraction as sequence labeling. In *Proceedings of the 2020 Conference on Empirical Methods in Natural Language Processing (EMNLP)*, pages 5357–5367, Online. Association for Computational Linguistics.

Jinghui Si, Xutan Peng, Chen Li, Haotian Xu, and Jianxin Li. 2022. Generating disentangled arguments with prompts: A simple event extraction framework that works. In *ICASSP 2022-2022 IEEE International Conference on Acoustics, Speech and Signal Processing (ICASSP)*, pages 6342–6346. IEEE.

Yixuan Su, Zaiqiao Meng, Simon Baker, and Nigel Collier. 2021. Few-shot table-to-text generation with prototype memory. In *Findings of the Association for Computational Linguistics: EMNLP 2021*, pages 910–917, Punta Cana, Dominican Republic. Association for Computational Linguistics.

Ananya Subburathinam, Di Lu, Heng Ji, Jonathan May, Shih-Fu Chang, Avirup Sil, and Clare Voss. 2019. Cross-lingual structure transfer for relation and event extraction. In *Proceedings of the 2019 Conference on Empirical Methods in Natural Language Processing and the 9th International Joint Conference on Natural Language Processing (EMNLP-IJCNLP)*, pages 313–325, Hong Kong, China. Association for Computational Linguistics.

David Wadden, Ulme Wennberg, Yi Luan, and Hannaneh Hajishirzi. 2019. Entity, relation, and event extraction with contextualized span representations. In *Proceedings of the 2019 Conference on Empirical Methods in Natural Language Processing and the 9th International Joint Conference on Natural Language Processing (EMNLP-IJCNLP)*, pages 5784–5789, Hong Kong, China. Association for Computational Linguistics.

C. Walker and Linguistic Data Consortium. 2005. *ACE 2005 Multilingual Training Corpus*. LDC corpora. Linguistic Data Consortium.

Thomas Wolf, Lysandre Debut, Victor Sanh, Julien Chaumond, Clement Delangue, Anthony Moi, Pierric Cistac, Tim Rault, Rémi Louf, Morgan Funtowicz, et al. 2019. Huggingface's transformers: State-of-the-art natural language processing. *ArXiv preprint*, abs/1910.03771.

Linting Xue, Noah Constant, Adam Roberts, Mihir Kale, Rami Al-Rfou, Aditya Siddhant, Aditya Barua, and Colin Raffel. 2021. mT5: A massively multilingual pre-trained text-to-text transformer. In *Proceedings of the 2021 Conference of the North American Chapter of the Association for Computational Linguistics: Human Language Technologies*, pages 483–498, Online. Association for Computational Linguistics.

Hang Yang, Dianbo Sui, Yubo Chen, Kang Liu, Jun Zhao, and Taifeng Wang. 2021. Document-level event extraction via parallel prediction networks. In *Proceedings of the 59th Annual Meeting of the Association for Computational Linguistics and the 11th International Joint Conference on Natural Language Processing (Volume 1: Long Papers)*, pages 6298–6308, Online. Association for Computational Linguistics.

Sen Yang, Dawei Feng, Linbo Qiao, Zhigang Kan, and Dongsheng Li. 2019. Exploring pre-trained language models for event extraction and generation. In *Proceedings of the 57th Annual Meeting of the Association for Computational Linguistics*, pages 5284–5294, Florence, Italy. Association for Computational Linguistics.

Kyra Yee, Yann Dauphin, and Michael Auli. 2019. Simple and effective noisy channel modeling for neural machine translation. In *Proceedings of the 2019 Conference on Empirical Methods in Natural Language Processing and the 9th International Joint Conference on Natural Language Processing (EMNLP-IJCNLP)*, pages 5696–5701, Hong Kong, China. Association for Computational Linguistics.

Junchi Zhang, Yanxia Qin, Yue Zhang, Mengchi Liu, and Donghong Ji. 2019. Extracting entities and events as a single task using a transition-based neural model. In *Proceedings of the Twenty-Eighth International Joint Conference on Artificial Intelligence, IJCAI 2019, Macao, China, August 10-16, 2019*, pages 5422–5428. ijcai.org.

Ningyu Zhang, Hongbin Ye, Shumin Deng, Chuanqi Tan, Mosha Chen, Songfang Huang, Fei Huang, and Huajun Chen. 2021. Contrastive information extraction with generative transformer. *IEEE/ACM Transactions on Audio, Speech, and Language Processing*, 29:3077–3088.

Senhui Zhang, Tao Ji, Wendi Ji, and Xiaoling Wang. 2022. Zero-shot event detection based on ordered contrastive learning and prompt-based prediction. In *Findings of the Association for Computational Linguistics: NAACL 2022*, pages 2572–2580, Seattle, United States. Association for Computational Linguistics.

Ming Zhong, Pengfei Liu, Yiran Chen, Danqing Wang, Xipeng Qiu, and Xuanjing Huang. 2020. Extractive summarization as text matching. In *Proceedings of the 58th Annual Meeting of the Association for Computational Linguistics*, pages 6197–6208, Online. Association for Computational Linguistics.

Yang Zhou, Yubo Chen, Jun Zhao, Yin Wu, Jiexin Xu, and Jinlong Li. 2021. What the role is vs. what plays the role: Semi-supervised event argument extraction via dual question answering. In *Proceedings of the AAAI conference on artificial intelligence*, volume 35, pages 14638–14646.

A Appendices

A.1 Implementation Details

Our pipeline training comprises two stages: generation model fine-tuning and re-ranking model fine-tuning. The T5-base model (Raffel et al., 2020) fine-tuning is achieved through the HuggingFace Transformers library (Wolf et al., 2019) on an RTX3090 GPU, using an AdamW optimizer (Loshchilov and Hutter, 2017), with a learning rate of 0.0001 with a decay schedule of 1e-5. We set a batch size of 8 and maximum input/output sequence lengths at 650/200.

For inference, we generate candidate triggers using a beam search strategy with 10 beams. These candidates are then re-ranked and filtered by the selector $\mathcal{S}$, based on optimal thresholds and weights derived through grid search.

In the second stage, we fine-tune a RoBERTa-base model (Liu et al., 2019) for re-ranking. This stage reduces the maximum input length to 512 and sets the number of negative candidates for contrastive learning to 5, with a learning rate of 0.005.

Upon refining triggers, they are concatenated to the context and reintroduced to the generator for argument generation via a greedy search. The final extraction of entities and roles is conducted using regular expressions. Our COFFEE generator and selector take approximately 4 hours and 2 hours to train, respectively.

Performance evaluation of the trigger and argument extraction is based on regular expressions to detect entities extracted from the placeholders. The results can be observed in Table 2.

Corpus-Based Task-Specific Relation Discovery

Karthik Venkat Ramanan
University of Illinois Urbana-Champaign
kv16@illinois.edu

Abstract

Relation extraction is a crucial language processing task for various downstream applications, including knowledge base completion, question answering, and summarization. Traditional relation-extraction techniques, however, rely on a predefined set of relations and model the extraction as a classification task. Consequently, such closed-world extraction methods are insufficient for inducing novel relations from a corpus. Unsupervised techniques like OpenIE, which extract `<head, relation, tail>` triples, generate relations that are too general for practical information extraction applications. In this work, we contribute the following: 1) We motivate and introduce a new task, corpus-based task-specific relation discovery. 2) We adapt existing data sources to create Wiki-Art, a novel dataset for task-specific relation discovery. 3) We develop a novel framework for relation discovery using zero-shot entity linking, prompting, and type-specific clustering. Our approach effectively connects unstructured text spans to their shared underlying relations, bridging the data-representation gap and significantly outperforming baselines on both quantitative and qualitative metrics. Our code and data are available in our GitHub repository.[1]

1 Introduction

Relation extraction (RE) aims to identify semantic relationships between entities in text in order to obtain triples of the form `<head, relation, tail>`, for instance, `<Washington D.C., capital_of, USA>`. RE is an important Information Extraction (IE) technique primarily used to complete knowledge bases (such as YAGO[2] and NELL[3]) and construct semantic graphs (Vashishth et al., 2018). Knowledge bases and semantic graphs see wide application in tasks such as question-answering (Saxena et al., 2020; Das et al., 2017), recommendation (Zhang et al., 2016), and natural language inference (Peters et al., 2019).

Traditional relation extraction techniques approach the problem as a multi-class classification problem, and hence assume a predefined set of relations. Open Information Extraction (OpenIE) approaches (Angeli et al., 2015; Mausam et al., 2012) seek to remedy this problem by extracting relations from text without a predefined schema. But recent work (Schneider et al., 2017) has shown that in the absence of a schema, OpenIE results tend to be uninformative or redundant. Moreover, OpenIE systems are tuned for high recall and hence extract a very general set of tuples and defer the problem of sifting through the generated triples to find meaningful ones to subsequent analysis.

We now introduce the problem of task-specific relation discovery. Discovering unseen relations from a corpus serves two functions. Firstly, it serves as a starting point to fine-tune relation extraction models on novel relations and unseen domains. Secondly, it is intuitively appealing as a data mining task to gather actionable insights from a large unstructured corpus. Say, for instance, we are presented with a collection of recent documents reporting on the COVID-19 pandemic. Discovering all the relationships between *viral variants* and *cities in Ohio* in the corpus would allow us to detect relations such as "declining in", "spreading in" and "endemic in". This would allow us to automatically identify if there are areas of concern where viral spread is increasing. We define a task as a pair of semantic types (such as Humans, Geographic Locations, Sports Teams, etc.) between which we are interested in relations. A few concrete examples of this formulation can be seen in figure 1.

In this work, we propose a novel solution to this problem in three steps. First, we identify candidate spans for relation discovery using zero-shot entity

[1] https://github.com/karthik63/relation-discovery
[2] https://yago-knowledge.org/
[3] http://rtw.ml.cmu.edu/rtw/kbbrowser/

Proceedings of the First Workshop on Matching From Unstructured and Structured Data (MATCHING 2023), pages 45–57
July 13, 2023 ©2023 Association for Computational Linguistics

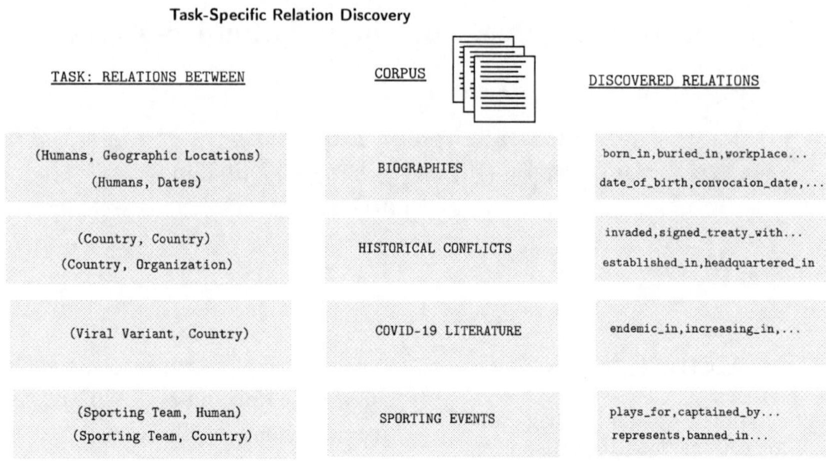

Figure 1: The formulation of corpus-based task-specific relation discovery.

linking and typing. Then we use a self-supervised prompting technique using an encoder-decoder transformer architecture (Lewis et al., 2019) to discover relation phrases that describe the relationship between the two entities. Finally, we cluster these discovered phrases while keeping the head and tail semantic types of our relations in mind.

We briefly summarize our contributions below

- We introduce a new task of corpus-based task-specific relation discovery and modify existing data sources to make available Wiki-Art, a new dataset for the same
- We propose a novel approach to extract candidate sentences, then discover and cluster unseen relations that significantly outperforms our baselines on both qualitative and quantitative metrics.

2 Related Work

The three lines of work most relevant to our approach are relation extraction, open information extraction, and prompting.

2.1 Relation Extraction

Most traditional relation extraction approaches model RE as a sequence classification task with specific accommodations for challenges arising from distant supervision. Models using piecewise CNNs (Zeng et al., 2015), reinforcement learning (Feng et al., 2018), and relationship side information have been proposed to mitigate the noise from sentences where ground-truth relations are not expressed.

2.2 Open Information Extraction

OpenIE seeks to produce domain-agnostic, unsupervised `<head, relation, tail>` extractions from a text span. Traditional approaches (Angeli et al., 2015; Mausam et al., 2012) to OpenIE use a combination of automatically mined and hand-crafted templates for relation extraction from the syntactic features and surface-forms of a sentence. These patterns are often mined using bootstrapping (Kolluru et al., 2020) where the triple extractions from multiple OpenIE approaches are aggregated to form a supervised training set using statistical rules.

2.3 Prompting

Prompting approaches (Liu et al., 2021) solve language processing tasks by eliciting natural language responses from language models rather than by training a classification layer. Relevant to our work, prompting has been successfully adapted to solve challenges such as few-shot event detection (Li et al., 2022) and event argument extraction (Ma et al., 2022; Li et al., 2021). Prompting can also be used to probe the inherent relational knowledge of pretrained language models by aggregating the masked language model generations from multiple hand-crafted prompts (Jiang et al., 2021).

3 Problem Definition

In this section, we formally define corpus-based task-specific relation discovery.

A corpus is a collection of documents from any domain. For simplicity, let our corpus $\mathcal{S} = [S_1, S_2, ..S_{|\mathcal{S}|}]$ be a sequence of sentences

S_i. A sentence $S_i = [w_{i,1}, w_{i,2}, ... w_{i,|S_i|}]$ is a sequence of words $w_i \in \mathcal{V}$. Our task $\mathcal{P} = \{(\mathcal{H}_1, \mathcal{T}_1), (\mathcal{H}_2, \mathcal{T}_2), ..(\mathcal{H}_{|\mathcal{P}|}, \mathcal{T}_{|\mathcal{P}|})\}$ is a set of $\mathcal{H}_i$ **head**, $\mathcal{T}_i$ **tail** semantic type tuples. $\mathcal{T} = \{(h_1, r_1, t_1), ...(h_{|\mathcal{T}|}, r_{|\mathcal{T}|}, t_{|\mathcal{T}|})\}$ represents the set of ground-truth head-relation-tail **triples** expressed in $\mathcal{S}$ such that $(h_i, t_i) \in \{(x_j, y_j)|(x_j, y_j) \in (\mathcal{H}_1, \mathcal{T}_1) \cup ... \cup (\mathcal{H}_{|\mathcal{P}|}, \mathcal{T}_{|\mathcal{P}|})\}$. That is, they only correspond to the task outlined using the head and tail semantic types.

Our end task is to discover the set of relations $\mathcal{R} = \{r_1, r_2, ... r_{|\mathcal{R}|}\}$ that occur in $\mathcal{T}$, without assuming any prior knowledge about the relations in $\mathcal{T}$ other than the head and tail semantic types.

4 Methodology

Our overall architecture is illustrated in figure 2. Our procedure for relation discovery comprises three steps that we detail below- 1. We identify relevant entities and extract candidate spans of sentences to perform discovery on. 2. We discover the relation phrases that explain the relation between the head and tail entities. 3. We cluster the extracted relation phrases.

4.1 Extracting Candidate Spans for Discovery

Extracting candidate spans for relation discovery requires that we identify when semantic types of interest, outlined by our task $\mathcal{P}$, co-occur in a paragraph. We require this entity typing process to have both high precision in order to avoid incorrect relation discoveries and high recall, so we don't miss infrequent relations in our corpus. We propose the following procedure (illustrated in Figure 3) that meets both of these requirements. We utilize the BLINK(Ott et al., 2019) framework for both named entity recognition and zero-shot entity linking to Wikipedia. The advantage of using a zero-shot entity linker is that we can swap the Wikipedia index out for a more recent one, if needed, in order to handle newer entities. We then make use of the Wikipedia API[4] in order to identify the Wikidata[5] ID of the linked entity. With an entity's Wikidata ID we first identify its type using the P31 *"instance of"* edge in the Wikidata KB. We then establish if it belongs to one of our pre-specified semantic classes by traversing the Wikidata taxonomy through the P279 *"subclass of"* edge until we reach the root node. If the concept node corresponding to one of our semantic classes (e.g. human, country, film) is an ancestor of the type node, we identify the entity as such. If entities from both the head and tail semantic classes co-occur in a paragraph, it is selected as a candidate span to perform relation discovery on.

[4]https://en.wikipedia.org/w/api.php

[5]https://www.wikidata.org/

Property Name	Property Definition	Property Aliases
discoverer or inventor (P61)	subject who discovered, first described, invented, or developed this discovery or invention	inventor, discoverer, inventor or discoverer, developer, coined, first described, invented by, created by, invented, discovered by, developed by, introduced by, devised by

Table 1: Example relation aliases for the relation *"discoverer or inventor"* (P61)

4.2 Identifying Novel Relation Phrases

We propose a prompting strategy to identify relation phrases between head and tail entities. We use the encoder-decoder transformer model BART (Lewis et al., 2019) and bootstrap from existing data sources in order to fine-tune the model for relation generation. Wikidata catalogs relation (property) aliases along with relations (example in table 1). We use the distant supervision setting explained in section 5 to identify paragraphs in which entities that have a relation in the Wikidata KB. Among these paragraphs, we filter out ones in which one of the aliases of the relation between the two entities does not occur. The semi-supervised data to train our prompting models comprises this filtered set of paragraphs and their corresponding head, tail entities, and relation surface-forms.

We experiment with a number of different prompting strategies. The optimal prompt variation, as determined by the results, is illustrated in Figure 4. The remaining three prompting strategies are presented in the appendix (Figure 6). Comparisons of the results of the different strategies on relation identification and unsupervised relation discovery are presented in tables 3 and 4, respectively. We briefly explain these different strategies below. `<ARG>`, `</ARG>`, `<HEAD>`, `</HEAD>`, `<TAIL>`, `</TAIL>`, `<PRED>` and `</PRED>` are all additional trainable embeddings that are fine-tuned with the rest of the model. `<MASK>` is the same mask token embedding used in BART's pre-training tasks.

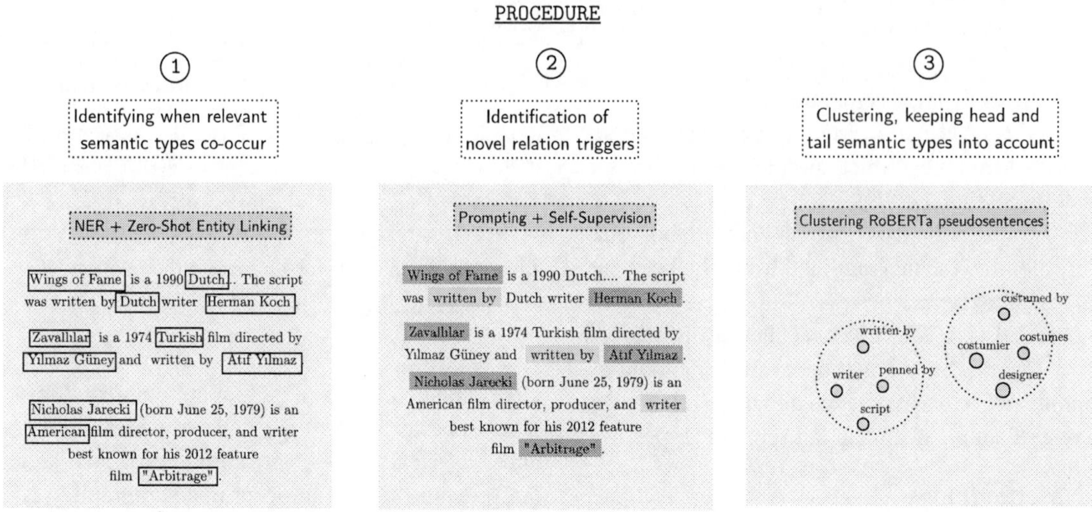

Figure 2: The overall architecture of our relation discovery model.

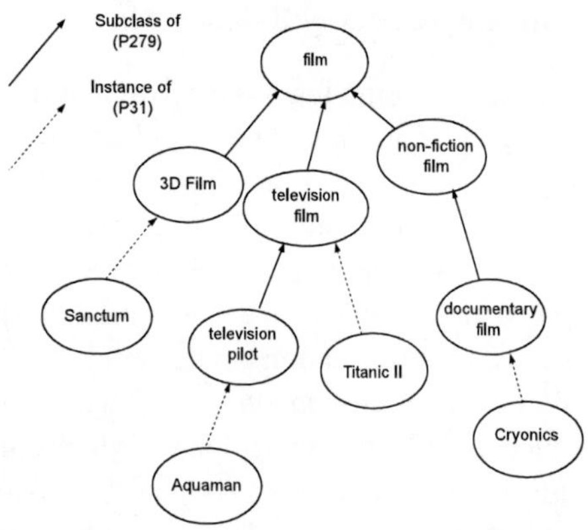

Figure 3: An illustration of our entity typing procedure.

4.2.1 Prompt Variations

Vanilla Prompt: The input to the encoder and the decoder target of BART are illustrated in fig. 6a. The input to the encoder is the candidate paragraph concatenated with the surface forms of the head and tail entities separated by the <MASK> token. The decoder is expected to reconstruct the input and generate the relation alias in place of <MASK>

d1 & d2: These variations are illustrated in figures 6b and 6c. In these variations, the decoder is only expected to generate the relation and entity surface-forms.

del: This variation is illustrated in figure 4. We introduce six additional trainable token vectors to delimit the head and tail in the encoder input and the head, tail and predicate in the decoder target. These trainable vectors serve a dual role. They act as an additional signal to the language model to help identify the head and tail entities for relation extraction and make the relation phrase easier to isolate during post-processing.

4.3 Clustering

Once we obtain the generated relation phrases, we aim to cluster phrases that denote the same underlying relation together in embedding space. Crucial to this step is the disambiguation between relations with the same surface form. For instance, the phrase *"written by"* corresponds to the relation *screenwriter* if it occurs between a human and a movie and the relation *author* if it occurs between a human and a comic book. To address this, we construct pseudosentences using the head and tail semantic types and the relation phrase. For instance, the generated relation phrase *"voiced by"* between a head of semantic type human and a tail of semantic type movie would result in the sentence *"Film voiced by human."*. We obtain the mean-pooled RoBERTa(Liu et al., 2019) embeddings of these pseudosentences and perform k-means clustering on them. The effect of including the head and tail types to our clustering process is shown in table 5. The results of clustering for unsupervised relation discovery is shown in table 4.

5 Dataset

In this section, we briefly describe our dataset Wiki-Art. We utilize the paragraphs scraped us-

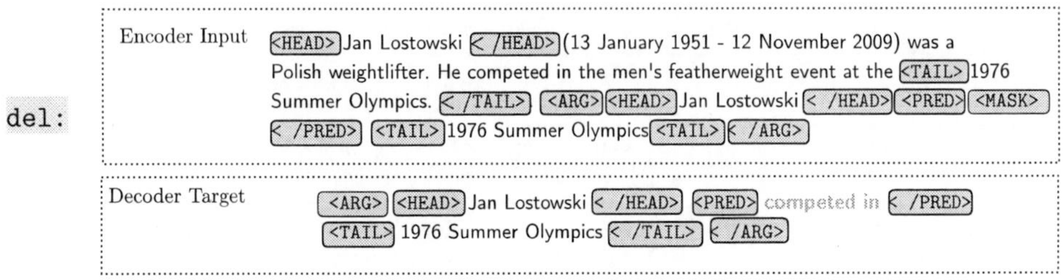

Figure 4: The highest-performing prompting strategy, **Prompt-del**; additional approaches are discussed in §4.2.1 and illustrated in Figure 6.

ing distant supervision from the REBEL dataset (Huguet Cabot and Navigli, 2021). Under the distant supervision setting, a paragraph containing a head and tail entity is assumed to express a relation between two entities if the two entities are related in a background knowledge base (Wikidata in our case). Head and tail entities are identified using the links from anchor texts. We extract 326 documents (Wikipedia abstracts) from the Wikipedia pages of movies and comic books. The statistics of our dataset are shown in table 2.

We briefly explain the difference between the two settings- *unsupervised relation discovery* and *corpus-based relation discovery*.

Unsupervised Relation Discovery: To compare different IE models on discovery using fully quantitative metrics, we require a uniform number of test instances. So we only evaluate discovery on paragraphs that contain head and tail entities that we know to have a ground-truth relation between them. That is, we ignore paragraphs that contain entities with the head and tail semantic types outlined by our task if the entities do not have a relation between them in Wikidata. The six relations in table 2 are the relations that occur with the highest frequency in our corpus with at least forty occurrences.

Corpus-Based Relation Discovery: Clearly, for realistic relation discovery from a corpus, we can not assume pre-existing knowledge base information to filter out false-positive paragraphs where our task's semantic types co-occur but a relation isn't expressed. So, in this case, we perform discovery on all the paragraphs that contain both task semantic types. In this setting, the model is required to discover all nineteen task-specific relations expressed in the corpus, not just the six most common ones.

6 Experimental Setup

We describe our baselines, metrics and the details of the three experimental settings for relation identification, unsupervised relation discovery and corpus-based relation discovery.

Compared Models We compare the performance of our model against two SOTA OpenIE approaches.

- `Stanford-OpenIE` (Angeli et al., 2015) uses fourteen hand-crafted patterns defined over a dependency parse of the input text sequence in order to identify relational triples.
- `OpenIE5`[6] combines four approaches- CALMIE(Saha and Mausam, 2018), BONIE(Saha et al., 2017), RelNoun(Pal and Mausam, 2016) and SRLIE(Christensen et al., 2011) to extract relational triples. It uses a combination of hand-crafted and automatically mined patterns using syntactic and surface-form information.

6.1 Relation Identification

The purpose of this experiment is to evaluate the relative performance of different models on identifying a relation between two entities directly. As the same relation between two entities can be expressed in a number of ways, we perform this evaluation manually. We report the proportion of instances where the relation is identified accurately among the same 30 randomly sampled paragraphs. The results are shown in table 3.

6.2 Unsupervised Relation Discovery

The distinction between unsupervised relation discovery and corpus-based relation discovery is explained in section 5. The purpose of this experiment is to determine relative performance on relation discovery quantitatively. We report three

[6] `github:dair-iitd/openie-standalone`

Task	#Data	#Relations	Target Relations
Unsupervised Relation Discovrery	813 Paragraphs	6	colorist, prod. designer, dir. of photography, after a work by, screewriter, director
Corpus-Based Relation Discovrery	326 Documents	19	librettist, inspired by, screenwriter, main subject, participant, director, producer, author, after a work by, production designer, choreographer, director of photography, voice actor, film editor, creator, based on, illustrator, cast member, notable work. composer, colorist

Table 2: Dataset Statistics

commonly used clustering metrics. Adjusted Rand Index (**ARI**) measures the number of item pairs in the same vs. different clusters compared to the ground truth label assignment. Normalized Mutual Information (**NMI**) measures the mutual information between assigned and ground-truth cluster assignments. Permutation Accuracy (**ACC**) measures the accuracy between assigned clusters and ground-truth class labels with the best possible permutation matching clusters to labels. The results are shown in table 4.

6.3 Corpus-Based Relation Discovery

This experiment measures the proportion of ground truth relations (table 2) in a corpus we identify using our end-to-end procedure. We follow the same procedure outlined by Huang et al. to evaluate our models. We cluster the relation phrase embeddings of all compared methods into 100 clusters. We isolate the instance closest to the cluster centroid of all 100 clusters. We then manually inspect the isolated instances to determine if the extracted relation phrase corresponds to one of the ground truth relations in the corpus. The results are shown in table 6.

7 Results and analysis

7.1 Relation Identification

The results of our approach on relation identification are tabulated in table 3. Throughout, we indicate the size of our pretraining set in parenthesis. We outperform OpenIE on relation identification by 76 points. From tables 3 and 4 we observe that increasing the size of our pretraining step to 250,000 instances does not improve performance. For future analysis it would be useful to determine how much we can decrease the size of our pre-training step without significantly affecting performance. We also observe that the improved prompting variations outperform the vanilla prompt by 46 points on average. A comparison between the errors of

Approach	Accuracy
Baselines	
Stanford OpenIE	0.11
OpenIE5	0.17
Prompting	
Prompt-pointer n/w (10k)	0.23
Prompt-v (10k)	0.43
Prompt-d1 (10k)	**0.93**
Prompt-d1 (250k)	0.87
Prompt-d2 (10k)	0.87
Prompt-del (10k)	**0.90**

Table 3: Comparing the performance of different techniques on relation identification

Approach	NMI	ARI	ACC
Baselines			
Stanford OpenIE	.25	.03	.36
OpenIE5	.19	.04	.35
Prompting			
Prompt-v (10k)	.32	.16	.47
Prompt-d1 (10k)	.67	.66	.84
Prompt-d1 (250k)	.55	.50	.74
Prompt-d2 (10k)	.65	.64	.81
Prompt-del (10k)	**.68**	**.69**	**.85**

Table 4: Comparing the performance of different approaches on unsupervised relation discovery.

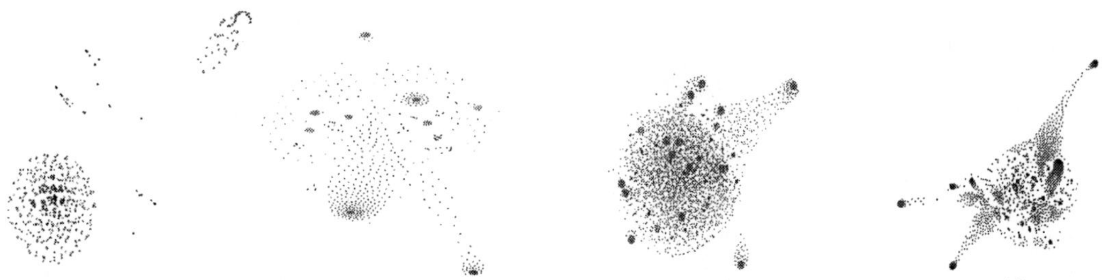

(a) (b) (c) (d)

Figure 5: t-SNE visualizations of the relations discovered under the unsupervised relation discovery (a & b) and the corpus-based relation discovery settings (c & d) (sec. 5). Fig. (a) shows the relations discovered using Stanford-OpenIE. Different colors indicate different ground-truth labels. (b) shows the relations discovered using `Prompt-del(10k)` under the same setting. Fig. (c) shows the relations discovered using OpenIE5 and Fig. (d) shows the relations discovered by `Prompt-del(10k)` under the same setting. In this case we do not have ground-truth label assignments as all extracted relation triples are clustered.

Approach	NMI	ARI	ACC
without entity type information			
Stanford OpenIE	.15	-.02	.32
Prompt-v(10k)	.21	.10	.37
Prompt-del(10k)	.60	.62	.77
with entity type information			
Stanford OpenIE	.25	.03	.36
Prompt-v(10k)	.32	.16	.47
Prompt-del(10k)	.68	.69	.85

Table 5: Ablation study comparing the performance of different models with and without head and tail semantic type information taken into account while clustering. The performance of different models is compared on unsupervised relation discovery. For more information about our clustering procedure please refer to section 4.3

Approach	#Relns. Disc.	Relations Missed
OpenIE5	12 / 19	*inspired by* *choreographer* *based on* *notable work* *voice actor* *illustrator* *colorist*
Prompt-del(10k)	15 / 19	*after a work by* *choreographer* *created by* *notable work*

Table 6: Comparing the performance of different models on corpus-based relation discovery. For more details about the evaluation setting please refer to section 6.3

the improved variations and the vanilla prompt can be observed in table 8 in the appendix. Restricting the decoder's output mitigates the problems of poor quality extractions and spelling errors. The improved prompting models generate incorrect extractions when there are multiple relations between the head and the tail or when the relation expressed is semantically complex.

7.2 Clustering & Discovery

The results of our model on unsupervised relation extraction are shown in table 4. `Prompt-del(10k)` outperforms Stanford-OpenIE by 49 points on permutation accuracy. t-SNE visualizations of these results are presented in figures 5a and 5b. We find that all six relations are discovered by our prompting approach and our clustering approach produces coherent, well-separated clusters. The improvements to our clustering strategy by taking head and tail semantic types into account are shown in table 5. Stanford-OpenIE on the other hand, only discovers relations expressed frequently as verbs such as *"written by"* and *"directed by"* with high precision.

Table 6 reports our results on corpus-based relation discovery. Our end-to-end pipeline discovers 15 out of the 19 ground-truth relations in our corpus. Figures 5c and 5d present t-SNE visualizations of our clustering results. We observe that most relations discovered by our framework coalesce into well-separated clusters. The majority of the relations extracted by OpenIE on the other hand, are too general to form well separated clusters.

A clearer illustration of the differences between our approach and OpenIE can be seen in table 7. We observe that both OpenIE baselines perform

Input	Relation Discovery Methods	
	OpenIE5	Prompt-del(10k)
The Iron Giant is a 1999 American... The film stars the voices of Vin Diesel (voicing the titular character)...	(It, was scripted, by Tim McCanlies) (It, was published, in the United States)	<arg> <head> Iron Giant </head> <pred> voiced by </pred> <tail> Vin Diesel </tail>. </arg>
Obelix and Co. is the twenty-third volume of the Asterix comic book series, by Rene Goscinny (stories) and Albert Uderzo (illustrations).	(Co., is, the twenty - third volume of the Asterix comic book series) (Co. is, the twenty - third volume of the Asterix comic book series , by Rene Goscinny) (Obelix, is, the twenty - third volume of the Asterix comic book series , by Rene Goscinny)	<arg> <head> Asterix </head> <pred> illustrator </pred> <tail> Albert Uderzo </tail> . </arg>

Table 7: A comparison between OpenIE and Prompt-del(10k) on the same text spans.

poorly on relations not expressed as verb phrases. As a result, OpenIE5 fails to discover *"colorist"* and *"voiced by"*, two relations frequently expressed as nouns.

8 Conclusions

We formulate a new task of corpus-based task-specific relation discovery and introduce a new dataset for the same. We empirically demonstrate that existing art are inadequate to tackle this task. To address this, we propose an end-to-end self-supervised pipeline for relation discovery that significantly outperforms our baselines on both quantitative and qualitative metrics. In the future, we plan on extending our approach to multiple domains in order to identify and correct possible gaps in our methodology.

Limitations

Domain Shift: In the current implementation, our prompting model relies on the availability of a training set. This assumption may not hold in cases where the relations to be discovered exhibit a significant domain shift from the training set. To address this limitation, future work should explore fully unsupervised prompting approaches that can better adapt to new domains and mitigate the impact of domain shift.

Limited Number of Relations: In this study, our analysis is restricted to a total of 25 relations. While this allows for a focused exploration of these specific relations, it also limits the scope and potential applications of our model. To broaden the applicability and effectiveness of our approach, future work should aim to utilize Wikidata more comprehensively, incorporating a larger number of relations for more extensive and diverse analysis.

Ethics Statement

We conform to the ACL ethics policy. Our research utilizes data from Wikipedia, which is governed by the Creative Commons Attribution-ShareAlike License, and Wikidata, which is governed by the CC0 Public Domain Dedication License. Importantly, we have taken care to ensure that no personal information of any user is used in our study.

References

Gabor Angeli, Melvin Jose Johnson Premkumar, and Christopher D. Manning. 2015. Leveraging linguistic structure for open domain information extraction. In *Proceedings of the 53rd Annual Meeting of the Association for Computational Linguistics and the 7th International Joint Conference on Natural Language Processing (Volume 1: Long Papers)*, pages 344–354, Beijing, China. Association for Computational Linguistics.

Janara Christensen, Mausam, Stephen Soderland, and Oren Etzioni. 2011. An analysis of open information extraction based on semantic role labeling. In *K-CAP '11*.

Rajarshi Das, Manzil Zaheer, Siva Reddy, and Andrew McCallum. 2017. Question answering on knowledge bases and text using universal schema and memory networks. In *Proceedings of the 55th Annual Meeting of the Association for Computational Linguistics (Volume 2: Short Papers)*, pages 358–365, Vancouver, Canada. Association for Computational Linguistics.

Jun Feng, Minlie Huang, Li Zhao, Yang Yang, and Xiaoyan Zhu. 2018. Reinforcement learning for relation classification from noisy data. In *AAAI*.

Lifu Huang, Taylor Cassidy, Xiaocheng Feng, Heng Ji, Clare R. Voss, Jiawei Han, and Avirup Sil. 2016. Liberal event extraction and event schema induction. In *Proceedings of the 54th Annual Meeting of the Association for Computational Linguistics (Volume 1: Long Papers)*, pages 258–268, Berlin, Germany. Association for Computational Linguistics.

Pere-Lluís Huguet Cabot and Roberto Navigli. 2021. REBEL: Relation extraction by end-to-end language generation. In *Findings of the Association for Computational Linguistics: EMNLP 2021*, pages 2370–2381, Punta Cana, Dominican Republic. Association for Computational Linguistics.

Zhengbao Jiang, Jun Araki, Haibo Ding, and Graham Neubig. 2021. How can we know when language models know? on the calibration of language models for question answering. *Transactions of the Association for Computational Linguistics*, 9:962–977.

Keshav Kolluru, Samarth Aggarwal, Vipul Rathore, Mausam, and Soumen Chakrabarti. 2020. IMoJIE: Iterative memory-based joint open information extraction. In *Proceedings of the 58th Annual Meeting of the Association for Computational Linguistics*, pages 5871–5886, Online. Association for Computational Linguistics.

Mike Lewis, Yinhan Liu, Naman Goyal, Marjan Ghazvininejad, Abdelrahman Mohamed, Omer Levy, Veselin Stoyanov, and Luke Zettlemoyer. 2019. BART: denoising sequence-to-sequence pre-training for natural language generation, translation, and comprehension. *CoRR*, abs/1910.13461.

Sha Li, Heng Ji, and Jiawei Han. 2021. Document-level event argument extraction by conditional generation. In *Proceedings of the 2021 Conference of the North American Chapter of the Association for Computational Linguistics: Human Language Technologies*, pages 894–908, Online. Association for Computational Linguistics.

Sha Li, Liyuan Liu, Yiqing Xie, Heng Ji, and Jiawei Han. 2022. Piled: An identify-and-localize framework for few-shot event detection. *arXiv preprint arXiv:2202.07615*.

Pengfei Liu, Weizhe Yuan, Jinlan Fu, Zhengbao Jiang, Hiroaki Hayashi, and Graham Neubig. 2021. Pretrain, prompt, and predict: A systematic survey of prompting methods in natural language processing. *ArXiv*, abs/2107.13586.

Yinhan Liu, Myle Ott, Naman Goyal, Jingfei Du, Mandar Joshi, Danqi Chen, Omer Levy, Mike Lewis, Luke Zettlemoyer, and Veselin Stoyanov. 2019. Roberta: A robustly optimized bert pretraining approach. *arXiv preprint arXiv:1907.11692*.

Yubo Ma, Zehao Wang, Yixin Cao, Mukai Li, Meiqi Chen, Kun Wang, and Jing Shao. 2022. Prompt for extraction? paie: Prompting argument interaction for event argument extraction. *arXiv preprint arXiv:2202.12109*.

Mausam, Michael Schmitz, Stephen Soderland, Robert Bart, and Oren Etzioni. 2012. Open language learning for information extraction. In *Proceedings of the 2012 Joint Conference on Empirical Methods in Natural Language Processing and Computational Natural Language Learning*, pages 523–534, Jeju Island, Korea. Association for Computational Linguistics.

Myle Ott, Sergey Edunov, Alexei Baevski, Angela Fan, Sam Gross, Nathan Ng, David Grangier, and Michael Auli. 2019. fairseq: A fast, extensible toolkit for sequence modeling. In *Proceedings of NAACL-HLT 2019: Demonstrations*.

Harinder Pal and Mausam. 2016. Demonyms and compound relational nouns in nominal open ie. In *AKBC@NAACL-HLT*.

Matthew E. Peters, Mark Neumann, Robert L Logan, Roy Schwartz, Vidur Joshi, Sameer Singh, and Noah A. Smith. 2019. Knowledge enhanced contextual word representations. In *EMNLP*.

Swarnadeep Saha and Mausam. 2018. Open information extraction from conjunctive sentences. In *Proceedings of the 27th International Conference on Computational Linguistics*, pages 2288–2299, Santa Fe, New Mexico, USA. Association for Computational Linguistics.

Swarnadeep Saha, Harinder Pal, and Mausam. 2017. Bootstrapping for numerical open IE. In *Proceedings of the 55th Annual Meeting of the Association for Computational Linguistics (Volume 2: Short Papers)*, pages 317–323, Vancouver, Canada. Association for Computational Linguistics.

Apoorv Saxena, Aditay Tripathi, and Partha Talukdar. 2020. Improving multi-hop question answering over knowledge graphs using knowledge base embeddings. In *Proceedings of the 58th Annual Meeting of the Association for Computational Linguistics*, pages 4498–4507, Online. Association for Computational Linguistics.

Rudolf Schneider, Tom Oberhauser, Tobias Klatt, Felix A. Gers, and Alexander Löser. 2017. Analysing errors of open information extraction systems. In *Proceedings of the First Workshop on Building Linguistically Generalizable NLP Systems*, pages 11–18, Copenhagen, Denmark. Association for Computational Linguistics.

Shikhar Vashishth, Prince Jain, and Partha Pratim Talukdar. 2018. Cesi: Canonicalizing open knowledge bases using embeddings and side information. *Proceedings of the 2018 World Wide Web Conference*.

Daojian Zeng, Kang Liu, Yubo Chen, and Jun Zhao. 2015. Distant supervision for relation extraction via piecewise convolutional neural networks. In *Proceedings of the 2015 Conference on Empirical Methods in Natural Language Processing*, pages 1753–1762, Lisbon, Portugal. Association for Computational Linguistics.

Fuzheng Zhang, Nicholas Jing Yuan, Defu Lian, Xing Xie, and Wei-Ying Ma. 2016. Collaborative knowledge base embedding for recommender systems. In *Proceedings of the 22nd ACM SIGKDD International Conference on Knowledge Discovery and Data Mining*, KDD '16, page 353–362, New York, NY, USA. Association for Computing Machinery.

A Comparative Error Analysis of Prompting Strategies

In our evaluation, we conducted an error analysis to compare the relative performance of different prompting models, which provided insights into their strengths and weaknesses. Qualitative results are displayed in Table 8.

B Prompting Strategies

In our exploration of prompting strategies for identifying relation phrases, we examined three additional alternative approaches, as illustrated in figure 6.

Example	Category
Vanilla Prompt (Prompt-v)	
Encoder Input: The cinematography was done by R. Rathnavelu, and the film was edited by Suresh Urs. The film score and soundtrack were composed by V. Harikrishna. "Gaalipata" was the first in Kannada to be shot in Super 35 format. <arg> Gaalipata <MASK> R. Rathnavelu </arg> Decoder Output: The cinematography was done by R. Rathnavelu, and the film was edited by Suresh Urs. The film score and soundtrack were composed by V. Harikrishna. "Gaalipata" was the first in Kannada to be shot in Super 35 format. <arg> Gaalipata written by Rathavelu </arg>	Poor quality extraction, Relation not present in input paragraph.
Encoder Input: ... Aagadu marked S. Thaman's 50th film as a music composer. K. V. Guhan provided the cinematography ... Decoder Output: ... <arg> Aagadatu provided cinematography K. J. Vhan. </arg>	Spelling errors, Hard to isolate relation phrase for clustering.
Encoder Input: ...Love from Paris (German: Monpti) is a 1957 West German romantic comedy-drama film dir... <arg> Love from Paris <MASK> Heinz Pehlke </arg> Decoder Output: ...unds of Paris. Love from Paris writer Heinz Penhlke.	Relation delimiters not generated, Hard to isolate relation phrase for clustering.
Prompt-d1	
Encoder Input: House of Bamboo is a 1955 American film noir shot in CinemaScope and DeLuxe Color. It was directed and co-written by Samuel Fuller. <arg> House of Bamboo <MASK> Samuel Fuller </arg> Decoder Output: <arg> House of Bamboo written by Samuel Fuller </arg>	Multiple relations between head and tail entities
Encoder Input: Road to Perdition is a 2002 American crime drama film directed by Sam Mendes. The screenplay was adapted by David Self from the graphic novel of the same name written by Max Allan Collins and illustrated by Richard Piers Rayner. <arg> Road to Perdition <MASK> Max Allan Collins </arg> Decoder Output: <arg> Road to Perdition written by Max Allan Collins. </arg>	Hard relations with multiple qualifiers
Encoder Input: Pavithram () is a 1994 Indian Malayalam-language drama film directed by T. K. Rajeev Kumar and written by P. Balachandran from a story by Balachandran and Kumar. <arg> Pavithram <MASK> T. K. Rajeev Kumar. </arg> Decoder Output: <arg> Pavithram written by T. K. Rajeev Kumar. </arg>	

Table 8: Error analysis comparing the relative performance of different prompting models.

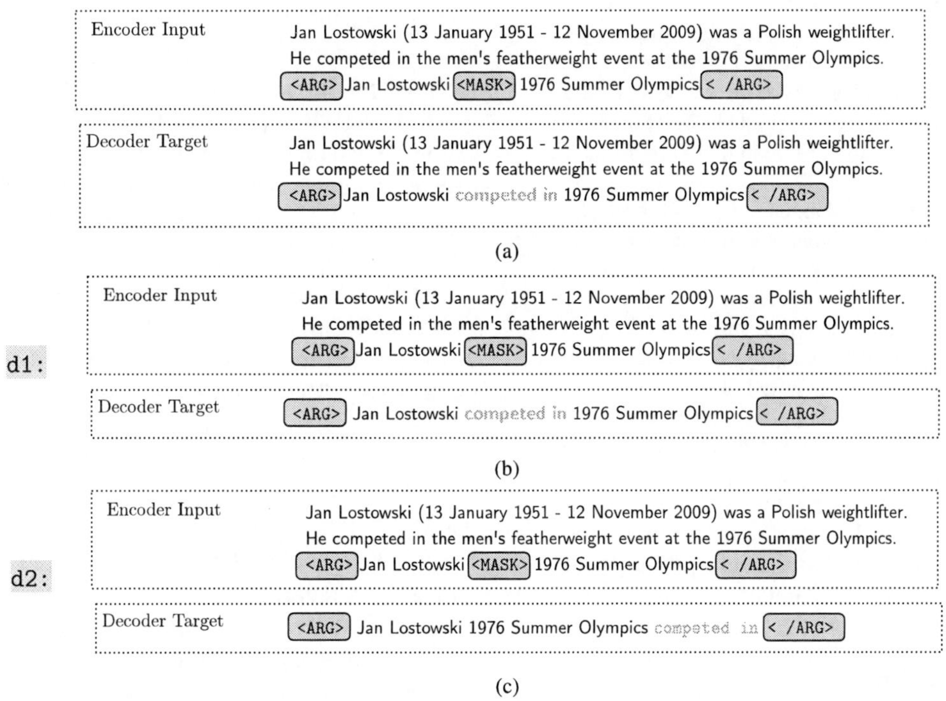

Figure 6: Three Alternative Prompting Strategies for Identifying Relation Phrases: The Optimal Strategy, **Prompt-del**, is Displayed in Table 4. The Strategies, Arranged from Top to Bottom, Include **Prompt-v** (Top), **Prompt-d1** (Middle), and **Prompt-d2** (Bottom).

On the Surprising Effectiveness of Name Matching Alone in Autoregressive Entity Linking

Elliot Schumacher **James Mayfield** **Mark Dredze**
Johns Hopkins University
eschuma7@jhu.edu mayfield@jhu.edu mdredze@cs.jhu.edu

Abstract

Fifteen years of work on entity linking has established the importance of different information sources in making linking decisions: mention and entity name similarity, contextual relevance, and features of the knowledge base. Modern state-of-the-art systems build on these features, including through neural representations (Wu et al., 2020). In contrast to this trend, the autoregressive language model GENRE (De Cao et al., 2021) generates normalized entity names for mentions and beats many other entity linking systems, despite making no use of knowledge base (KB) information. How is this possible? We analyze the behavior of GENRE on several entity linking datasets and demonstrate that its performance stems from memorization of name patterns. In contrast, it fails in cases that might benefit from using the KB. We experiment with a modification to the model to enable it to utilize KB information, highlighting challenges to incorporating traditional entity linking information sources into autoregressive models.

1 Introduction

Early work in entity linking in Wikipedia (Cucerzan, 2007; Bunescu and Paşca, 2006) followed by the formulation of the task at the TAC KBP shared task (McNamee and Dang, 2009; Ji et al., 2010; Li et al., 2011) has led to more than a decade of research into how to match textual mentions of entities to grounded entities in a knowledge base (KB). This large body of research has led to some clear findings (Dredze et al., 2010; Durrett and Klein, 2014; Gupta et al., 2017; Lample et al., 2016; Francis-Landau et al., 2016; Cao et al., 2018; Wang et al., 2015; Witten and Milne, 2008; Piccinno and Ferragina, 2014). Entity linking is commonly modeled as a ranking task, in which a triaged set of KB entities is ranked by comparison to a textual entity mention. These ranking systems rely on different information sources. First, the entity mention is compared to the entity name in the KB (name matching), with allowances for aliases, acronyms, etc. Second, the context of the mention is compared to entity descriptions in the KB to select the correct entity among a set of similarly named candidates. Third, other relevant information from the KB (type information, links to related entities, popularity, etc.) can help disambiguate between candidates. This information is formulated as features (either engineered or learned) into the ranking system.

The recent emergence of autoregressive large language models as multi-task learners (Radford et al., 2019) has led to numerous new applications of these models. These models have been particularly effective in few-shot learning settings (Brown et al., 2020; Chowdhery et al., 2022), but typically fall behind supervised training of traditional systems that can flexibly incorporate a range of features. Despite this trend, De Cao et al. (2021) presented GENRE, an autoregressive language model that uses supervised training to link textual mentions to entities in a KB. Given a sentence and a previously-identified mention span, the model generates an entity name selected from a set of (triaged) candidates, with the option to generate entities without any constraints (with worse performance). Surprisingly, aside from the entity name, GENRE uses no information from the KB, in contrast to other high-performing entity linking systems that rely on textual entity descriptions (Wu et al., 2020) or type information (Orr et al., 2020). We may expect an autoregressive LM to do well, but how can it beat the best available feature-based entity linking systems?

We explore the benefits and drawbacks of autoregressive entity linking. First, we ask – why GENRE performs so well? Our answer comes from an analysis of the behavior of GENRE across several different entity linking datasets. Specifically, we measure the generalization ability of the

Proceedings of the First Workshop on Matching From Unstructured and Structured Data (MATCHING 2023), pages 58–69
July 13, 2023 ©2023 Association for Computational Linguistics

model by looking at performance on new datasets and knowledge bases. We find that GENRE relies heavily on memorization of name patterns, meaning that it struggles to generalize to new entities and KBs. KB information is often found to be useful in these cases, but its absence from GENRE means it struggles when name matching fails. Therefore, our second question is: can GENRE make use of information from the KB when available? Specifically, we provide descriptive information about an entity from the KB to GENRE and measure its resulting performance in various settings. We find that while it sometimes can make use of this information, it still struggles to learn generalizable patterns. Our analysis shows opportunities for incorporating KB information into an autoregressive entity linker, but also the challenges of doing so given current model architectures.

2 Autoregressive Entity Linking

GENRE (De Cao et al., 2021) is an autoregressive language model that links textual mentions to entities in Wikipedia through text generation. Autoregressive language models, such as BART (Lewis et al., 2020), are trained to generate text, as opposed to other non-autoregressive based models (*e.g.,* BERT (Devlin et al., 2019)), which are better suited for classification or scoring tasks. BART and similar models do very well at text generation tasks (Johner et al., 2021).

GENRE formulates entity linking as text generation as follows. Given the selected entity mention and its left context within the sentence, the model is trained to predict the next tokens as the normalized entity name. Consider the example in Figure 1. The model encodes the context *Two of the party's European*, and is trained to generate the correct normalized entity name *European Parliament* for this context. During training, the model is trained to minimize the smoothed cross-entropy loss between the generated entity name and the correct (normalized) entity name, where the normalized entity name matches the title of the associated node in the KB (Wikipedia page title). In this setup, negative sampling is not required. GENRE starts with a pretrained BART model and continues training on 9 million example entity mentions selected from Wikipedia, where the entity name is appended after each entity mention (see Section 5).

Asking GENRE to freely generate a normalized name is both extremely challenging and unnecessary. In practice, a pre-filtering (triage) step can be used to automatically select the most likely entity candidates for a textual reference via a name matching algorithm.[1] De Cao et al. (2021) evaluated GENRE under several conditions. First, a free decoding step whereby the model could output any string; this did not do well. Second, constraining the model to generate a valid entity name from the KB. Third, constraining the model to generate an entity from the small set of triaged candidates. For the constrained generation case, the authors constructed a trie $\mathcal{T}$, where each node of the trie consists of a vocabulary entry, with a specialized token in the root. For each subword $t \in \mathcal{T}$, its children are allowed subword continuations.

In an evaluation on the several entity linking datasets, including Wikipedia and MSNBC (Derczynski et al., 2015), GENRE achieved state-of-the-art results compared to traditional entity linking systems. Yet the shocking thing about this result is what GENRE lacks. First, GENRE uses no information from the KB. Typical entity linking systems consider contextual overlap between the mention string and the KB entity description; GENRE does not. For example, when linking the textual mention *America*, a system would measure overlap with the KB description *The United States of America is a transcontinental country primarily located in North America* (United States) or *Americans are the citizens and nationals of the United States of America.* (American). Another popular feature is entity type, for example, *country* (United States) or *nationality* (American). Other feature such as entity popularity, entity type, and related entities, are not available to GENRE. This information has long been used to disambiguate entities, and recent systems continue to show their ongoing effectiveness. Orr et al. (2020) use type information to help disambiguate entities that do not occur frequently. BLINK (Wu et al., 2020) build contexualized embeddings for each entity using entity descriptions. None of this information is available to GENRE.

Furthermore, due to the generation nature of BART, GENRE only uses the left context of the entity mention. In sentences such as that in Figure 1, a very limited left context is availble to provide any information. While GENRE can memorize associations between the limited left context and the entity name, it cannot generalize even this limited

[1]This task itself is a challenge, and relying on a candidate set that contains the correct entity is often unrealistic.

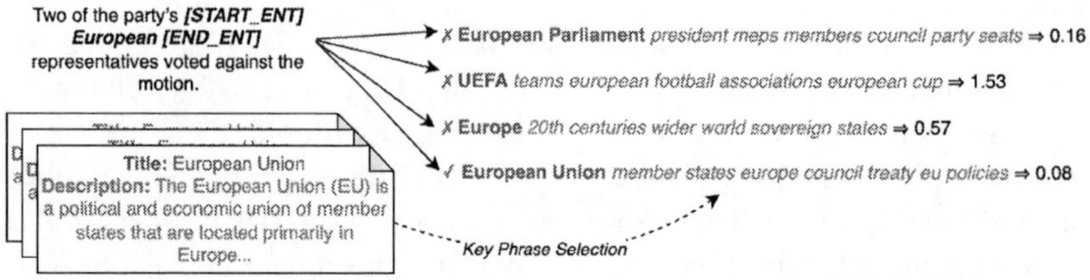

Figure 1: An example mention taken from the TAC training set. In the original GENRE model, constrained decoding would be performed over only the **normalized entity names** (in blue, bolded) in the candidate list, given the mention and the sentence context. In our proposed GENRE-KB, we perform constrained decoding over the **normalized entity names** and *keywords* taken from entity descriptions in the knowledge base.

information to new settings. Despite these limitations, GENRE represents a state-of-the-art entity linker.

3 GENRE and Generalization

How does GENRE achieve great entity linking results with such limited information? We explore this through the issue of generalization: how well does the model do on new unseen data?

Since the model does not have access to the KB, its predictions on new data are based entirely on what it can learn about entities fron training data.

De Cao et al. (2021) suggested that GENRE predicts entities with contextualized name matching by leveraging large amounts of entity linking annotations during training. For example, while the original authors show that the model performs acceptably on rare entities (*e.g.,* approximately 80% accuracy on Wikipedia entities seen once in the training data), the accuracy for entities unseen in the training data is only 50%. Bhargav et al. (2022) show that GENRE is very data-intensive to train; reducing training to 0.01% of the original size performs 11% worse than BLINK. Constrained decoding is also necessary for accurate predictions. Generating without triaged candidates drops the accuracy by 9.2%. However, the importance of training data is clearly central, as triage could be adapted to new settings separately.

What is GENRE learning from the massive training data? One possibility is that it learns how to normalize entity name (*Bill Clinton* to *William Clinton*) from annotated data. Pretraining on massive amounts of unannotated text followed by a large amount of entity linking annotations may also allow it to learn how to normalize certain informal names (*America*) to formal ones (*The United States*). Furthermore, pretraining may allow for robust modeling of the context before mentions. Finally, as in other NLP tasks, the effect of using the encoding of the context provided by the sentence is likely valuable.

If GENRE exhibits these behaviors, it can generalize certain abilities to new domains. However, if instead it is memorizing the training data, e.g. learning specific entities that appear in training, it cannot generalize. For example, Wikipedia titles and mentions follow conventions, which may be learnable by the model, but will not generalize to settings that do not use Wikipedia data or KBs. Additionally, De Cao et al. (2021) report results on examples where the gold entity is found in the triage step, which biases toward lexical matches. Examples that can be lexically matched are likely more likely to be solved by name matching. These links are far more common in Wikipedia than other domains.

In short, while generalization is a challenge for any machine learning model, it may be especially challenging for the mechanisms used by GENRE to learn from the training data. Our first question is: Does GENRE learn generalizable patterns or does it memorize the entities in the training data? We answer by probing how GENRE leverages its training data to perform linking. We evaluate GENRE on new datasets (Section 5) more challenging than those reported in the original paper. We begin with datasets linked to Wikipedia KBs, the proceed to datasets with different KBs. These new KBs contain entities unobserved in training, especially difficult for GENRE because it cannot access the KB.

4 GENRE and the Knowledge Base

GENRE faces challenges in generalization from its lack of access to the KB, which contains information about unseen entities. If GENRE was able to access the KB, could it better generalize to new data? A long line of entity linking research suggests that the answer should be "yes". In this Section, we modify the training data to provide this information to GENRE.

The key idea is to augment the training data with short descriptions of information in the KB. Specifically, we add several keywords that summarize an entity's description in the KB to each training instance. GENRE is then asked (and trained) to generate the entity title followed by these keywords after each entity mention. This approach uses an unchanged GENRE model architecture to both learn to normalize names and bias the model towards entity descriptions (via keywords) that are most triggered by the (left) context of the mention.

We choose to use keywords instead of the full text description for several reasons. First, in many KBs (especially Wikipedia) entity descriptions are quite long, often multiple paragraphs. This stretches the context beyond what GENRE can reasonably model. Even selecting a short snippet, e.g. the first sentence, also pushes the model beyond what is reasonable. Instead, selecting a few important phrases from the description allows us to easily control the length of the produced string. Furthermore, if selected correctly, these keyword can highlight topically related content, signaling a match with the left context of the entity.

Context enables GENRE to match the topic of the context with that of the candidate entity. In Figure 1, which entity best matches the the term *European* is ambigious. Although the correct entity *European Union* has a partial lexical match, other entities do as well (*e.g., European Parliament*), and others are close lexical variants (*Europe*). GENRE's ability to link this mention correctly would likely solely be based on whether it is seen in the training data, given the ambigiuity in the knowledge base. Adding additional keywords can signal that *European Union* and *European Parliament* are potentially related, given political-related keywords such as *party* and *council*, whereas *Europe* is less related. The same approach may be helpful to other mentions that could be amibigously linked in the knowledge base, such as *Washington*. The keywords for *Washington D.C.*, *district city congress united states metropolitan area*, can help differentiate that entity from *Washington (State)*, which is paired with keywords *seattle united states british columbia cascade range*. This idea is in the same spirit as Bevilacqua et al. (2022), which uses autoregressive language models for search, but decodes entire spans from a corpus, as opposed to keywords.

4.1 Keyword Selection

We use the PKE toolkit (Boudin, 2016) to select keywords from the entity description. After a careful examination of several of the unsupervised methods in the toolkit, we found that Topic Rank (Bougouin et al., 2013) produced the most descriptive keywords. We selected the top n keywords (phrases) and multiplied the Topic Rank score s by a frequency factor from the KB. For each keyword in the KB, we took a summation over their inverse rank ($\frac{1}{rank+1}$) within each entity-specific set. The final score for a keyword k for a given entity is

$$s_k * (1 + \log(\sum_{e \in \text{KB}, k \in e} \frac{1}{\text{rank}_k + 1})) \quad (1)$$

The keywords are ordered by their score. The addition of the frequency factor removed some highly-scored esoteric keywords (*e.g., Punic Wars* for *Spain*) that may not generalize well. We also experimented with the number of keywords to include, and found that adding at least five words was best. Many keywords are phrases with multiple words, which results in some sequences being just over five words. This selection procedure can generalize to other sources of information in KBs.

To avoid GENRE memorizing this training data, we use a different selection method during the training step. During training, we sample five words from the entire keyword list proportional to the Topic Rank score, and resample for each training instance. Scores less than zero are set to a small value (0.0001), then normalized to form a probability distribution. At inference, we use the same top scoring keywords for every instance of an entity. Examples of selected keywords are shown in Appendix Table 4.

4.2 Training and Inference

We closely follow the training procedure in De Cao et al. (2021). Beginning with the pretrained GENRE model, we train GENRE-KB to maximize the entity title and keyword sequence given the sentence context: maximize $logp_\theta(y|x)$ with respect to the model's parameters θ. We closely follow their choices of training methods and parameter selections, and use teacher forcing, dropout, and label smoothing. The authors originally add a special token to the beginning of each target sequence. In

Dataset	Wikipedia		TAC	
	acc.	mrr	acc.	mrr
GENRE	92.1 $\pm$.67	.952	92.4 $\pm$.56	.950
+KB	81.1 $\pm$.97	.874	91.8 $\pm$.58	.950
GENRE*	90.9 $\pm$.69	.943	80.7 $\pm$.75	.856
+KB*	77.5 $\pm$1.0	.846	80.9 $\pm$.75	.862

Table 1: Datasets with Wikipedia as the KB. The first two rows show examples with correct entity in the triaged set. The rows with an asterisk show the oracle setting, where all examples with the correct candidate added if not present. Confidence Intervals (at 95%) are included for accuracy.

addition to using this token, we add special tokens before and after the keywords to indicate where keywords are present. We do not add these as tokens to the vocabulary due to Fairseq (Ott et al., 2019) constraints. We believe the performance difference is likely small.

Similarly, we use GENRE's candidate scoring with constrained beam search. For Wikipedia-based datasets, we use the same beam size (10) as in their work. However, for other datasets, we found that a smaller beam size works better (5). Additionally, since we are scoring longer strings that likely vary much more in length than in the title-only model, we explored normalizing the likelihood of a candidate by its length (in number of byte pair encoding tokens). In some datasets, we found this provided a small improvement. Training these models from scratch exceeded our computational resources, so we initialized training using the existing models. We trained each model on a single NVIDIA GeForce RTX 2080 for 32 hours, iterating over all the data.

5 Data

Wikipedia GENRE was trained on the BLINK-created version of a Wikipedia dataset (Wu et al., 2020) based on a May 2019 English Wikipedia dump with 5.9 million entities. They use a 9 million-sized subset of Wikipedia-linked mentions (*e.g.,* links within Wikipedia pages to other Wikipedia pages). The KB consists of all pages within that snapshot of Wikipedia. We exclusively use this dataset to train GENRE-KB. While we also report evaluation results on this dataset, we primarily target more challenging datasets. For evaluation, we use the provided candidate sets.

TAC The 2015 TAC KBP Entity Linking dataset (Ji et al., 2015) consists of newswire and discussion forum posts linked to an English KB. The discussion forum posts with informal entity mentions are especially challenging. Chinese and Spanish data are also included, but we only consider English. While this dataset does not directly link to Wikipedia, almost all entities linked in the English dataset include a Wikipedia title in their metadata. Therefore, we convert all entities with Wikipedia links to their respective entry in the Wikipedia KB and convert all others to NIL (no relevant entity). To generate a candidate set at inference time, we use the system of Upadhyay et al. (2018), which is largely based on work in Tsai and Roth (2016). This approach uses Wikipedia cross-links to generate a prior probability $\mathtt{P_{prior}}(e_i|m)$ by estimating counts from those mentions. This prior is used to provide the top k English Wikipedia page titles for each mention.

Wikia To explore how GENRE and GENRE-KB work on datasets where Wikipedia is not the KB, we include the Wikia dataset (Logeswaran et al., 2019). Wikia was constructed from the Wikia.com website (now Fandom), which consists of community-written encyclopedias on a particular subject or theme. This was constructed in the same manner as the Wikipedia dataset – mentions were taken from in-page hyperlinks, and each document served as an entity. The authors collect 16 Wikias, each with a different topic and KB, thus serving as a challenging adaptation for our Wikipedia-trained models. The authors exclude all NIL entities and provide candidate sets for each mention of size 64, retrieved via BM25.

Topics are partitioned across training, validation, and test sets so that each appears in only one set. Each mention is categorized by the amount of token overlap between the mention text and the normalized entity title. The categories include *high overlap* (5% of mentions), which represent exact matches; *multiple categories* (28% of mentions), where the entity title is the mention text plus a disambiguation phrase (*e.g.,* mention *Batman*, entity title *Batman (Lego)*); and *ambiguous substring* (8% of mentions), where the mention is a substring of the title. The category *other* (59% of mentions) includes all remaining mentions. We believe the original label of *low overlap* is misleading, as many examples in that category have a high degree of lexical similarity. For example, of the *other* examples that have a candidate identified in the validation set, 28.96% of mention span - entity title pairs have a Jaro-Winkler lexical similarity (Winkler, 1990) of over 0.794.

6 Experimental Setup

For GENRE-KB, we train all models on the Wikipedia dataset alone and select the best-performing model using the Wikipedia validation set's loss. In all cases, we do not use the Wikia or TAC training data for training but only as a validation set. For Wikia and TAC data, we provide the model with the sentence where the mention occurs. Sentence boundaries are identified with Spacy (Honnibal and Montani, 2017). We adopt the method of reporting results from Logeswaran et al. (2019), which reports normalized accuracy, which is calculated over the set of examples that are non-NIL and have the gold standard entity in their candidate set. As this restricts the types of examples to those that have mentions which are lexically similar to the entity name, we also report oracle results for some datasets, where we add the gold standard entity to all non-NIL examples if not already present.

7 Results

Our experiments address two questions. First, why does GENRE perform so well? We answer this through evaluating generalization to new datasets. Second, can GENRE utilize KB information to improve generalization (GENRE-KB)?

7.1 GENRE Generalization

To probe GENRE's reliance on the mention string matching the normalized entity name, we performed two experiments with the TAC training dataset using the original GENRE model. First, we remove the available context around the tntity and replace it with a generic prompt: *This entity is called **mention**.* In this setting, no context is available for linking decisions. Second, we keep the original context but remove the actual mention string. In this setting, GENRE relies on context alone.

How important to GENRE are each type of information: name matching and context? Compared to the normal model's performance of 49.1% on TAC data (unnormalized, *i.e.,* including NIL entities), using only the mention string GENRE did nearly as well (41.6%). By comparison, using only context drops accuracy significantly (26.8%). This suggests that GENRE largely relies on the training data to learn transformations between the mention and the entity name alone. The context adds a bit to the model's ability.

Despite this result, GENRE performs well on the more challenging datasets. Table 1 shows the performance of the GENRE model on the Wikipedia and TAC datasets. While it is unsurprising that GENRE performs well on Wikipedia, the performance on the TAC dataset is surprisingly high for the setting with only retrieved candidates. However, the performance on TAC in the oracle setting is significantly lower. As detailed in Section 6, we add the gold standard entity to the candidate set for any example where it isn't already present. Focusing only on the retrieved candidates restricts examples to those that can be lexically matched, as triage systems frequently rely on surface forms alone. The oracle setting highlights the fact that many of these more challenging matches cannot be linked by GENRE.

The results for Wikia are shown in Table 2. Previous work (Logeswaran et al., 2019) report results on several baselines for the validation set. We include the best-performing baselines that also have not been trained on Wikia data.[2] We report macro accuracy (accuracy is calculated separately on each domain, and divided by the number of domains), and micro accuracy (accuracy is calculated on the corpus as a whole), in addition to mean reciprocal rank (MRR) and top-K accuracy ($k = 5$). In absolute terms, the performance on the Wikia dataset is worse, as it is not trained to link mentions to the Wikia knowledge bases. However, it does outperform two previously reported baselines by a small margin, suggesting that even in this challenging setting GENRE is surprisingly effective.

The reason behind this effectiveness varies in each setting. For linking mentions to the Wikipedia KB, the sheer amount of data GENRE is trained on enables it to recall which entity is likely best. Therefore, when the data allows for such a strategy, memorization can be effective when paired with a model that can also model the context.

7.2 GENRE-KB

We evaluate GENRE-KB (GENRE augmented in training by keywords) on all of our datasets dis-

[2]The authors of that paper also include several baselines that are trained on Wikia data, but are an unfair comparison for this setting.

Method	Validation macro	Validation micro	Validation mrr	Validation top-K	Test macro	Test micro	Test mrr	Test top-K
TF-IDF*	26.06							
Gupta et al*	27.03							
GENRE	29.09	26.89 $\pm$1.0	.42	52.88	31.99	33.16 $\pm$1.1	.44	43.01
GENRE-KB	29.53	29.63 $\pm$1.0	.46	55.65	28.11	27.83 $\pm$1.1	.42	44.64
Comb. (par)	35.54	35.14 $\pm$1.1	.49	54.48	35.63	36.14 $\pm$1.1	.47	43.89
Comb. (jw)	32.36	30.97 $\pm$1.0	.46	58.82	34.48	35.00 $\pm$1.1	.46	47.00

Table 2: Results on Wikia Datasets. Results for methods marked with an asterisk are taken from Logeswaran et al. (2019). The combination models are built off of the predictions of GENRE-KB and GENRE described in Chapter 4. Confidence Intervals (at 95%) are included for micro accuracy.

degree of similarity	validation accuracy #	validation accuracy GENRE	validation accuracy GENRE-KB	test accuracy #	test accuracy GENRE	test accuracy GENRE-KB
mult. categories	4106	11.93	26.04	2341	16.66	25.72
amb. substring	543	54.70	36.46	419	47.02	28.88
high overlap	501	89.22	71.66	825	91.03	62.30
other	2434	33.07	25.55	3227	28.54	20.42

Table 3: Results on Wikia by degree of similarity category.

cussed in the previous section. For the Wikipedia dataset in Table 1, GENRE performs consistently better than GENRE-KB. This is unsurprising, given the model's ability to memorize training examples and that it has been trained on other Wikipedia data. As reported in the previous section, GENRE relies heavily on name matching, which is sufficient when the model stays within the same domain. In addition, 82.9% of examples in the test set have a Jaro-Winkler score of 0.8 or higher, indicating they are largely lexically similar.

However, performance on the TAC dataset is much closer. On the set of examples where the correct entity is present in the triage candidate set, GENRE performs slightly better on accuracy, while both models tie in MRR. However, in the oracle setting, GENRE-KB performs marginally better in both metrics. This suggests that when trying to link these more challenging examples, which a lexical triage system could not identify, GENRE-KB has an advantage. In short, when context matters, GENRE-KB is better. However, it is still challenging to overcome the memorization capacity of the original GENRE model, and GENRE-KB is still based on the same architecture.

As shown in Table 1, the confidence intervals for accuracy ($\alpha = 0.05$) suggest that the differences in top-predictions are not significant for TAC, but are for Wikipedia. However, to test whether GENRE and GENRE-KB produce rankings that are significantly different, we use a Wilcoxon signed-rank test. For the TAC dataset, the difference between the two models on the Retrieved Candidates setting ($p = 0.005$) and the Oracle setting ($p = 0.005$) are both significant. This suggests the two models produce different rankings despite their similar top-level predictions.

Table 2 shows results on the Wikia validation and test sets. Again, the differences between GENRE and GENRE-KB are small and depend on the dataset. In the validation set, GENRE-KB performs better in all metrics. In test set, GENRE performs better with the exception of top-K accuracy, where GENRE-KB performs better. Comparing the rankings produced by the two models using a Wilcoxon signed-rank test, we find that the difference in the GENRE and GENRE-KB validation rankings is significant ($p = 2.1e - 36$), but not significant for the test rankings ($p = 0.13$). In terms of micro accuracy, the confidence intervals show that the differences between GENRE and GENRE-KB are significant.

At first glance, this suggests that the validation data was overfitted. However, we believe this has more to do with the distribution of examples in each set. Table 3 breaks down accuracy by similarity categories (detailed in Section 5). In the validation set, the largest category is *multiple categories*, which are linked to entities that have a parenthetical in their name. In both sets, GENRE-KB performs consistently better than GENRE, but the portion of these examples is smaller in the test set. Conversely, it is unsurprising that in the cases of *high overlap* and *amb. substring* GENRE performs better since those are categories with high lexical similarity between mention and entity title.

For the *other* category, GENRE performs well on examples with high lexical similarity. For example, in the validation set, while only 28.96% of textitother examples have a high lexical similarity, those examples consist of 52.9% of the examples that GENRE gets correct. GENRE performs better on test and GENRE-KB better on validation because the sets have a different distribution over example types.

GENRE and GENRE-KB are useful for different types of examples. GENRE is excellent when name string alone is sufficient. GENRE-KB improves when context matters. Therefore, we explore combining the two systems. Table 2 shows two methods for model combination. First, we propose a model (labeled *paren*) where we use the prediction from GENRE-KB if it predicts a parenthetical, and GENRE otherwise. Second, we combine scores of GENRE and GENRE-KB with the Jaro-Winkler lexical similarity between the GENRE model's top predicted entity and the mention serving as a scalar between the two scores (labeled as *jw*)[3]. This puts more weight on examples where GENRE thinks there is a lexically similar entity name to the mention, but more weight on GENRE-KB in dissimilar cases.

Neither model changes predictions based on the gold standard entity label – they only operate off of the top prediction of one of the two models. In both cases, across both data sets and metrics, both combination models outperform GENRE-KB and GENRE. The confidence intervals included in Table 2 suggest that while the difference between the *jw* model and the best-performing individual model is not significant, the difference between the *par* model and the best-performing individual model is significant. In summary, adding KB information to GENRE helps, but only where such information is informative to the correct prediction. A simple metric (Jaro Winkler) can successfully identify those cases.

8 Related Work

Entity linking has been broadly studied (Dredze et al., 2010; Durrett and Klein, 2014; Gupta et al., 2017; Lample et al., 2016; Cao et al., 2018; Wang et al., 2015; Wu et al., 2020). Recent work (Bhargav et al., 2022; Orr et al., 2020) highlights the utility of type information in making linking decisions for rarer entities. Other work has applied autoregressive models to other information extraction tasks (De Cao et al., 2022; Josifoski et al., 2022). De Cao et al. (2021) seeks to alleviate some of the performance challenges with GENRE during inference, although initial experiments found this performed worse in new domains. Aghajanyan et al. (2022) proposed a method that allows both the left and right context surrounding an entity mention to be modeled by producing the link at the end of the sequence.

[3]We divide the GENRE score by the candidate's length, to match the length normalization procedure of GENRE-KB, as described in Section 4.1.

9 Conclusion

Autoregressive transformer-based sequence-to-sequence models, such as BART, have found increasing success in information extraction tasks. The GENRE model, which applies autoregressive sequence-to-sequence approaches to entity linking, has high performance on many datasets linked to the Wikipedia domain. However, its performance on other domains with different challenges produces mixed results.

We suggest that adding previously-explored entity linking features to GENRE can address some of these pitfalls. Specifically, descriptions are a commonly used source of text to make linking decisions. While we see performance decreases in the original Wikipedia datasets, we see some improvements in both newswire text and in applying GENRE-KB to previously unseen knowledge bases for more challenging matches. Yet, the ability of GENRE to work in even challenging settings suggests that it can memorize patterns useful for mention-entity pairs with high lexical similarity.

There are several unexplored directions for our model. Specifically, we used an off-the-shelf keyword selection method. Selecting keywords in a more targeted fashion – perhaps by selecting keywords for an entity that best separates it from another entity – may improve performance. Having the computational resources to train a model from scratch would also likely improve performance, as opposed to training from a GENRE checkpoint. Moreover, we focus on integrating descriptive information within the original GENRE framework. Future work may consider an autoregressive entity linker with a novel architecture that can integrate and learn representations of entities would better utilize this information in learning.

10 Ethics and Limitations

Our experiments focus solely on English-language entity linking. Similar models have been trained to perform entity linking in multiple languages (De Cao et al., 2022), but we do not consider performance beyond English. The issues faced in other languages are likely to be similar, but the multilingual element of other models might lead to different results. Further, how to select keywords in the multilingual setting is unclear.

In addition, we are limited by the available annotated entity linking datasets. Given that we need a large amount of data to train these models, they are inherently reliant on Wikipedia. These entity linking datasets are skewed towards specific types of matches, including ones that are frequently exact matches. The effectiveness of this model might change when trained on a dataset with different characteristics, even with a large amount of data.

Finally, the computational resources required to train these models are large, and our final results do not reflect numerous other preliminary experiments. This restricts our ability to run multiple experiments, train models from scratch easily, and potentially leads to underfitting of our final models.

References

Armen Aghajanyan, Bernie Huang, Candace Ross, Vladimir Karpukhin, Hu Xu, Naman Goyal, Dmytro Okhonko, Mandar Joshi, Gargi Ghosh, Mike Lewis, and Luke Zettlemoyer. 2022. Cm3: A causal masked multimodal model of the internet.

Michele Bevilacqua, Giuseppe Ottaviano, Patrick Lewis, Wen tau Yih, Sebastian Riedel, and Fabio Petroni. 2022. Autoregressive search engines: Generating substrings as document identifiers. In *arXiv pre-print 2204.10628*.

G P Shrivatsa Bhargav, Dinesh Khandelwal, Saswati Dana, Dinesh Garg, Pavan Kapanipathi, Salim Roukos, Alexander Gray, and L Venkata Subramaniam. 2022. Zero-shot entity linking with less data. In *Findings of the Association for Computational Linguistics: NAACL 2022*, pages 1681–1697, Seattle, United States. Association for Computational Linguistics.

Florian Boudin. 2016. pke: an open source python-based keyphrase extraction toolkit. In *Proceedings of COLING 2016, the 26th International Conference on Computational Linguistics: System Demonstrations*, pages 69–73, Osaka, Japan.

Adrien Bougouin, Florian Boudin, and Béatrice Daille. 2013. TopicRank: Graph-based topic ranking for keyphrase extraction. In *Proceedings of the Sixth International Joint Conference on Natural Language Processing*, pages 543–551, Nagoya, Japan. Asian Federation of Natural Language Processing.

Tom Brown, Benjamin Mann, Nick Ryder, Melanie Subbiah, Jared D Kaplan, Prafulla Dhariwal, Arvind Neelakantan, Pranav Shyam, Girish Sastry, Amanda Askell, et al. 2020. Language models are few-shot learners. *Advances in neural information processing systems*, 33:1877–1901.

Razvan Bunescu and Marius Paşca. 2006. Using encyclopedic knowledge for named entity disambiguation. In *11th Conference of the European Chapter of the Association for Computational Linguistics*, pages 9–16, Trento, Italy. Association for Computational Linguistics.

Yixin Cao, Lei Hou, Juanzi Li, and Zhiyuan Liu. 2018. Neural collective entity linking. In *Proceedings of the 27th International Conference on Computational Linguistics*, pages 675–686, Santa Fe, New Mexico, USA. Association for Computational Linguistics.

Aakanksha Chowdhery, Sharan Narang, Jacob Devlin, Maarten Bosma, Gaurav Mishra, Adam Roberts, Paul Barham, Hyung Won Chung, Charles Sutton, Sebastian Gehrmann, et al. 2022. Palm: Scaling language modeling with pathways. *arXiv preprint arXiv:2204.02311*.

Silviu Cucerzan. 2007. Large-scale named entity disambiguation based on Wikipedia data. In *Proceedings of the 2007 Joint Conference on Empirical Methods in Natural Language Processing and Computational Natural Language Learning (EMNLP-CoNLL)*, pages 708–716, Prague, Czech Republic. Association for Computational Linguistics.

Nicola De Cao, Wilker Aziz, and Ivan Titov. 2021. Highly parallel autoregressive entity linking with discriminative correction. In *Proceedings of the 2021 Conference on Empirical Methods in Natural Language Processing*, pages 7662–7669, Online and Punta Cana, Dominican Republic. Association for Computational Linguistics.

Nicola De Cao, Gautier Izacard, Sebastian Riedel, and Fabio Petroni. 2021. Autoregressive entity retrieval. In *International Conference on Learning Representations*.

Nicola De Cao, Ledell Wu, Kashyap Popat, Mikel Artetxe, Naman Goyal, Mikhail Plekhanov, Luke Zettlemoyer, Nicola Cancedda, Sebastian Riedel, and Fabio Petroni. 2022. Multilingual autoregressive entity linking. *Transactions of the Association for Computational Linguistics*, 10:274–290.

Leon Derczynski, Diana Maynard, Giuseppe Rizzo, Marieke Van Erp, Genevieve Gorrell, Raphaël Troncy, Johann Petrak, and Kalina Bontcheva. 2015. Analysis of named entity recognition and linking for tweets. *Information Processing & Management*, 51(2):32–49.

Jacob Devlin, Ming-Wei Chang, Kenton Lee, and Kristina Toutanova. 2019. BERT: Pre-training of deep bidirectional transformers for language understanding. In *Proceedings of the 2019 Conference of the North American Chapter of the Association for Computational Linguistics: Human Language Technologies, Volume 1 (Long and Short Papers)*, pages 4171–4186, Minneapolis, Minnesota. Association for Computational Linguistics.

Mark Dredze, Paul McNamee, Delip Rao, Adam Gerber, and Tim Finin. 2010. Entity disambiguation for knowledge base population. In *Conference on Computational Linguistics (COLING)*, pages 277–285. Association for Computational Linguistics.

Greg Durrett and Dan Klein. 2014. A joint model for entity analysis: Coreference, typing, and linking. *Transactions of the Association for Computational Linguistics*, 2:477–490.

Matthew Francis-Landau, Greg Durrett, and Dan Klein. 2016. Capturing semantic similarity for entity linking with convolutional neural networks. In *Proceedings of the 2016 Conference of the North American Chapter of the Association for Computational Linguistics: Human Language Technologies*, pages 1256–1261, San Diego, California. Association for Computational Linguistics.

Nitish Gupta, Sameer Singh, and Dan Roth. 2017. Entity linking via joint encoding of types, descriptions, and context. In *Proceedings of the 2017 Conference on Empirical Methods in Natural Language Processing*, pages 2681–2690, Copenhagen, Denmark. Association for Computational Linguistics.

Matthew Honnibal and Ines Montani. 2017. spaCy 2: Natural language understanding with Bloom embeddings, convolutional neural networks and incremental parsing. To appear.

Heng Ji, Ralph Grishman, Hoa Trang Dang, Kira Griffitt, and Joe Ellis. 2010. Overview of the tac 2010 knowledge base population track. In *Third text analysis conference (TAC 2010)*, volume 3, pages 3–3.

Heng Ji, Joel Nothman, Ben Hachey, and Radu Florian. 2015. Overview of TAC-KBP2015 Tri-lingual Entity Discovery and Linking. *TAC*.

Timo Johner, Abhik Jana, and Chris Biemann. 2021. Error analysis of using BART for multi-document summarization: A study for English and German language. In *Proceedings of the 23rd Nordic Conference on Computational Linguistics (NoDaLiDa)*, pages 391–397, Reykjavik, Iceland (Online). Linköping University Electronic Press, Sweden.

Martin Josifoski, Nicola De Cao, Maxime Peyrard, Fabio Petroni, and Robert West. 2022. GenIE: Generative information extraction. In *Proceedings of the 2022 Conference of the North American Chapter of the Association for Computational Linguistics: Human Language Technologies*, pages 4626–4643, Seattle, United States. Association for Computational Linguistics.

Guillaume Lample, Miguel Ballesteros, Sandeep Subramanian, Kazuya Kawakami, and Chris Dyer. 2016. Neural architectures for named entity recognition. In *Proceedings of the 2016 Conference of the North American Chapter of the Association for Computational Linguistics: Human Language Technologies*, pages 260–270, San Diego, California. Association for Computational Linguistics.

Mike Lewis, Yinhan Liu, Naman Goyal, Marjan Ghazvininejad, Abdelrahman Mohamed, Omer Levy, Veselin Stoyanov, and Luke Zettlemoyer. 2020. BART: Denoising sequence-to-sequence pre-training for natural language generation, translation, and comprehension. In *Proceedings of the 58th Annual Meeting of the Association for Computational Linguistics*, pages 7871–7880, Online. Association for Computational Linguistics.

Xuansong Li, Joe Ellis, Kira Griffitt, Stephanie M Strassel, Robert Parker, and Jonathan Wright. 2011. Linguistic resources for 2011 knowledge base population evaluation. In *TAC*.

Lajanugen Logeswaran, Ming-Wei Chang, Kenton Lee, Kristina Toutanova, Jacob Devlin, and Honglak Lee. 2019. Zero-shot entity linking by reading entity descriptions. In *Proceedings of the 57th Annual Meeting of the Association for Computational Linguistics*, pages 3449–3460, Florence, Italy. Association for Computational Linguistics.

Paul McNamee and Hoa Trang Dang. 2009. Overview of the tac 2009 knowledge base population track. In *Text analysis conference (TAC)*, volume 17, pages 111–113.

Laurel Orr, Megan Leszczynski, Simran Arora, Sen Wu, Neel Guha, Xiao Ling, and Christopher Re. 2020. Bootleg: Chasing the tail with self-supervised named entity disambiguation.

Myle Ott, Sergey Edunov, Alexei Baevski, Angela Fan, Sam Gross, Nathan Ng, David Grangier, and Michael Auli. 2019. fairseq: A fast, extensible toolkit for sequence modeling. In *Proceedings of the 2019 Conference of the North American Chapter of the Association for Computational Linguistics (Demonstrations)*, pages 48–53, Minneapolis, Minnesota. Association for Computational Linguistics.

Francesco Piccinno and P. Ferragina. 2014. From tagme to wat: a new entity annotator. In *ERD '14*.

Alec Radford, Jeffrey Wu, Rewon Child, David Luan, Dario Amodei, Ilya Sutskever, et al. 2019. Language models are unsupervised multitask learners. *OpenAI blog*, 1(8):9.

Chen-Tse Tsai and Dan Roth. 2016. Cross-lingual Wikification Using Multilingual Embeddings. In *Proceedings of the 2016 Conference of the North American Chapter of the Association for Computational*

Linguistics: Human Language Technologies, pages 589–598, Stroudsburg, PA, USA. Association for Computational Linguistics.

Shyam Upadhyay, Nitish Gupta, and Dan Roth. 2018. Joint multilingual supervision for cross-lingual entity linking. In *Proceedings of the 2018 Conference on Empirical Methods in Natural Language Processing*, pages 2486–2495, Brussels, Belgium. Association for Computational Linguistics.

Han Wang, Jin Guang Zheng, Xiaogang Ma, Peter Fox, and Heng Ji. 2015. Language and domain independent entity linking with quantified collective validation. In *Proceedings of the 2015 Conference on Empirical Methods in Natural Language Processing*, pages 695–704, Lisbon, Portugal. Association for Computational Linguistics.

William E Winkler. 1990. String comparator metrics and enhanced decision rules in the fellegi-sunter model of record linkage. *ERIC*.

Ian H Witten and David N Milne. 2008. An effective, low-cost measure of semantic relatedness obtained from wikipedia links.

Ledell Wu, Fabio Petroni, Martin Josifoski, Sebastian Riedel, and Luke Zettlemoyer. 2020. Scalable zero-shot entity linking with dense entity retrieval. In *Proceedings of the 2020 Conference on Empirical Methods in Natural Language Processing (EMNLP)*, pages 6397–6407, Online. Association for Computational Linguistics.

Entity Title	Keywords
Germany	german states country member berlin france
Church of England	local parishes christianity common people bishop
General officer	army air forces countries different systems
Flowering plant	plants families species pollen embryo
Civil liberties	religion european convention constitution personal freedoms
Julia Gillard	leader education australia university labor
1924 World Series	games washington ninth walter johnson giants
John Hodgman	radio episode death role appearance
Humoral immunity	function phagocytosis cellular components presence antibodies
Camino Real (play)	time tennessee williams esmeralda marguerite camille
Bumper Tormohlen	december known seasons nba draft record
Craig Wiseman	tim mcgraw blake shelton songs year
Carroll Gardens Historic District	brooklyn common new york city smith
Dallas	city southern united states universities texas
Phanagoria	town site augustus black sea auxiliary bishop
Pierre Berton	time books canada ontario canadian history
Military advisor	afghanistan capabilities marines infantry vietnam
Francesca Schiavone	fourth round italy semifinals french open
Show Boat (1951 film)	julie stage play characters song magnolia
Los Angeles County, California	pasadena arts san bernardino port cities
Metatheria	years earliest marsupials placentals north america
The New York Times	articles report publisher newspaper paper
Tamil Nadu	india coimbatore parts british chennai
Government of Hong Kong	chief secretary systems chief executive head
Roberto Matta	europe surrealist art life work le corbusier
DC Comics	series line picture stories second title
The Outer Limits (1995 TV series)	tales season science fiction time monster
Marvel Comics	year american comic books titles series
Berkshire Hathaway	years share cash general decline stock
Portugal	lisbon portuguese government country territory spain
Methanosphaera	carbon dioxide taxonomy genus formate methanol

Table 4: Example keywords for the shuffled scoring selection method detailed in Section 4.1.

Knowledge-Augmented Language Model Prompting for Zero-Shot Knowledge Graph Question Answering

Jinheon Baek[1*] **Alham Fikri Aji**[2] **Amir Saffari**[3]
KAIST[1] MBZUAI[2] Amazon[3]
jinheon.baek@kaist.ac.kr alham.fikri@mbzuai.ac.ae amsafari@amazon.com

Abstract

Large Language Models (LLMs) are capable of performing zero-shot closed-book question answering tasks, based on their internal knowledge stored in parameters during pre-training. However, such internalized knowledge might be insufficient and incorrect, which could lead LLMs to generate factually wrong answers. Furthermore, fine-tuning LLMs to update their knowledge is expensive. To this end, we propose to augment the knowledge directly in the input of LLMs. Specifically, we first retrieve the relevant facts to the input question from the knowledge graph based on semantic similarities between the question and its associated facts. After that, we prepend the retrieved facts to the input question in the form of the prompt, which is then forwarded to LLMs to generate the answer. Our framework, Knowledge-Augmented language model PromptING (KAPING), requires no model training, thus completely zero-shot. We validate the performance of our KAPING framework on the knowledge graph question answering task, that aims to answer the user's question based on facts over a knowledge graph, on which ours outperforms relevant zero-shot baselines by up to 48% in average, across multiple LLMs of various sizes.

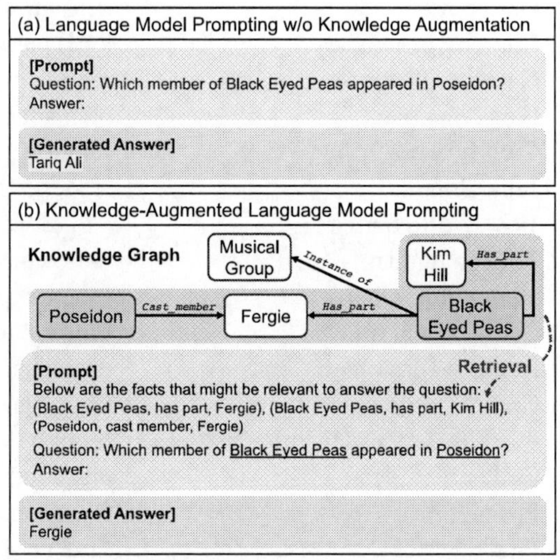

Figure 1: (a) For the input question in the prompt, the large language model, GPT-3 (Brown et al., 2020), can generate the answer based on its internal knowledge in parameters, but hallucinates it which is highlighted in yellow. (b) Our Knowledge-Augmented language model PrompTING (KAPING) framework first retrieves the relevant facts in the knowledge graph from the entities in the question, and then augments them to the prompt, to generate the factually correct answer.

1 Introduction

Pre-trained Language Models (LMs) (Devlin et al., 2019; Raffel et al., 2020), which are trained on a large amount of text corpora with self-supervised learning, can perform closed-book Question Answering (QA) tasks that aim to answer the user's question based only on their internal knowledge in parameters, without using any external knowledge (Petroni et al., 2019; Roberts et al., 2020). Also, when we increase the LM sizes, Large Language Models (LLMs) can generate the answer for the question without any additional fine-tuning steps, called *LM prompting* (Brown et al., 2020; Liu et al., 2021). However, since the knowledge in LLMs might be incomplete, incorrect, and outdated, they often generate factually wrong answers, known as *hallucination* (Rohrbach et al., 2018) (See Figure 1a). Also, refining the knowledge in LLMs with parameter updates is costly, especially when knowledge is constantly changing (e.g., exchange rates of money). Lastly, whether LLMs are fetching the correct knowledge for QA is unclear.

To overcome those limitations, we propose to retrieve and inject the relevant knowledge directly as an input, called a *prompt*, to LLMs (Figure 1b). As a knowledge source, we use a Knowledge Graph (KG) consisting of symbolic knowledge in the form of a triple: (head entity, relation, tail entity). Therefore, to extract the relevant facts to the input question, we first match entities in the question with entities in the KG. After that, triples associated to

* Work done while interning at Amazon. Corresponding author: Jinheon Baek (jinheon.baek@kaist.ac.kr)

Proceedings of the First Workshop on Matching From Unstructured and Structured Data (MATCHING 2023), pages 70–98
July 13, 2023

entities in the KG are verbalized (i.e., transforming the symbolic relational knowledge to the textual string) and prepended to the input question, which are then forwarded to LLMs to generate the answer. Consequently, LLMs conditioned on the factual knowledge are able to generate the factual answers, alleviating the hallucination issue, while keeping LLMs' parameters unchanged: fine-tuning is not required for knowledge updates. We refer to our overall framework as **K**nowledge-**A**ugmented language model **P**rompt**ING** (**KAPING**), which is completely *zero-shot* and can be done with any off-the-shelf LLMs, without additional training.

While the above scheme looks simple yet effective, there is a couple of challenges. First, most retrieved triples associated with the question entities are unrelated to answer the given question. For example, when we retrieve the associated triples for the question entity (e.g., Poseidon) in Figure 1 in the Wikidata KG (Vrandecic and Krötzsch, 2014), there exist 60 triples, and most of them (e.g., genre, publication date, to name a few) are irrelevant to answer the question. Therefore, they might mislead the model into generating incorrect answers. On the other hand, the number of triples for the question entities is occasionally large (e.g., 27% samples for the WebQSP dataset (Yih et al., 2016) have more than 1,000 triples), thereby encoding all triples including unnecessary ones yields high computational costs, especially on LLMs.

To overcome such challenges, we further propose to filter out unnecessary triples based on their semantic similarities to the input question, inspired by the information retrieval (Bast et al., 2016). To be specific, we first represent the question and its associated verbalized triples in the embedding space. Then, we retrieve the small number of triples whose embeddings are more close to the input question's embedding than others. By doing so, we can prepend only the more relevant triples to the given question, which can effectively prevent LLMs from generating irrelevant answers with high computational efficiencies, unlike the one that augments all triples. Note that, our filtering approach uses off-the-shelf sentence embedding models (Song et al., 2020; Hofstätter et al., 2021); thus no additional training is required in every part of our pipeline.

We then validate our KAPING framework on Knowledge Graph Question Answering (KGQA) tasks. The results show that our KAPING significantly outperforms relevant zero-shot baselines. Also, the detailed analyses support the importance of knowledge retrieval and augmentation schemes.

Our contributions in this work are threefold:

- We present a new knowledge-augmented LM prompting framework that leverages the factual knowledge from KGs, for zero-shot QA.
- We propose to retrieve and augment relevant facts from KGs, based on semantic similarities between the question and its associated triples.
- We validate our KAPING on KGQA benchmark datasets, on which ours impressively outperforms relevant zero-shot baselines.

2 Related Work

Language Model Prompting Language model pre-training, which trains Transformers (Vaswani et al., 2017) on unannotated text corpora with auto-encoding (Devlin et al., 2019; Liu et al., 2019) or auto-regressive (Yang et al., 2019; Radford et al., 2018) objectives, becomes an essential approach for natural language tasks. Also, Large Language Models (LLMs) (Brown et al., 2020; Raffel et al., 2020; Chowdhery et al., 2022; Soltan et al., 2022) are able to perform zero-shot learning, for example, generating the answer for the input textual prompt, based on the knowledge stored in pre-trained parameters (Petroni et al., 2019; Roberts et al., 2020; Sung et al., 2021), without additional parameter updates as well as labeled datasets. To further improve their performances, some work (Rubin et al., 2022; Liu et al., 2022a) proposes retrieving relevant samples to the input question from the training dataset and prepending them in the prompt under few-show learning. Recent few work (Sanh et al., 2022; Wei et al., 2022a) further shows that, when LLMs are fine-tuned on a collection of instructions phrased from natural language tasks, they can have strong generalization performance on unseen zero-shot tasks. However, the knowledge inside LMs might be insufficient to tackle factual questions, which gives rise to knowledge-augmented LMs. Notably, our LM prompting is different from prompt-tuning literature (Lester et al., 2021a; Chen et al., 2022a) that additionally tunes LMs with model training (See Appendix C for discussions).

Knowledge-Augmented LMs Recent work proposes to integrate the knowledge, such as documents from unstructured corpora (e.g., Wikipedia) and facts from Knowledge Graphs (KGs), into LMs. To mention a few, REALM (Guu et al., 2020) and

RAG (Lewis et al., 2020) learn to retrieve documents and augment LMs with them. In addition, KGs could be another knowledge source, where the knowledge is succinctly encoded in the most compact form, and some methods augment such facts in KGs into LMs (Galetzka et al., 2021; Rony et al., 2022; Kang et al., 2022). However, all aforementioned approaches require massive amount of training data and model updates for downstream tasks. While more recent work (Izacard et al., 2022) shows retrieval-augmented LM can have strong performance with few-shot learning, it still requires extra training steps, which is different from ours focusing on *LM prompting* for entirely zero-shot.

Recently, there are few studies augmenting the knowledge in the LM prompting scheme. At first, some work proposes to extract the knowledge in the parameters of LLMs themselves via prompting, and then use the extracted knowledge to answer the question (Kojima et al., 2022; Liu et al., 2022b; Wei et al., 2022b; Wang et al., 2022). However, since LLMs' parameters might be insufficient to store all the world knowledge, the extracted knowledge and generated answers might be inaccurate. On the other hand, most recently, Lazaridou et al. (2022) propose to use the Google Search to retrieve documents on the Web, and then prepend the retrieved documents to the input question along with few-shot demonstrations, to answer the question under few-shot LLM prompting schemes. However, our focus on *zero-shot prompting with KGs* is orthogonal to the previous study working on documents with few-shot prompting, and leveraging KGs can bring additional advantages. Specifically, since KGs can succinctly encode the knowledge in the compact triple form, for QA tasks, ours makes LLM prompting more efficient (i.e., reducing the input sequence length compared to the document case), as well as more effective on the zero-shot QA scheme: LLMs need to select one triple containing the answer entity in the prompt, instead of looking through lengthy documents having various entities.

Knowledge Graph Question Answering The goal of our target Knowledge Graph Question Answering (KGQA) tasks is to answer the input question based on a set of facts over KGs (Chakraborty et al., 2019; Fu et al., 2020). Previous approaches are broadly classified into neural semantic parsing-based methods (Yih et al., 2015; Bao et al., 2016; Luo et al., 2018), information retrieval-based methods (Sun et al., 2018; Saxena et al., 2020; Yasunaga et al., 2021), and differentiable KG-based methods (Cohen et al., 2020; Saffari et al., 2021; Sen et al., 2021), which, however, require annotated data with additional model training. While Zhou et al. (2021) aim to transfer the KGQA model to the target language domains without any training data on them, this work indeed needs the labeled data to train the model on data-rich source domains first before transferring the model to the target domains. In contrast to all the aforementioned methods, we explore the novel zero-shot KGQA mechanism, which does not require any annotated QA pairs and additional training, leveraging LM prompting.

3 Method

We now describe our Knowledge-Augmented language model PromptING (KAPING) framework.

3.1 LM Prompting for Zero-Shot QA

We begin with the zero-shot question answering, and then explain the language model prompting.

Zero-Shot Question Answering Given an input question $\boldsymbol{x}$, the Question Answering (QA) system returns an answer $\boldsymbol{y}$, where $\boldsymbol{x}$ and $\boldsymbol{y}$ consist of sequences of tokens: $\boldsymbol{x} = [w_1, w_2, \dots, w_{|\boldsymbol{x}|}]$. Let P be a QA model based on the generative Language Model (LM) (Raffel et al., 2020; Brown et al., 2020), which generates the conditional probability of answer $\boldsymbol{y}$ for question $\boldsymbol{x}$ as follows: $P(\boldsymbol{y}|\boldsymbol{x})$. Then, in contrast to supervised learning that trains model P with a set of annotated ($\boldsymbol{x}$, $\boldsymbol{y}$) pairs, zero-shot learning does not use any labeled samples and model training. Notably, we are interested in this zero-shot QA, since collecting the dataset and then fine-tuning the existing LMs for every new domain are known to be expensive and sometimes infeasible (Houlsby et al., 2019; Lester et al., 2021b).

LM Prompting LMs are often pre-trained by predicting the next token based on previous tokens, which is known as auto-regressive language modeling (Radford et al., 2018; Raffel et al., 2020). Then, thanks to this pre-training objective, LLMs can perform zero-shot instruction learning. Specifically, when we provide a question as well as an instruction (e.g., "Please answer the question: Who is the author of Lady Susan?") to the LLM (i.e., P), such the LLM, conditioned by the input text, can sequentially generate the probability of output tokens, which might be an answer, "Jane Austen".

To be more formal, for every input question $\boldsymbol{x}$, we first modify it with a particular instruction template T into a textual string x' called a *prompt*, as follows: $T : x \mapsto x'$. For example, if we have the previous question x = "Who is the author of Lady Susan?" along with the previous instruction template "Please answer the question:", the resulting prompt x' would be $T(x)$ = "Please answer the question: Who is the author of Lady Susan?". Then, we forward the prompt x' to the LLM (i.e., P), which then generates the answer (i.e., y) through $P(y|x')$. Note that this LM prompting scheme does not require any additional model parameter updates (i.e., fine-tuning) on the labeled data, thus appropriate for the target zero-shot QA task.

However, there are multiple challenges in this naive zero-shot prompting for QA. First, LLMs, which rely on the knowledge in parameters, are vulnerable from generating the factually incorrect answer, since the knowledge in LLMs might be inaccurate, and outdated: knowledge can be emerged and changed over time. Also, refining the internalized knowledge with additional parameter updates is expensive, while it is necessary to reflect the wrong and ever growing knowledge. Lastly, which knowledge LLMs memorize and utilize when generating the answer to the question prompt is unclear, which limits their explainability on the outputs.

3.2 Knowledge-Augmented LM Prompting

In order to tackle the aforementioned limitations of the existing LM prompting scheme, we propose to inject the relevant knowledge to the input question from the Knowledge Graph (KG), which we refer to as Knowledge-Augmented language model PromptING (KAPING). In this subsection, we first define the main objective of our KAPING framework, and then introduce the ingredients for augmenting the knowledge over KGs to LM prompts.

LM Prompting with Knowledge Graphs Instead of relying on the knowledge internalized in parameters, we propose to additionally access and inject the knowledge from the external KG, which contains accurate and up-to-date facts helpful to answer the question. Formally, a knowledge graph $\mathcal{G}$ consists of a set of factual triples $\{(s, r, o)\}$, where s and o denote subject and object entities, and r is a specific type of a relation between them. For example, one relational knowledge "Lady Susan was written by Jane Austen" can be represented as a triple consisting of two entities s = "Lady Susan" and o = "Jane Austen" along with a relation r = "written by". Then, for the question prompt x' transformed from the example question x = "Who is the author of Lady Susan?" via the template T, we additionally augment its relevant triple: (Lady Susan, written by, Jane Austen), to the LM prompting scheme. By doing so, LLMs can generate the correct answer with regard to the augmented knowledge from KGs, formalized as follows: $P(y|x', \mathcal{G})$. Note that, since we can provide specific and valid facts in KGs to LLMs whenever they exist, our framework can alleviate hallucination issue, originated from inaccurate and outdated knowledge in LLMs, without costly updating their model parameters. Furthermore, we can confirm whether LLMs generate answers based on augmented facts, thus improving the explainability of LM prompting.

The remaining questions are then how to *access* the relational symbolic facts over the KG from the input question, *verbalize* the symbolic knowledge to the textual string, and *inject* the verbalized knowledge into the LM prompting scheme. We explain them one by one in the following paragraphs.

Knowledge Access In order to utilize the related facts to the input question, we first extract the entities in the question. For example, for the question "Who is the author of *Lady Susan*?", we extract the entity "Lady Susan". Then, based on the extracted entity, we find its corresponding entity over the KG, whose incident triples then become associated facts to the input question. Note that entity matching can be done by existing entity linking techniques (Wu et al., 2020; Li et al., 2020; Ayoola et al., 2022).

Knowledge Verbalization LLMs are working on textual inputs, whereas factual triples are represented over the symbolic graph. Therefore, before injecting the symbolic fact from KGs to LLMs, we first transform the triple consisting of (s, r, o) into its textual string, called verbalization. While there exists recent methods (Oguz et al., 2022; Ma et al., 2022) that particularly design or even learn the graph-to-text transformation, in this work, we use the linear verbalization: concatenating the subject, relation, and object texts in the triple, which we observe works well in LM prompting (See Appendix B.5). For instance, one triple (Lady Susan, written by, Jane Austen) is used as is: "(Lady Susan, written by, Jane Austen)", for an LLM's input.

Knowledge Injection Based on verbalized facts associated with the input question, the remaining step is to realize the knowledge injection mechanism, which allows LLMs to be grounded on the external knowledge, useful to generate the answer. Let assume we have a set of N associated triples $\boldsymbol{k} = \{(s_i, r_i, o_i)\}_{i=1}^N$ for question $\boldsymbol{x}$. Then, similar to instruction template $T : \boldsymbol{x} \mapsto \boldsymbol{x}'$ described in Section 3.1, we modify N verbalized triples $\boldsymbol{k}$ along with the instruction for the knowledge injection into the knowledge prompt $\boldsymbol{k}'$, as follows: $T : \boldsymbol{k} \mapsto \boldsymbol{k}'$. One particular template we use for constructing the prompt is that, we first enumerate N verbalized triples line-by-line and then add the specific instruction: "Below are facts in the form of the triple meaningful to answer the question.", at the top of the prompt. After that, such the knowledge prompt string, $\boldsymbol{k}'$, is prepended to the question prompt $\boldsymbol{x}'$, and LLMs conditioned by knowledge and question prompts then sequentially generate the answer tokens, formalized as follows: $P(\boldsymbol{y}|[\boldsymbol{k}', \boldsymbol{x}'])$, where $[\cdot]$ denotes concatenation.

3.3 Question-Relevant Knowledge Retrieval

The proposed KAPING framework in Section 3.2, allows LLMs to leverage the knowledge from KGs for zero-shot QA. However, there are critical challenges that the number of triples associated to questions is often too large to forward in LLMs. Also, most of them are unrelated to the question, misleading LLMs into generating the irrelevant answer.

Knowledge Retriever To overcome those limitations, we further propose to retrieve and augment only the relevant triples to the question. Note that there exists a document-retrieval scheme (Lin et al., 2021), whose goal is to retrieve relevant documents for the given query based on their embedding similarities, which motivates us to retrieve, in our case, the triples for the user's question. In particular, thanks to the verbalizer defined in Section 3.2, we can play with triples, obtained from symbolic KGs, over the text space. Therefore, for the verbalized triple and the question, we first embed them onto the representation space with off-the-shelf sentence embedding models for text retrieval (Song et al., 2020; Karpukhin et al., 2020; Xiong et al., 2021), and then calculate their similarities. After that, we use only the top-K similar triples, instead of using all N triples, associated to the given question. Note that, unlike few recent studies (Oguz et al., 2022; Ma et al., 2022; Kang et al., 2022) that aim at improving KG retrievers themselves under supervised training, we focus on zero-shot LM prompting with KGs, thus we use any off-the-shelf retrievers as a tool to filter out unnecessary triples for questions.

4 Experimental Setups

We explain datasets, models, metrics, and implementations. For additional details, see Appendix A.

4.1 Datasets

We evaluate our Knowledge-Augmented language model PromptING (KAPING) framework on two Knowledge Graph Question Answering (KGQA) datasets, namely WebQuestionsSP and Mintaka.

WebQuestionsSP (WebQSP) This dataset (Berant et al., 2013; Yih et al., 2016) is designed with a Freebase KG (Bollacker et al., 2008). It consists of 1,639 test samples, which we use for zero-shot evaluation. Additionally, since Freebase is outdated, we further use the Wikidata KG (Vrandecic and Krötzsch, 2014) by using available mappings from Freebase ids to Wikidata (Diefenbach et al., 2017). This additional dataset consists of 1,466 samples.

Mintaka This dataset (Sen et al., 2022) is recently designed with the Wikidata KG for complex KGQA tasks. Among 8 different languages, we use English test sets consisting of 4,000 samples.

4.2 Large Language Models

To verify the performance of our KAPING framework on Large Language Models (LLMs), as well as benchmarking them on zero-shot KGQA, we use various LLMs with different sizes. Specifically, we use T5 (Raffel et al., 2020) (0.8B, 3B, 11B), T0 (Sanh et al., 2022) (3B, 11B), OPT (Zhang et al., 2022) (2.7B, 6.7B) and GPT-3 (Brown et al., 2020) (6.7B, 175B). We provide details in Appendix A.2.

4.3 Baselines and Our Model

In this subsection, we explain four zero-shot LM prompting baselines and our KAPING framework.

No Knowledge This is a naive LM prompting baseline, which generates answers from input questions without knowledge augmentation from KGs.

Random Knowledge This is an LM prompting baseline, which additionally augments the randomly sampled K triples, associated to the entities appeared in the question, to the prompt.

Popular Knowledge This is an LM prompting baseline, which augments K popular triples among all triples from the question entities, based on relations that appear the most frequently in the KG.

Generated Knowledge This is an LM prompting baseline, which first extracts the knowledge from LLMs themselves based on prompting, and then

Table 1: **Main results of language model prompting**, where we report the generation accuracy. The number inside the parentheses in the first row denotes the parameter size of language models, and best scores are emphasized in bold.

Datasets	Methods	T5 (0.8B)	T5 (3B)	T5 (11B)	OPT (2.7B)	OPT (6.7B)	OPT (13B)	T0 (3B)	T0 (11B)	GPT-3 (6.7B)	GPT-3 (175B)	AlexaTM (20B)	Average
WebQSP w/ Freebase	No Knowledge	6.95	13.40	9.48	19.85	29.77	28.38	21.43	40.77	44.63	63.59	46.79	29.55
	Random Knowledge	21.55	19.15	17.57	28.07	31.73	33.31	32.62	51.20	51.01	65.87	57.37	37.22
	Popular Knowledge	15.30	16.88	18.39	28.32	28.13	24.21	27.05	47.22	45.58	62.26	54.91	33.48
	Generated Knowledge	6.19	7.84	6.76	7.46	11.50	8.22	19.41	38.81	45.89	62.14	35.13	22.67
	KAPING (Ours)	**34.70**	**25.41**	**24.91**	**41.09**	**43.93**	**40.20**	**52.28**	**62.85**	**60.37**	**73.89**	**67.67**	**47.94**
WebQSP w/ Wikidata	No Knowledge	10.30	18.42	15.21	23.94	33.77	32.40	24.56	44.20	48.50	67.60	42.41	32.85
	Random Knowledge	17.94	22.78	24.28	37.24	35.61	38.27	28.85	47.68	52.05	60.64	55.63	38.27
	Popular Knowledge	15.35	20.80	20.74	30.83	30.01	27.83	24.83	48.02	47.41	63.37	53.92	34.83
	Generated Knowledge	11.94	13.30	12.28	11.26	17.53	14.19	22.92	41.34	48.77	65.89	31.16	26.42
	KAPING (Ours)	**23.67**	**40.38**	**35.47**	**49.52**	**53.34**	**51.57**	**49.86**	**58.73**	**60.44**	**69.58**	**65.04**	**50.69**
Mintaka w/ Wikidata	No Knowledge	11.23	14.25	17.06	19.76	27.19	26.83	14.75	23.74	34.65	56.33	41.97	26.16
	Random Knowledge	17.59	18.19	18.83	28.11	26.58	28.36	16.10	26.15	32.98	51.56	46.02	28.22
	Popular Knowledge	17.56	18.09	18.73	26.97	27.08	23.10	16.74	27.15	32.48	53.16	46.41	27.95
	Generated Knowledge	13.61	14.61	14.29	11.87	14.96	16.24	14.46	23.13	33.12	55.65	34.58	22.41
	KAPING (Ours)	**19.72**	**22.00**	**22.85**	**32.94**	**32.37**	**33.37**	**20.68**	**29.50**	**35.61**	**56.86**	**49.08**	**32.27**

		1-Hop Retrieval				2-Hop Retrieval			
Datasets	**Retrievers**	**MRR**	**Top-1**	**Top-10**	**Top-30**	**MRR**	**Top-1**	**Top-10**	**Top-30**
WebQSP w/ Freebase	Random	12.50	7.21	25.09	34.64	1.50	0.70	2.65	5.37
	Popular	8.58	5.31	15.93	24.53	1.59	0.95	2.72	4.68
	MPNet	**47.27**	**40.27**	**60.56**	**64.48**	**41.64**	**33.12**	**58.47**	**65.23**
WebQSP w/ Wikidata	Random	9.50	3.62	22.58	40.72	1.31	0.00	2.80	8.59
	Popular	8.52	4.57	15.89	35.47	4.63	4.02	5.53	6.62
	MPNet	**43.46**	**33.36**	**64.39**	**70.67**	**40.42**	**30.56**	**62.62**	**71.56**
Mintaka w/ Wikidata	Random	4.80	1.85	11.48	22.03	0.91	0.14	1.78	5.15
	Popular	6.09	3.09	12.51	20.47	0.24	0.04	0.28	1.24
	MPNet	**13.01**	**7.50**	**25.44**	**35.43**	**13.00**	**6.82**	**26.65**	**40.01**

Table 2: **Retriever results.** We compare random model, popular model, and MPNet (Song et al., 2020), on 1- and 2-hop retrievals.

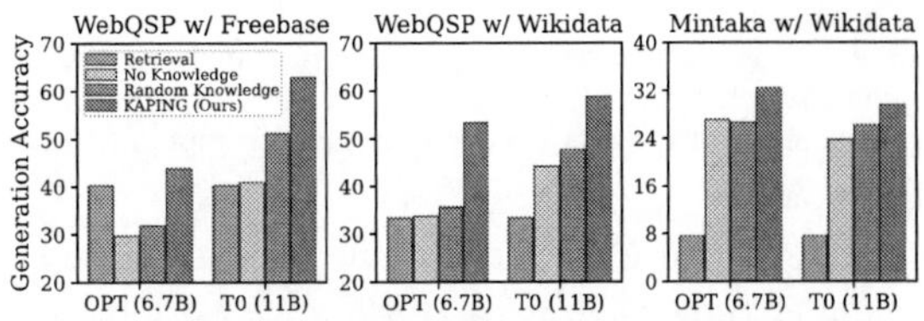

Figure 2: **Comparisons of retrieval and LM prompting.** Retrieval is the Top-1 result of the MPNet (Song et al., 2020).

augments them as the form of the prompt (Liu et al., 2022b), which is similar to Kojima et al. (2022).

KAPING (Ours) This is our Knowledge Augmented language model PromptING (KAPING) framework, which first retrieves the top-K similar triples to the question with the knowledge retriever, and then augments them as the form of the prompt.

4.4 Evaluation Metrics

Generation Following the evaluation protocol of generative KGQA (Yin et al., 2016; Sen et al., 2022; Mavi et al., 2022), we use accuracy, which measures whether the generated tokens from the given prompt include one of the answer entities. Note that we further consider *aliases* – a set of alternative names – of answer entities available in Freebase and Wikidata KGs, for evaluation.

Retrieval We also measure the retriever performance, to see how much the retrieved triples are helpful for answer generation. As metrics, we use Mean Reciprocal Rank (MRR) and Top-K accuracy (Top-K), which are calculated by ranks of correctly retrieved triples containing answer entities among all triples associated to question entities.

4.5 Implementation Details

For the knowledge injection, we set the number of retrieved facts as 10 ($K = 10$), and the hop for triple retrieval as one. For the text-based retriever, we experiment with MPNet (Song et al., 2020) that uses the same encoder for embedding question and triples. See Appendix A.4 for additional details.

5 Experimental Results and Analyses

We provide the overall results of our KAPING framework along with its comprehensive analyses.

Main Results As shown in Table 1, our KAPING framework significantly outperforms all LM prompting baselines, on zero-shot KGQA tasks. In particular, the generated knowledge model mostly degenerates the performance compared to the no knowledge model, since the extracted knowledge from LLMs themselves might be inaccurate. On the other hand, the random and popular knowledge baselines bring performance improvements, since the augmented knowledge from KGs are sometimes useful to answer the question. However, ours outperforms them, which suggests that, for zero-shot LM prompting for QA, the knowledge internalized in LLMs is insufficient to generate factual answers, and it is important to use only the relevant facts.

In addition, we also observe larger performance improvements when LMs are relatively small. In other words, since smaller models have insufficient parameter spaces to memorize the knowledge during pre-training, they are more likely to generate factually incorrect answers. However, when the appropriate knowledge is given to them, their performances sometimes become similar to larger models (e.g., different sizes of OPT have similar performances by our KAPING). Therefore, for tasks that require factual knowledge under low-resource setups (e.g., production), augmenting the knowledge would be beneficial, instead of increasing model sizes to handle the huge volume of knowledge.

Figure 3: **Comparisons of correct and incorrect retrieval** for the generation performance on the GPT-3 (6.7B) model.

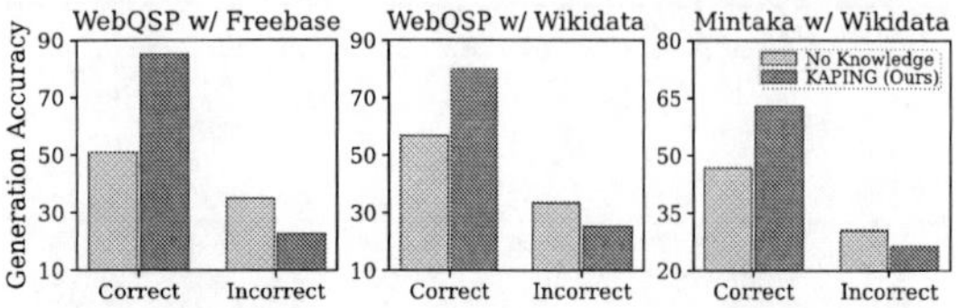

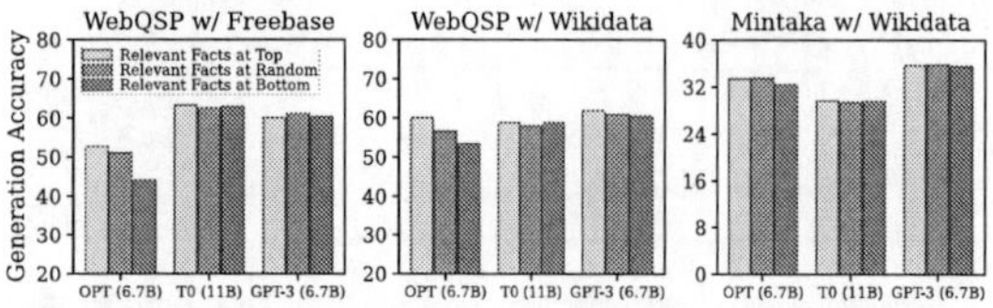

Figure 4: **Performances with varying the knowledge order**, where we change the location – top, bottom, or random – of more relevant triples for the question in the prompt of LLMs.

Figure 5: **Performances with varying knowledge amount**, where we change the number of retrieved triples to augment.

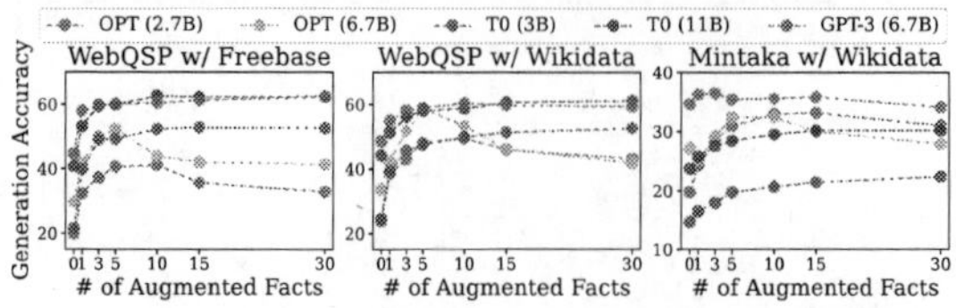

Models	# of Retrieved Facts	Relative Time	
		T0 (3B)	**OPT (2.7B)**
No Knowledge	0	1.00	1.00
KAPING (Ours)	1	0.49	1.12
	5	0.73	1.48
	10	1.07	1.89
	15	1.54	2.36
	30	2.49	3.77

Table 3: **Efficiencies with varying the knowledge amount**, where we measure the wall-clock time of every model for generating the answer on the WebQSP w/ Wikidata dataset.

Retriever Results To see how relevant the augmented knowledge is, we further measure the retrieval performances. As shown in Table 2, the existing retrieval model (i.e., MPNet) shows superior performances against naive models: random and popular retrievers. This result suggests that our simple graph-to-text verbalization works well with the existing retriever, which further confirms that our KAPING augments useful facts in the LM prompt. Regarding the number of hops for the candidate triples to retrieve, we observe that, when we increase the hop-size from one to two, the retriever is more likely to retrieve irrelevant triples that does not include answer entities, as shown in Table 2. Therefore, in our experiments, we retrieve knowledge among 1-hop triples of question entities.

Additionally, since we can alternatively answer the input question based on entities in the Top-1 triple from the retriever, we compare the generation performance of LLMs to the retrieval performance. As shown in Figure 2, LM prompting schemes even without knowledge augmentation (i.e., no knowledge) are superior than simply answering with the entity in the retrieved triple, except for the WebQSP w/ Freebase dataset. Also, we observe huge gaps between our KAPING framework and the simple retrieval scheme on all datasets. These results suggest that, for zero-shot KGQA, it would be helpful to leverage LLMs to generate answers based on their internalized and external facts, instead of directly searching answer entities over KGs.

Impact of Correct & Incorrect Retrievals We conduct analyses on how much the correctly retrieved triples, having answer entities, bring performance improvements, and how performances are affected by the incorrectly retrieved triples, which do not include answer entities. As shown in Figure 3, when retrieved triples contain answer entities, performances of LLMs are significantly improved, compared to models without knowledge augmentation. However, when retrievers fail, performances are lower than models of no knowledge augmentation. These results suggest, when relevant knowledge is augmented, LLMs can contextualize and generate answers accurately. Meanwhile, incorrectly retrieved knowledge makes LLMs condition on irrelevant facts, and generate wrong answers.

Varying the Amount of Knowledge We change the number of facts, to see which triple amounts are optimal to augment in the prompt, by comparing trade-off between the generation performance and the wall-clock time. First of all, as shown in Figure 5, most LLMs reach the somewhat highest performance, when the number of triples is 5 or 10. Also, when we further increase the augmented triple size to 15 and 30, performances of OPT models are largely decreasing. This result suggests that some LMs might be distracted by irrelevant triples when their volumes are high, therefore, failing to select and generate the answer entity.

We then measure the wall-clock time of the answer generation, for the encoder-decoder (T0) and decoder-only (OPT) models with varying the number of augmented triples in the prompt. As shown in Table 3, regarding the encoder-decoder model, our KAPING framework with less than 10 triples is faster than the model without knowledge augmentation. We observe this is because, when the knowledge is augmented to the model, the model tends to generate shorter answers, which can reduce the decoding time. More specifically, the length of generated tokens for the T0 model with 10 triples is

Table 4: **Generation examples** of the prompted GPT-3 for the input question with augmented triples from the retriever, where, in the last row, we change the knowledge of augmented facts to see whether the model is able to adapt to the changed knowledge.

Question: Where did Alex Chilton die?
Retrieved triples: (Alex Chilton, place of death, New Orleans), (Alex Chilton, manner of death, natural causes), (Alex Chilton, cause of death, myocardial infarction), (Alex Chilton, date of death, time: +2010-03-17), ...
Answer: New Orleans

	Prompts	Outputs
No Knowledge	Question: Where did Alex Chilton die? Answer:	Alex Chilton died in a ~~car accident~~ on ~~February 10, 1979~~.
KAPING (Ours)	Below are facts in the form of the triple meaningful to answer the question. ... (Alex Chilton, date of death, time: +2010-03-17) (Alex Chilton, cause of death, myocardial infarction) (Alex Chilton, manner of death, natural causes) (Alex Chilton, place of death, New Orleans) Question: Where did Alex Chilton die? Answer:	Alex Chilton died on March 17, 2010 in New Orleans, Louisiana due to a myocardial infarction.
KAPING (Ours) w/ Knowledge Change	Below are facts in the form of the triple meaningful to answer the question. ... (Alex Chilton, date of death, time: +2000-09-01) (Alex Chilton, cause of death, pancreatic cancer) (Alex Chilton, manner of death, natural causes) (Alex Chilton, place of death, Los Angeles) Question: Where did Alex Chilton die? Answer:	Alex Chilton died in Los Angeles, California on September 1, 2000 from pancreatic cancer.

Models	T5 (3B)	T5 (11B)	OPT (2.7B)	OPT (13B)	T0 (3B)	T0 (11B)
No Knowledge	14.25	17.06	19.76	26.83	14.75	23.74
Random Knowledge	18.19	18.83	28.11	28.36	16.10	26.15
Random Knowledge w/ EL	15.99	17.98	23.10	26.47	15.60	24.66
KAPING	22.00	22.85	32.94	33.37	20.68	29.50
KAPING w/ EL	18.94	20.58	26.87	28.39	18.51	27.11

Table 5: **Results with entity linking**, where the model w/ EL uses entities extracted from the entity linking technique (Ayoola et al., 2022), instead of using labeled ones, on Mintaka.

15, whereas, the no knowledge model generates 32 tokens in average. However, for the decoder-only model (OPT), the more knowledge we augment, the slower the model becomes, because of its auto-regressive characteristic for digesting the input.

Impact of Orders of Retrieved Triples In few-shot LM prompting where LLMs additionally observe few examples in the prompt, they are known to be sensitive to the order of examples (Lu et al., 2022), and they tend to follow the answer in the last example (Zhao et al., 2021). Based on those observations, we also conduct an analysis on whether the order of retrieved triples affects the performance. In particular, we vary the location of more similar triples for the question, by locating them at the Top, Bottom, or Random position of the prompt. As shown in Figure 4, our KAPING is not sensitive to the location of retrieved triples, except for the OPT model on the WebQSP dataset. In other words, the OPT model tends to generate the entity located at the first part of the prompt input. Meanwhile, other LLMs can contextualize the entire prompt input, and generate the entity regardless of its position.

Effectiveness with Entity Linking Following the conventional KGQA evaluation (Cohen et al., 2020), we use question entities labeled in datasets, to retrieve facts in KGs. However, to see the performance with entities identified by Entity Linking (EL) technique, we further conduct experiments with the EL model, namely ReFinED (Ayoola et al., 2022). As shown in Table 5, while the performance of KAPING w/ EL is slightly decreasing from the model with labeled entities due to the performance of EL, we consistently observe meaningful performance improvements from a No Knowledge model.

Case Study We conduct a case study in Table 4. In particular, when the knowledge is not given to the LM, it hallucinates the factually incorrect answer. However, when related facts are retrieved and augmented in the prompt, it can generate the correct answer. In addition, we analyze whether our KAPING can adapt to the updated knowledge, motivated by that some knowledge can be changed over time, while the knowledge in LMs remains static. To do so, as shown in the last row of Table 4, we replace object entities of triples, and then forward the prompt with the modified facts to the LM. Then, the result shows that the LM can generate the output based on the updated facts, which suggests the potential of adapting LMs without costly updating their parameters.

Additional Results Note that we further provide additional experimental results in Appendix B. In particular, we compare the performance of retrievers in Appendix B.1, conduct the sensitivity analysis on template texts in Appendix B.2, provide the results with additional metrics including human evaluation in Appendix B.3, validate our KAPING under few-shot setups in Appendix B.4, provide the analysis on verbalization in Appendix B.5, and provide the efficiencies in Appendix B.6.

6 Conclusion

In this work, we focused on the limitation of existing LM prompting schemes, which rely on the static knowledge internalized in parameters; therefore, when such knowledge are incomplete, inaccurate, and outdated, LLMs may generate factually incorrect answers. To tackle this challenge, we introduced a novel Knowledge-Augmented language model PrompTING (KAPING) framework, which augments the knowledge for the input question from KGs directly in the input prompt of LLMs, with the fact retriever to inject only the relevant knowledge. The proposed framework is completely zero-shot, and versatile with any LMs, without additional parameter updates and training datasets. We validated that our KAPING yields huge performance gaps from the LM prompting model relying on its internal knowledge, especially with smaller LMs, on the KGQA tasks. We believe our new mechanism for augmenting facts from KGs to the LM prompt will bring substantial practical impacts in generating knowledge-grounded answers.

Limitations

In this section, we faithfully discuss the current limitations and potential avenues for future research.

First of all, the generation performance of our knowledge-augmentation framework largely depends on the efficacy of retrievers. In other words, if the retriever fails to retrieve the relevant facts to the input question, the prompted LLM, conditioned on the irrelevant facts, is likely to generate the incorrect answer (See Figure 3). Similarly, if the retriever is not designed to retrieve the facts in 2-hop neighborhoods of the question entities, LLMs are less likely to generate the answer requiring 2-hop knowledge. Note that, for the Mintaka dataset (Sen et al., 2022), the number of answerable questions with 1-hop facts is only 40% of total samples. However, when we include 2-hop triples, the number of answerable questions becomes 62%, which suggests the necessity of 2-hop retrievals, which is yet challenging (See Table 2). Thus, future work may improve the retrieval scheme itself to provide more accurate facts including multi-hops to the LLM, or may develop the mechanism to prevent the LLM from being misled by unrelated facts.

On the other hand, the evaluation metric for the generation performance of prompted LLMs may be further improved. Specifically, regarding our target KGQA tasks, the answer for the question is the entity in KGs. However, the prompted LLMs without additional training (i.e., zero-shot) tend to generate the answer as the sentence. For instance, the label entity for the question (e.g., Where did Alex Chilton die?) in Table 4 is "New Orleans", however, the LLMs often generate the sentence-level output: "Alex Chilton died on March 17, 2010 in New Orleans, Louisiana due to a myocardial infarction". We currently evaluate the model performance by measuring whether generated tokens contain the answer entity or not; however, it would be worthwhile to develop the additional metric to compare the sentence-level output from LLMs to the word-level answer in KGs in a more effective way. Note that we also try other available metrics (See Appendix B.3), such as F1 and Exact Match (EM) scores (Rajpurkar et al., 2016), however, they largely penalize the longer sentences (e.g., EM of correct examples in Table 4 are 0), thus may not be appropriate for evaluating LM prompting schemes.

Lastly, since we focus on the improvement of knowledge injection in LM prompting, we use the labeled entities in KGQA datasets when evaluating models, following the existing KGQA evaluation setups (Cohen et al., 2020; Sen et al., 2021). However, in real-world applications where the entities in the question are mostly not provided, we first need to extract entities in the question with existing entity linking techniques; therefore, our model performance depends on the efficacy of entity linking. In particular, regarding the result with entity linking in Table 5, the portion of answerable questions from labeled entities in the dataset is 40%, however, the portion of them with entities from the entity linking model (Ayoola et al., 2022) is 22%. Therefore, since the improved entity linking performance would contribute to the performance gain of our KAPING framework, for KGQA tasks, future work may advance such the entity linking scheme.

Ethics Statement

For a user's question, our knowledge-augmentation scheme can allow prompted LMs generate a factually correct answer, grounded by the provided knowledge, for KGQA tasks. However, the performance of our KAPING framework is still far from perfect, due to potential failures in entity linking, fact retrieval, and knowledge generation itself. Thus, we should be aware whether LMs generate correct answers, especially on high-risk domains.

Acknowledgements

We thank the members of the End-to-End Reasoning team of Alexa AI at Amazon and the anonymous reviewers for their constructive comments.

References

Tom Ayoola, Shubhi Tyagi, Joseph Fisher, Christos Christodoulopoulos, and Andrea Pierleoni. 2022. Refined: An efficient zero-shot-capable approach to end-to-end entity linking. *arXiv preprint arXiv:2207.04108*.

Junwei Bao, Nan Duan, Zhao Yan, Ming Zhou, and Tiejun Zhao. 2016. Constraint-based question answering with knowledge graph. In *COLING*. ACL.

Hannah Bast, Björn Buchhold, and Elmar Haussmann. 2016. Semantic search on text and knowledge bases. *Found. Trends Inf. Retr.*

Jonathan Berant, Andrew Chou, Roy Frostig, and Percy Liang. 2013. Semantic parsing on freebase from question-answer pairs. In *Proceedings of the 2013 Conference on Empirical Methods in Natural Language Processing, EMNLP 2013, 18-21 October 2013, Grand Hyatt Seattle, Seattle, Washington, USA, A meeting of SIGDAT, a Special Interest Group of the ACL*. ACL.

Kurt D. Bollacker, Colin Evans, Praveen K. Paritosh, Tim Sturge, and Jamie Taylor. 2008. Freebase: a collaboratively created graph database for structuring human knowledge. In *Proceedings of the ACM SIGMOD International Conference on Management of Data, SIGMOD 2008, Vancouver, BC, Canada, June 10-12, 2008*. ACM.

Tom B. Brown, Benjamin Mann, Nick Ryder, Melanie Subbiah, Jared Kaplan, Prafulla Dhariwal, Arvind Neelakantan, Pranav Shyam, Girish Sastry, Amanda Askell, Sandhini Agarwal, Ariel Herbert-Voss, Gretchen Krueger, Tom Henighan, Rewon Child, Aditya Ramesh, Daniel M. Ziegler, Jeffrey Wu, Clemens Winter, Christopher Hesse, Mark Chen, Eric Sigler, Mateusz Litwin, Scott Gray, Benjamin Chess, Jack Clark, Christopher Berner, Sam McCandlish, Alec Radford, Ilya Sutskever, and Dario Amodei. 2020. Language models are few-shot learners. In *NeurIPS*.

Nilesh Chakraborty, Denis Lukovnikov, Gaurav Maheshwari, Priyansh Trivedi, Jens Lehmann, and Asja Fischer. 2019. Introduction to neural network based approaches for question answering over knowledge graphs. *arXiv preprint arXiv:1907.09361*.

Xiang Chen, Lei Li, Ningyu Zhang, Xiaozhuan Liang, Shumin Deng, Chuanqi Tan, Fei Huang, Luo Si, and Huajun Chen. 2022a. Decoupling knowledge from memorization: Retrieval-augmented prompt learning. *arXiv preprint arXiv:2205.14704*.

Xiang Chen, Ningyu Zhang, Xin Xie, Shumin Deng, Yunzhi Yao, Chuanqi Tan, Fei Huang, Luo Si, and Huajun Chen. 2022b. Knowprompt: Knowledge-aware prompt-tuning with synergistic optimization for relation extraction. In *WWW*, pages 2778–2788. ACM.

Aakanksha Chowdhery, Sharan Narang, Jacob Devlin, Maarten Bosma, Gaurav Mishra, Adam Roberts, Paul Barham, Hyung Won Chung, Charles Sutton, Sebastian Gehrmann, Parker Schuh, Kensen Shi, Sasha Tsvyashchenko, Joshua Maynez, Abhishek Rao, Parker Barnes, Yi Tay, Noam Shazeer, Vinodkumar Prabhakaran, Emily Reif, Nan Du, Ben Hutchinson, Reiner Pope, James Bradbury, Jacob Austin, Michael Isard, Guy Gur-Ari, Pengcheng Yin, Toju Duke, Anselm Levskaya, Sanjay Ghemawat, Sunipa Dev, Henryk Michalewski, Xavier Garcia, Vedant Misra, Kevin Robinson, Liam Fedus, Denny Zhou, Daphne Ippolito, David Luan, Hyeontaek Lim, Barret Zoph, Alexander Spiridonov, Ryan Sepassi, David Dohan, Shivani Agrawal, Mark Omernick, Andrew M. Dai, Thanumalayan Sankaranarayana Pillai, Marie Pellat, Aitor Lewkowycz, Erica Moreira, Rewon Child, Oleksandr Polozov, Katherine Lee, Zongwei Zhou, Xuezhi Wang, Brennan Saeta, Mark Diaz, Orhan Firat, Michele Catasta, Jason Wei, Kathy Meier-Hellstern, Douglas Eck, Jeff Dean, Slav Petrov, and Noah Fiedel. 2022. Palm: Scaling language modeling with pathways. *arXiv preprint arXiv:2204.02311*.

William W. Cohen, Haitian Sun, R. Alex Hofer, and Matthew Siegler. 2020. Scalable neural methods for reasoning with a symbolic knowledge base. In *ICLR*.

Jacob Devlin, Ming-Wei Chang, Kenton Lee, and Kristina Toutanova. 2019. BERT: pre-training of deep bidirectional transformers for language understanding. In *NAACL*. Association for Computational Linguistics.

Dennis Diefenbach, Thomas Pellissier Tanon, Kamal Deep Singh, and Pierre Maret. 2017. Question answering benchmarks for wikidata. In *Proceedings of the ISWC 2017 Posters & Demonstrations and Industry Tracks co-located with 16th International Semantic Web Conference (ISWC 2017), Vienna, Austria, October 23rd - to - 25th, 2017*, CEUR Workshop Proceedings. CEUR-WS.org.

Bin Fu, Yunqi Qiu, Chengguang Tang, Yang Li, Haiyang Yu, and Jian Sun. 2020. A survey on complex question answering over knowledge base: Recent advances and challenges. *arXiv preprint arXiv:2007.13069*.

Fabian Galetzka, Jewgeni Rose, David Schlangen, and Jens Lehmann. 2021. Space efficient context encoding for non-task-oriented dialogue generation with graph attention transformer. In *Proceedings of the 59th Annual Meeting of the Association for Computational Linguistics and the 11th International Joint Conference on Natural Language Processing, ACL/IJCNLP 2021, August 1-6, 2021*. Association for Computational Linguistics.

Kelvin Guu, Kenton Lee, Zora Tung, Panupong Pasupat, and Ming-Wei Chang. 2020. REALM: retrieval-augmented language model pre-training. *arXiv preprint arXiv:2002.08909*.

Sebastian Hofstätter, Sheng-Chieh Lin, Jheng-Hong Yang, Jimmy Lin, and Allan Hanbury. 2021. Efficiently teaching an effective dense retriever with balanced topic aware sampling. In *SIGIR '21: The 44th International ACM SIGIR Conference on Research and Development in Information Retrieval, Canada, July 11-15, 2021*. ACM.

Neil Houlsby, Andrei Giurgiu, Stanislaw Jastrzebski, Bruna Morrone, Quentin de Laroussilhe, Andrea Gesmundo, Mona Attariyan, and Sylvain Gelly. 2019. Parameter-efficient transfer learning for NLP. In *ICML*, Proceedings of Machine Learning Research. PMLR.

Shengding Hu, Ning Ding, Huadong Wang, Zhiyuan Liu, Jingang Wang, Juanzi Li, Wei Wu, and Maosong Sun. 2022. Knowledgeable prompt-tuning: Incorporating knowledge into prompt verbalizer for text classification. In *ACL*, pages 2225–2240, Dublin, Ireland. Association for Computational Linguistics.

Gautier Izacard, Patrick Lewis, Maria Lomeli, Lucas Hosseini, Fabio Petroni, Timo Schick, Jane Dwivedi-Yu, Armand Joulin, Sebastian Riedel, and Edouard Grave. 2022. Few-shot learning with retrieval augmented language models. *arXiv preprint arXiv:2208.03299*.

Minki Kang, Jin Myung Kwak, Jinheon Baek, and Sung Ju Hwang. 2022. Knowledge-consistent dialogue generation with knowledge graphs. In *ICML 2022 Workshop on Knowledge Retrieval and Language Models*.

Vladimir Karpukhin, Barlas Oguz, Sewon Min, Patrick S. H. Lewis, Ledell Wu, Sergey Edunov, Danqi Chen, and Wen-tau Yih. 2020. Dense passage retrieval for open-domain question answering. In *Proceedings of the 2020 Conference on Empirical Methods in Natural Language Processing, EMNLP 2020, November 16-20, 2020*. Association for Computational Linguistics.

Takeshi Kojima, Shixiang Shane Gu, Machel Reid, Yutaka Matsuo, and Yusuke Iwasawa. 2022. Large language models are zero-shot reasoners. *arXiv preprint arXiv:2205.11916*.

Angeliki Lazaridou, Elena Gribovskaya, Wojciech Stokowiec, and Nikolai Grigorev. 2022. Internet-augmented language models through few-shot prompting for open-domain question answering. *arXiv preprint arXiv:2203.05115*.

Brian Lester, Rami Al-Rfou, and Noah Constant. 2021a. The power of scale for parameter-efficient prompt tuning. In *Proceedings of the 2021 Conference on Empirical Methods in Natural Language Processing, EMNLP 2021, Virtual Event / Punta Cana, Dominican Republic, 7-11 November, 2021*, pages 3045–3059. Association for Computational Linguistics.

Brian Lester, Rami Al-Rfou, and Noah Constant. 2021b. The power of scale for parameter-efficient prompt tuning. In *Proceedings of the 2021 Conference on Empirical Methods in Natural Language Processing, EMNLP 2021 / Punta Cana, Dominican Republic, 7-11 November, 2021*. Association for Computational Linguistics.

Patrick S. H. Lewis, Ethan Perez, Aleksandra Piktus, Fabio Petroni, Vladimir Karpukhin, Naman Goyal, Heinrich Küttler, Mike Lewis, Wen-tau Yih, Tim Rocktäschel, Sebastian Riedel, and Douwe Kiela. 2020. Retrieval-augmented generation for knowledge-intensive NLP tasks. In *NeurIPS*.

Belinda Z. Li, Sewon Min, Srinivasan Iyer, Yashar Mehdad, and Wen-tau Yih. 2020. Efficient one-pass end-to-end entity linking for questions. In *Proceedings of the 2020 Conference on Empirical Methods in Natural Language Processing, EMNLP 2020, November 16-20, 2020*. Association for Computational Linguistics.

Jimmy Lin, Rodrigo Nogueira, and Andrew Yates. 2021. *Pretrained Transformers for Text Ranking: BERT and Beyond*. Synthesis Lectures on Human Language Technologies. Morgan & Claypool Publishers.

Jiachang Liu, Dinghan Shen, Yizhe Zhang, Bill Dolan, Lawrence Carin, and Weizhu Chen. 2022a. What makes good in-context examples for gpt-3? In *Proceedings of Deep Learning Inside Out: The 3rd Workshop on Knowledge Extraction and Integration for Deep Learning Architectures, DeeLIO@ACL 2022, Dublin, Ireland and Online, May 27, 2022*, pages 100–114. Association for Computational Linguistics.

Jiacheng Liu, Alisa Liu, Ximing Lu, Sean Welleck, Peter West, Ronan Le Bras, Yejin Choi, and Hannaneh Hajishirzi. 2022b. Generated knowledge prompting for commonsense reasoning. In *ACL*. Association for Computational Linguistics.

Pengfei Liu, Weizhe Yuan, Jinlan Fu, Zhengbao Jiang, Hiroaki Hayashi, and Graham Neubig. 2021. Pretrain, prompt, and predict: A systematic survey of prompting methods in natural language processing. *arXiv preprint arXiv:2107.13586*.

Yinhan Liu, Myle Ott, Naman Goyal, Jingfei Du, Mandar Joshi, Danqi Chen, Omer Levy, Mike Lewis, Luke Zettlemoyer, and Veselin Stoyanov. 2019. Roberta: A robustly optimized BERT pretraining approach. *arXiv preprint arXiv:1907.11692*.

Yao Lu, Max Bartolo, Alastair Moore, Sebastian Riedel, and Pontus Stenetorp. 2022. Fantastically ordered prompts and where to find them: Overcoming few-shot prompt order sensitivity. In *ACL*. Association for Computational Linguistics.

Kangqi Luo, Fengli Lin, Xusheng Luo, and Kenny Q. Zhu. 2018. Knowledge base question answering via encoding of complex query graphs. In *Proceedings of the 2018 Conference on Empirical Methods in Natural Language Processing, Brussels, Belgium, October 31 - November 4, 2018*. Association for Computational Linguistics.

Kaixin Ma, Hao Cheng, Xiaodong Liu, Eric Nyberg, and Jianfeng Gao. 2022. Open domain question answering with A unified knowledge interface. In *ACL*. Association for Computational Linguistics.

Vaibhav Mavi, Anubhav Jangra, and Adam Jatowt. 2022. A survey on multi-hop question answering and generation. *arXiv preprint arXiv:2204.09140*.

Tri Nguyen, Mir Rosenberg, Xia Song, Jianfeng Gao, Saurabh Tiwary, Rangan Majumder, and Li Deng. 2016. MS MARCO: A human generated machine reading comprehension dataset. In *Proceedings of the Workshop on Cognitive Computation: Integrating neural and symbolic approaches 2016 co-located with the 30th Annual Conference on Neural Information Processing Systems (NIPS 2016), Barcelona, Spain, December 9, 2016*, CEUR Workshop Proceedings. CEUR-WS.org.

Barlas Oguz, Xilun Chen, Vladimir Karpukhin, Stan Peshterliev, Dmytro Okhonko, Michael Sejr Schlichtkrull, Sonal Gupta, Yashar Mehdad, and Scott Yih. 2022. Unik-qa: Unified representations of structured and unstructured knowledge for open-domain question answering. In *Findings of the Association for Computational Linguistics: NAACL*. Association for Computational Linguistics.

Adam Paszke, Sam Gross, Francisco Massa, Adam Lerer, James Bradbury, Gregory Chanan, Trevor Killeen, Zeming Lin, Natalia Gimelshein, Luca Antiga, Alban Desmaison, Andreas Kopf, Edward Yang, Zachary DeVito, Martin Raison, Alykhan Tejani, Sasank Chilamkurthy, Benoit Steiner, Lu Fang, Junjie Bai, and Soumith Chintala. 2019. Pytorch: An imperative style, high-performance deep learning library. In *NeurIPS*. Curran Associates, Inc.

Ted Pedersen, Siddharth Patwardhan, and Jason Michelizzi. 2004. Wordnet: : Similarity - measuring the relatedness of concepts. In *Proceedings of the Nineteenth National Conference on Artificial Intelligence, Sixteenth Conference on Innovative Applications of Artificial Intelligence, July 25-29, 2004, San Jose, California, USA*, pages 1024–1025. AAAI Press / The MIT Press.

Fabio Petroni, Tim Rocktäschel, Sebastian Riedel, Patrick S. H. Lewis, Anton Bakhtin, Yuxiang Wu, and Alexander H. Miller. 2019. Language models as knowledge bases? In *Proceedings of the 2019 Conference on Empirical Methods in Natural Language Processing and the 9th International Joint Conference on Natural Language Processing, EMNLP-IJCNLP 2019, Hong Kong, China, November 3-7, 2019*. Association for Computational Linguistics.

Alec Radford, Karthik Narasimhan, Tim Salimans, Ilya Sutskever, et al. 2018. Improving language understanding by generative pre-training.

Colin Raffel, Noam Shazeer, Adam Roberts, Katherine Lee, Sharan Narang, Michael Matena, Yanqi Zhou, Wei Li, and Peter J. Liu. 2020. Exploring the limits of transfer learning with a unified text-to-text transformer. *J. Mach. Learn. Res.*

Pranav Rajpurkar, Jian Zhang, Konstantin Lopyrev, and Percy Liang. 2016. Squad: 100, 000+ questions for machine comprehension of text. In *Proceedings of the 2016 Conference on Empirical Methods in Natural Language Processing, EMNLP 2016, Austin, Texas, USA, November 1-4, 2016*. The Association for Computational Linguistics.

Adam Roberts, Colin Raffel, and Noam Shazeer. 2020. How much knowledge can you pack into the parameters of a language model? In *EMNLP*.

Anna Rohrbach, Lisa Anne Hendricks, Kaylee Burns, Trevor Darrell, and Kate Saenko. 2018. Object hallucination in image captioning. In *Proceedings of the 2018 Conference on Empirical Methods in Natural Language Processing, Brussels, Belgium, October 31 - November 4, 2018*. Association for Computational Linguistics.

Md. Rashad Al Hasan Rony, Ricardo Usbeck, and Jens Lehmann. 2022. Dialokg: Knowledge-structure aware task-oriented dialogue generation. In *Findings of the Association for Computational Linguistics: NAACL*. Association for Computational Linguistics.

Ohad Rubin, Jonathan Herzig, and Jonathan Berant. 2022. Learning to retrieve prompts for in-context learning. In *Proceedings of the 2022 Conference of the North American Chapter of the Association for Computational Linguistics: Human Language Technologies, NAACL 2022, Seattle, WA, United States, July 10-15, 2022*, pages 2655–2671. Association for Computational Linguistics.

Amir Saffari, Armin Oliya, Priyanka Sen, and Tom Ayoola. 2021. End-to-end entity resolution and question answering using differentiable knowledge graphs. In *Proceedings of the 2021 Conference on Empirical Methods in Natural Language Processing, EMNLP 2021 / Punta Cana, Dominican Republic, 7-11 November, 2021*. Association for Computational Linguistics.

Victor Sanh, Albert Webson, Colin Raffel, Stephen Bach, Lintang Sutawika, Zaid Alyafeai, Antoine Chaffin, Arnaud Stiegler, Arun Raja, Manan Dey, M Saiful Bari, Canwen Xu, Urmish Thakker, Shanya Sharma Sharma, Eliza Szczechla, Taewoon Kim, Gunjan Chhablani, Nihal V. Nayak, Debajyoti Datta, Jonathan Chang, Mike Tian-Jian Jiang, Han Wang, Matteo Manica, Sheng Shen, Zheng Xin Yong, Harshit Pandey, Rachel Bawden, Thomas Wang, Trishala Neeraj, Jos Rozen, Abheesht Sharma, Andrea Santilli, Thibault Févry, Jason Alan Fries, Ryan Teehan, Teven Le Scao, Stella Biderman, Leo Gao, Thomas Wolf, and Alexander M. Rush. 2022. Multitask prompted training enables zero-shot task generalization. In *ICLR*.

Apoorv Saxena, Aditay Tripathi, and Partha P. Talukdar. 2020. Improving multi-hop question answering over knowledge graphs using knowledge base embeddings. In *ACL*. Association for Computational Linguistics.

Priyanka Sen, Alham Fikri Aji, and Amir Saffari. 2022. Mintaka: A complex, natural, and multilingual dataset for end-to-end question answering. In *COLING*. International Committee on Computational Linguistics.

Priyanka Sen, Armin Oliya, and Amir Saffari. 2021. Expanding end-to-end question answering on differentiable knowledge graphs with intersection. In *Proceedings of the 2021 Conference on Empirical Methods in Natural Language Processing, EMNLP 2021 / Punta Cana, Dominican Republic, 7-11 November, 2021*. Association for Computational Linguistics.

Taylor Shin, Yasaman Razeghi, Robert L. Logan IV, Eric Wallace, and Sameer Singh. 2020. Autoprompt: Eliciting knowledge from language models with automatically generated prompts. In *Proceedings of the 2020 Conference on Empirical Methods in Natural Language Processing, EMNLP 2020, Online, November 16-20, 2020*, pages 4222–4235. Association for Computational Linguistics.

Saleh Soltan, Shankar Ananthakrishnan, Jack FitzGerald, Rahul Gupta, Wael Hamza, Haidar Khan, Charith Peris, Stephen Rawls, Andy Rosenbaum, Anna Rumshisky, Chandana Satya Prakash, Mukund Sridhar, Fabian Triefenbach, Apurv Verma, Gökhan Tür, and Prem Natarajan. 2022. Alexatm 20b: Few-shot learning using a large-scale multilingual seq2seq model. *arXiv preprint arXiv:2208.01448*.

Kaitao Song, Xu Tan, Tao Qin, Jianfeng Lu, and Tie-Yan Liu. 2020. Mpnet: Masked and permuted pre-training for language understanding. In *NeurIPS*.

Robyn Speer, Joshua Chin, and Catherine Havasi. 2017. Conceptnet 5.5: An open multilingual graph of general knowledge. In *Proceedings of the Thirty-First AAAI Conference on Artificial Intelligence, February 4-9, 2017, San Francisco, California, USA*, pages 4444–4451. AAAI Press.

Haitian Sun, Bhuwan Dhingra, Manzil Zaheer, Kathryn Mazaitis, Ruslan Salakhutdinov, and William W. Cohen. 2018. Open domain question answering using early fusion of knowledge bases and text. In *Proceedings of the 2018 Conference on Empirical Methods in Natural Language Processing, Brussels, Belgium, October 31 - November 4, 2018*. Association for Computational Linguistics.

Mujeen Sung, Jinhyuk Lee, Sean S. Yi, Minji Jeon, Sungdong Kim, and Jaewoo Kang. 2021. Can language models be biomedical knowledge bases? In *EMNLP*. Association for Computational Linguistics.

Ashish Vaswani, Noam Shazeer, Niki Parmar, Jakob Uszkoreit, Llion Jones, Aidan N. Gomez, Lukasz Kaiser, and Illia Polosukhin. 2017. Attention is all you need. In *NeurIPS*.

Denny Vrandecic and Markus Krötzsch. 2014. Wikidata: a free collaborative knowledgebase. *Commun. ACM*, 57(10):78–85.

Xuezhi Wang, Jason Wei, Dale Schuurmans, Quoc V. Le, Ed H. Chi, and Denny Zhou. 2022. Self-consistency improves chain of thought reasoning in language models. *arXiv preprint arXiv:2203.11171*.

Jason Wei, Maarten Bosma, Vincent Y. Zhao, Kelvin Guu, Adams Wei Yu, Brian Lester, Nan Du, Andrew M. Dai, and Quoc V. Le. 2022a. Finetuned language models are zero-shot learners. In *ICLR*.

Jason Wei, Xuezhi Wang, Dale Schuurmans, Maarten Bosma, Ed H. Chi, Quoc Le, and Denny Zhou. 2022b. Chain of thought prompting elicits reasoning in large language models. *arXiv preprint arXiv:2201.11903*.

Thomas Wolf, Lysandre Debut, Victor Sanh, Julien Chaumond, Clement Delangue, Anthony Moi, Pierric Cistac, Tim Rault, Rémi Louf, Morgan Funtowicz, Joe Davison, Sam Shleifer, Patrick von Platen, Clara Ma, Yacine Jernite, Julien Plu, Canwen Xu, Teven Le Scao, Sylvain Gugger, Mariama Drame, Quentin Lhoest, and Alexander M. Rush. 2020. Transformers: State-of-the-art natural language processing. In *Proceedings of the 2020 Conference on Empirical Methods in Natural Language Processing: System Demonstrations*. Association for Computational Linguistics.

Ledell Wu, Fabio Petroni, Martin Josifoski, Sebastian Riedel, and Luke Zettlemoyer. 2020. Scalable zero-shot entity linking with dense entity retrieval. In *Proceedings of the 2020 Conference on Empirical Methods in Natural Language Processing, EMNLP 2020, November 16-20, 2020*. Association for Computational Linguistics.

Lee Xiong, Chenyan Xiong, Ye Li, Kwok-Fung Tang, Jialin Liu, Paul N. Bennett, Junaid Ahmed, and Arnold Overwijk. 2021. Approximate nearest neighbor negative contrastive learning for dense text retrieval. In *ICLR*.

Zhilin Yang, Zihang Dai, Yiming Yang, Jaime G. Carbonell, Ruslan Salakhutdinov, and Quoc V. Le. 2019. Xlnet: Generalized autoregressive pretraining for language understanding. In *NeurIPS*.

Michihiro Yasunaga, Hongyu Ren, Antoine Bosselut, Percy Liang, and Jure Leskovec. 2021. QA-GNN: reasoning with language models and knowledge graphs for question answering. In *NAACL*. Association for Computational Linguistics.

Wen-tau Yih, Ming-Wei Chang, Xiaodong He, and Jianfeng Gao. 2015. Semantic parsing via staged query graph generation: Question answering with knowledge base. In *ACL*. The Association for Computer Linguistics.

Wen-tau Yih, Matthew Richardson, Christopher Meek, Ming-Wei Chang, and Jina Suh. 2016. The value of semantic parse labeling for knowledge base question answering. In *ACL*. The Association for Computer Linguistics.

Jun Yin, Xin Jiang, Zhengdong Lu, Lifeng Shang, Hang Li, and Xiaoming Li. 2016. Neural generative question answering. In *Proceedings of the Twenty-Fifth International Joint Conference on Artificial Intelligence, IJCAI 2016, New York, NY, USA, 9-15 July 2016*, pages 2972–2978. IJCAI/AAAI Press.

Susan Zhang, Stephen Roller, Naman Goyal, Mikel Artetxe, Moya Chen, Shuohui Chen, Christopher Dewan, Mona Diab, Xian Li, Xi Victoria Lin, Todor Mihaylov, Myle Ott, Sam Shleifer, Kurt Shuster, Daniel Simig, Punit Singh Koura, Anjali Sridhar, Tianlu Wang, and Luke Zettlemoyer. 2022. OPT: open pretrained transformer language models. *arXiv preprint arXiv:2205.01068*.

Zihao Zhao, Eric Wallace, Shi Feng, Dan Klein, and Sameer Singh. 2021. Calibrate before use: Improving few-shot performance of language models. In *ICML*, Proceedings of Machine Learning Research. PMLR.

Yucheng Zhou, Xiubo Geng, Tao Shen, Wenqiang Zhang, and Daxin Jiang. 2021. Improving zero-shot cross-lingual transfer for multilingual question answering over knowledge graph. In *NAACL*. Association for Computational Linguistics.

A Additional Experimental Setups

Here we provide additional experimental setups.

A.1 Datasets

We provide the additional details for two Knowledge Graph Question Answering (KGQA) datasets, namely WebQuestionsSP and Mintaka, which we use for evaluating baselines and our model.

WebQuestionsSP (WebQSP) A question and its corresponding answer are annotated with Freebase entities (Bollacker et al., 2008), and refined with additional cleaning steps (Yih et al., 2016): filtering out samples with invalid annotations, from the original WebQuestions dataset (Berant et al., 2013).

Mintaka This dataset (Sen et al., 2022) is designed for complex KGQA tasks including superlative and comparative questions, where question-answer pairs are collected from crowdsourcing with Wikidata entities (Vrandecic and Krötzsch, 2014).

A.2 Large Language Models

We describe the specific details of Large Language Models (LLMs) that we use for LM prompting.

T5 This model (Raffel et al., 2020) is an encoder-decoder model, and, among different variants, we use the LM-adapted version[1], which is additionally pre-trained with auto-regressive language modeling objective (Radford et al., 2018) for LM prompting.

T0 This model (Sanh et al., 2022) is further fine-tuned from T5 (Raffel et al., 2020) over prompted text-to-text tasks, for improved zero-shot generalization performance with LM prompting.

GPT-3 This model (Brown et al., 2020) is a decoder only model, which we access via API[2].

OPT This model (Zhang et al., 2022) is a decoder only model, freely available for researchers.

AlexaTM This model (Soltan et al., 2022) is an encoder-decoder model, pre-trained with denoising, which reconstructs the context of 15% dropped tokens, and auto-regressive, which predicts the next tokens based on their previous tokens, objectives.

A.3 Evaluation Metrics

We provide more details for evaluation metrics.

Aliases For generative question answering tasks, there can be alternative names of entities, called aliases, and we consider them for evaluation. For example, one Wikidata entity, "William Shakespeare" (Q692), has alternative names, such as "Shakespeare" and "The Bard", and we consider them when measuring the generation performance.

Filtering Unnamed Entities For evaluating generative models, the name of entities are required. However, we sometime cannot find the name of the answer entities from their ids on Freebase and Wikidata KGs. This is because the annotated answer entities are sometimes not entities but categories, and the entity ids in KGs could be changed but we cannot find the KG dumps that are used to annotate datasets. Therefore, we filter out samples that do not have literal name texts for the answer entities. This filtering step results in 1,582 test samples for the WebQSP w/ Freebase dataset, 1,466 test samples for the WebQSP w/ Wikidata dataset, and 2,814 test samples for the Mintaka dataset.

A.4 Implementation Details

In this subsection, we provide additional details for implementing our KAPING framework.

Knowledge Injection Schemes There are different choices in knowledge injection schemes, from the number of facts to retrieve, to the number of hops for candidate triples, to the order of retrieved facts in the prompt (i.e., where the most relevant knowledge should be located in the prompt), to the template of prompts including their instruction texts. While search spaces of them are extremely huge, we aim to to find the optimal one (See analyses in Section 5). Specifically, as reported in Section 4.5, the best settings we find are the number of retrieved facts of 10, and the number of hops for the triples to retrieve from the question entities of one. Also, we locate more relevant triples to the input question closer to the question text in the prompt, inspired by the observation that the model tends to rewrite answers that appeared at the end of the prompt (Zhao et al., 2021). Further, we examine different instruction templates for generating answers, such as "Question: $\{x\}$ Answer: " or "Please answer the following question: $\{x\}$", where x is the literal question. Regarding instruction templates, we observe that the performances of LLMs are sensitive across different instructions (See Appendix B.2), therefore, we try both of them and then report the best result.

[1]https://github.com/google-research/text-to-text-transfer-transformer/blob/main/released_checkpoints.md

[2]https://openai.com/api/

Datasets	Retrievers	1-Hop Retrieval MRR	Top-1	Top-10	Top-30	2-Hop Retrieval MRR	Top-1	Top-10	Top-30
WebQSP w/ Freebase	MPNet	47.27	40.27	60.56	64.48	41.64	33.12	58.47	65.23
	TAS-B	51.62	45.76	61.76	64.41	37.08	25.85	58.66	64.48
WebQSP w/ Wikidata	MPNet	43.46	33.36	64.39	70.67	40.42	30.56	62.62	71.56
	TAS-B	46.68	37.65	65.08	70.67	41.92	32.20	62.21	72.17
Mintaka w/ Wikidata	MPNet	13.01	7.50	25.44	35.43	13.00	6.82	26.65	40.01
	TAS-B	13.21	7.57	25.20	35.04	12.36	6.79	24.13	36.07

Table 6: **Results of two different retrievers**, namely MPNet (Song et al., 2020) and TAS-B (Hofstätter et al., 2021).

Retrieval Models To augment only the relevant triples to the input question under the zero-shot setup, we use off-the-shelf text-based retriever models. Specifically, we experiment with two different types of retrievers: symmetric retriever that uses the same encoder for question and triples; asymmetric one that uses individual encoders for them. For the symmetric retriever, we use MPNet (Song et al., 2020), which is trained on 1B sentence pairs[3]. Also, for the asymmetric retriever, we use TAS-B (Hofstätter et al., 2021), which is trained on the MS-MARCO dataset (Nguyen et al., 2016). We mainly report the results with MPNet, unless noted, since there performances are similar (See Appendix B.1).

A.5 Hyperparameters and Resources

We evaluate all models with PyTorch (Paszke et al., 2019) and Transformers (Wolf et al., 2020) libraries. We set the maximum number of input token lengths of LMs as 1,024 and the maximum number of output token lengths as 128, for encoder-decoder models. For decoder-only models, we set the maximum token lengths as 1,152 (1,024 + 128). For computing resources, we run all models with 8 V100 GPUs, having 8 $\times$ 32GB GPU memory, in which every model is runnable within one day. Note that, due to the expensive computational costs for model prompting with LLMs, we run every model one time, and then report the results, without additional hyperparameter tuning unless noted.

B Additional Experiment Results

In this section, we provide additional experimental results, on the comparisons of available text-based retrieval models in Section B.1, the sensitive analyses on template texts of the prompt in Section B.2, and the extra evaluation metrics in Section B.3.

B.1 Performance Comparisons of Retrievers

In Table 6, we compare existing symmetric and asymmetric retrievers named MPNet (Song et al., 2020) and TAS-B (Hofstätter et al., 2021), explained in Section A.4, on 1- and 2-hop retrievals. As shown in Table 6, we observe similar performances between symmetric (MPNet) and asymmetric (TAS-B) retrievers, which suggests that our simple graph-to-text verbalization is robust across different text-based retrieval schemes. Note that, since retrieval performances of both are similar, we conduct experiments mainly with MPNet, to reduce expensive computational costs for GPU usages.

[3]https://huggingface.co/sentence-transformers/all-mpnet-base-v2

Datasets	Models	Templates	T5 (11B)	T0 (11B)	OPT (6.7B)	GPT-3 (6.7B)
WebQSP w/ Freebase	No Knowledge	Default	9.48	34.70	29.77	44.63
		Please	3.03	40.77	18.71	42.48
	KAPING	Default	24.91	62.58	43.93	60.37
		Please	17.45	61.19	34.07	60.43
WebQSP w/ Wikidata	No Knowledge	Default	15.21	38.88	33.77	48.50
		Please	5.12	44.20	22.71	48.29
	KAPING	Default	35.47	58.73	53.34	60.44
		Please	20.12	56.89	48.16	59.69
Mintaka w/ Wikidata	No Knowledge	Default	17.06	22.60	27.19	35.00
		Please	5.47	23.74	17.70	34.65
	KAPING	Default	22.85	29.50	32.37	33.55
		Please	14.68	29.18	28.18	35.61

Table 7: **Results with varying instruction templates**, for various LLMs on the WebQSP and Mintaka datasets.

B.2 Sensitivity Analyses on Template Texts

Following the observation in Zhao et al. (2021), the performances of LLMs vary across different templates in the prompt. In our experiments, since it is computationally infeasible to try all different prompt templates on various LLMs, we consider two types of question templates, described in Appendix A.4. In particular, for the question x, we use either "Question: $\{x\}$ Answer: ", which we refer to as *default* template, or "Please answer the following question: $\{x\}$", referred to as *please* template. As shown in Table 7, for the T5 model, the default template is superior than the please template. Meanwhile, for the OPT model, the please template is superior than the other. However, for T0 and GPT-3 models, performance differences between default and please templates are marginal. Therefore, these results suggest that we may need to select instruction templates carefully across different LLMs for achieving optimal performances.

Additionally, regarding the knowledge-injection template described in Section 3.2, we also observe that the generation performance of GPT-3 depends on the instruction text in the template. In particular, we mainly conduct experiments with the template: "Below are facts in the form of the triple meaningful to answer the question."; however, we observe the performance degeneration when the augmented triples are irrelevant to the given question as shown

Datasets	Methods	T5 (0.8B) Acc.	T5 (0.8B) F1	T5 (0.8B) EM	T5 (3B) Acc.	T5 (3B) F1	T5 (3B) EM	T5 (11B) Acc.	T5 (11B) F1	T5 (11B) EM	OPT (2.7B) Acc.	OPT (2.7B) F1	OPT (2.7B) EM	OPT (6.7B) Acc.	OPT (6.7B) F1	OPT (6.7B) EM	OPT (13B) Acc.	OPT (13B) F1	OPT (13B) EM
WebQSP w/ Freebase	No Knowledge	6.95	5.20	0.00	13.40	8.11	0.00	9.48	8.25	0.06	19.85	7.20	0.38	29.77	10.60	0.06	28.38	7.92	0.70
	Random Knowledge	21.55	9.74	0.00	19.15	8.08	0.00	17.57	7.50	0.19	28.07	13.33	0.06	31.73	13.01	0.00	33.31	12.41	0.00
	Popular Knowledge	15.30	8.75	0.06	16.88	8.19	0.00	18.39	8.95	0.19	28.32	13.78	0.06	28.13	12.21	0.00	24.21	9.86	0.00
	Generated Knowledge	6.19	7.96	0.00	7.84	7.56	0.06	6.76	6.51	0.00	7.46	4.59	0.00	11.50	4.95	0.00	8.22	4.59	0.00
	KAPING (Ours)	34.70	15.39	0.00	25.41	8.31	0.06	24.91	11.02	0.32	41.09	16.32	0.00	43.93	15.15	0.00	40.20	13.32	0.00
WebQSP w/ Wikidata	No Knowledge	10.30	5.60	0.00	18.42	8.48	0.00	15.21	8.94	0.07	23.94	7.90	0.48	33.77	11.41	0.07	32.40	8.45	0.75
	Random Knowledge	17.94	7.81	0.00	22.78	7.74	0.07	24.28	9.41	0.34	37.24	16.78	0.00	35.61	12.54	0.00	38.27	14.61	0.07
	Popular Knowledge	15.35	8.01	0.00	20.80	8.48	0.00	20.74	9.20	0.14	30.83	15.65	0.00	30.01	13.32	0.00	27.83	11.95	0.00
	Generated Knowledge	11.94	8.64	0.00	13.30	8.19	0.07	12.28	7.11	0.00	11.26	5.06	0.00	17.53	5.60	0.00	14.19	4.94	0.00
	KAPING (Ours)	23.67	10.46	0.00	40.38	13.25	0.00	35.47	11.50	0.34	49.52	20.17	0.00	53.34	16.62	0.00	51.57	16.73	0.14
Mintaka w/ Wikidata	No Knowledge	11.23	6.77	0.00	14.25	9.81	0.00	17.06	10.28	0.00	19.76	6.63	0.28	27.19	10.60	0.04	26.83	9.82	0.43
	Random Knowledge	17.59	10.48	0.18	18.19	9.24	0.00	18.83	9.82	0.57	28.11	14.47	0.00	26.58	12.80	0.00	28.36	14.02	0.11
	Popular Knowledge	17.56	9.88	0.00	18.09	10.47	0.07	18.73	10.07	0.53	26.97	13.76	0.00	27.08	12.95	0.07	23.10	11.28	0.00
	Generated Knowledge	13.61	9.23	0.00	14.61	8.85	0.00	14.29	7.51	0.04	11.87	6.34	0.00	14.96	5.81	0.04	16.24	7.14	0.00
	KAPING (Ours)	19.72	11.36	0.04	22.00	11.17	0.00	22.85	10.91	0.43	32.94	14.99	0.00	32.37	14.37	0.04	33.37	14.65	0.11

Datasets	Methods	T0 (3B) Acc.	T0 (3B) F1	T0 (3B) EM	T0 (11B) Acc.	T0 (11B) F1	T0 (11B) EM	AlexaTM (20B) Acc.	AlexaTM (20B) F1	AlexaTM (20B) EM	GPT-3 (6.7B) Acc.	GPT-3 (6.7B) F1	GPT-3 (6.7B) EM	GPT-3 (175B) Acc.	GPT-3 (175B) F1	GPT-3 (175B) EM	Average Acc.	Average F1	Average EM
WebQSP w/ Freebase	No Knowledge	21.43	22.70	9.99	40.77	46.10	34.39	46.79	17.65	0.00	44.63	21.12	1.77	63.59	32.75	8.47	29.55	17.05	5.07
	Random Knowledge	32.62	36.48	26.55	51.20	55.98	46.90	57.37	20.91	0.00	51.01	28.04	6.19	65.87	41.28	18.46	37.22	22.43	8.94
	Popular Knowledge	27.05	31.38	20.23	47.22	52.44	42.04	54.91	20.45	0.00	45.58	25.94	4.87	62.26	38.84	17.00	33.48	20.98	7.68
	Generated Knowledge	19.41	23.15	10.56	38.81	43.43	31.23	35.13	14.42	0.00	45.89	27.98	9.48	62.14	38.79	17.57	22.67	16.72	6.26
	KAPING (Ours)	52.28	55.27	48.04	62.85	66.11	58.53	67.67	23.16	0.00	60.37	32.89	8.34	73.89	43.15	20.67	**47.94**	**27.28**	**12.36**
WebQSP w/ Wikidata	No Knowledge	24.56	24.20	10.98	44.20	49.27	37.65	42.41	16.43	0.00	48.50	24.01	3.96	67.60	34.31	10.30	32.85	18.09	5.84
	Random Knowledge	28.85	33.08	22.37	47.68	52.34	42.50	55.63	19.88	0.06	52.05	25.37	2.18	60.64	36.88	13.92	38.27	21.49	7.41
	Popular Knowledge	24.83	27.89	16.03	48.02	52.84	41.88	53.92	19.77	0.00	47.41	24.36	3.75	63.37	37.08	14.73	34.83	20.78	6.96
	Generated Knowledge	22.92	25.28	11.80	41.34	45.70	33.83	31.16	13.36	0.00	48.77	29.72	11.19	65.89	39.52	17.87	26.42	17.56	6.80
	KAPING (Ours)	49.86	50.75	41.27	58.73	61.90	53.27	65.04	22.72	0.00	60.44	31.18	6.82	69.58	41.83	19.71	**50.69**	**27.01**	**11.05**
Mintaka w/ Wikidata	No Knowledge	14.75	20.84	11.34	23.74	28.69	20.86	41.97	17.05	0.00	34.65	17.67	2.31	56.33	26.77	6.11	26.16	14.99	3.76
	Random Knowledge	16.10	23.08	14.14	26.15	31.70	22.85	46.02	17.02	0.00	32.98	17.55	1.39	51.56	25.98	6.29	28.22	16.92	4.14
	Popular Knowledge	16.74	23.13	14.53	27.15	32.17	23.45	46.41	17.31	0.00	32.48	20.07	4.41	53.16	27.44	6.86	27.95	17.14	4.54
	Generated Knowledge	14.46	20.08	11.98	23.13	27.34	18.76	34.58	14.91	0.00	33.12	18.29	3.09	55.65	30.69	11.73	22.41	14.20	4.15
	KAPING (Ours)	20.68	27.80	18.12	29.50	34.83	26.23	49.08	17.90	0.00	35.61	20.80	5.79	56.86	28.63	7.64	**32.27**	**18.86**	**5.31**

Table 8: **LM prompting results with additional metrics: F1 and Exact Match (EM)**, along with accuracy (Acc.) scores.

in Figure 3. Therefore, to improve the performance on incorrect retrievals, we further experiment with the additional template: "Below are facts in the form of the triple that might be meaningful to answer the question.". Then, the GPT-3 (175B) model with the previous template achieves 74.16 and 42.80 accuracies for correct and incorrect retrievals, respectively. Meanwhile, the same model with the instruction template containing "might be" achieves 72.91 and 51.38 accuracies for correct and incorrect retrievals, respectively. Thus, these results suggest that the knowledge-injection template with "might be" statement makes the model less selective on the augmented triples while focusing more on the internalized knowledge in parameters, thus improving the incorrect retrieval performance while degenerating the correct retrieval.

B.3 Additional Evaluation Metrics

As described in Section 4.4, we evaluate the performance of LLMs based on whether generated tokens for the input question contain answer entities or not. This is because, as explained in Section 6 of the limitation, pre-trained LLMs without further finetuning tend to generate the answer as the sentence, while the answer for the KGQA task is the entity consisting of few tokens. In this subsection, we further provide experiment results with additional evaluation metrics (Rajpurkar et al., 2016), namely F1 and Exact Match (EM) scores. Note that they are frequently used for evaluating extractive QA models, whose goal is to classify the answer span in the given context, without generation. As shown in Table 8, since the F1 score penalizes the longer sentence too much, the performances of LLMs evaluated by F1 scores are largely decreasing, except for the T0 model that is further fine-tuned by prompted text-to-text tasks, including QA, thus capable of generating entity-level outputs. Similarly, except for the T0, it is highly suboptimal to evaluate the performance of prompted LMs with EM scores, due to differences in output lengths. Thus, it would be promising direction to further develop better evaluation metrics for KGQA under LM prompting schemes, which we leave as future work.

While such F1 and EM scores, used for extractive QA tasks, might be suboptimal to evaluate generative LM prompting schemes, our KAPING framework consistently outperforms all the other baselines based on averaged F1 and EM scores as well, by large margins. Note that the superior EM and F1 scores of the generated knowledge baseline with GPT-3 on few cases, even though they are rarely happen, is because, for this baseline, the GPT-3 model generates entity-level outputs, unlike ours that generates sentence-level outputs. In other words, the sentence-level outputs from our KAPING is often longer than the answer entities, since our model is grounded by retrieved facts from KGs as shown in Table 15; however, longer sentences penalize F1 and EM scores. More specifically, the average number of output sequence lengths of the

LLMs	Models	Correct	Semi-Correct	Incorrect
T0 (3B)	No Knowledge	7	1	22
	KAPING (Ours)	17	0	13
T0 (11B)	No Knowledge	14	0	16
	KAPING (Ours)	20	0	10
GPT-3 (6.7B)	No Knowledge	12	4	14
	KAPING (Ours)	19	4	17
GPT-3 (175B)	No Knowledge	22	1	7
	KAPING (Ours)	26	1	3

Table 9: **Human evaluation results**, where we randomly sample 30 examples from the WebQSP w/ Freebase dataset.

Models	Shots	T5 (3B)	OPT (6.7B)	T0 (11B)
No Knowledge	Zero-Shot	18.42	33.77	44.20
	One-Shot	18.28	36.90	41.13
	Three-Shots	17.87	37.65	37.38
KAPING (Ours)	Zero-Shot	40.38	53.34	58.73
	One-Shot	18.42	52.25	48.70
	Three-Shots	10.16	50.34	43.45

Table 10: **KGQA results with few-shot learning**. We vary the number of examples (i.e., shots) in the prompt, and report the performances on the WebQSP w/ Wikidata dataset.

generated knowledge model is 67.77, meanwhile, ours is 74.92. However, when we compare the generated knowledge baseline to our KAPING with other LLMs but also with other metrics, our KAPING significantly outperforms this baseline.

Human Evaluation Additionally, similar to the previous generative QA work (Roberts et al., 2020), we manually inspect 30 samples from the WebQSP w/ Freebase dataset, to see whether the generated sentence is factually correct to the input question. For this experiment, we evaluate four LLMs: T0 (3B), T0 (11B), GPT-3 (6.7B), and GPT-3 (175B), with no knowledge baseline and our KAPING. Also, we use three different ratings for each generation example: 1) we label it as correct if all information in the generated sentence is factually correct to the question; 2) we label it as semi-correct if some information in the generated sentence is factually incorrect which yet contains at least one answer entity; 3) we label it as incorrect for all the other cases. As shown in Table 9, we observe that our KAPING framework can generate the factually correct answer more, compared to the no knowledge baseline, which are consistent with the results from available evaluation metrics in Table 1 and Table 8. We provide generated answers, which we use for human evaluation in Table 9, for GPT-3 (175B) and T0 (3B) models in Table 15 and Table 16.

B.4 Performances of Few-Shot Learning

While the focus of our work is zero-shot as outlined in the main paper, in this subsection, we additionally extend this zero-shot setting to the few-shot

Retrievers	MRR	Top-1	Top-10	Top-30
Random Retrieval	9.50	3.62	22.58	40.72
Popular Retrieval	8.52	4.57	15.89	35.47
Retrieval with Free-Form Texts	41.33	31.11	62.07	69.92
Retrieval with Triple-Form Texts	43.46	33.36	64.39	70.67

Table 11: **Retrieval results with different verbalizers**. We use the graph-to-text transformation model proposed in Ma et al. (2022) for obtaining free-form texts. For triple-form texts, we use the verbalization technique described in Section 3.2. MPNet (Song et al., 2020) is used as the retriever, and the performance is reported on WebQSP w/ Wikidata.

Retrievers	T5 (3B)	OPT (6.7B)	T0 (3B)	T0 (11B)
No Knowledge	18.42	33.77	24.56	44.20
KAPING with Free-Form Texts	43.25	53.00	47.75	53.21
KAPING with Triple-Form Texts	40.38	53.34	49.86	58.73

Table 12: **KGQA results with different verbalizers**. We use the graph-to-text transformation model proposed in Ma et al. (2022) for obtaining free-form texts. For triple-form texts, we use the verbalization technique described in Section 3.2. We then inject the verbalized triples in the input prompt. We report the generation accuracy on WebQSP w/ Wikidata.

setting, where we prepend the few examples about the input-output pairs in the prompt of LLMs. As shown in Table 10, for the KGQA task, the performances are decreasing when we increase the number of samples (i.e., shots) in the input prompt, except for the OPT model. We suggest this might be because, the injected examples in the prompt are less relevant to the given factual question, misleading the model to focus on unrelated contexts on the injected examples. This phenomenon is even more severe in our KAPING framework; this is similarly because our KAPING augments the retrieved facts, and if the facts on the other few-shot examples are further injected in the input prompt, the model is more likely to be confused by those irrelevant facts. For the OPT model, we observe a slight performance improvement in the No Knowledge model, since few injected examples provide a hint on how the output format looks like. We leave further extending our zero-shot KAPING framework to the few-shot learning mechanism as future work.

B.5 Analyses on Knowledge Verbalization

As described in the Knowledge Verbalization paragraph of Section 3.2, we use the linear triple verbalization technique, which simply concatenates the tokens of subject, relation, and object in the triple, instead of using the sophisticated techniques that use the particular graph-to-text transformation methods (Oguz et al., 2022; Ma et al., 2022). This is because, we observe that our simple verbalization technique works well, and, in this subsection, we concretely show performance differences between our and existing verbalization techniques in

Models	# of Augmented Knowledge	Relative Time							
		T5 (0.8B)	T5 (3B)	T5 (11B)	OPT (2.7B)	OPT (6.7B)	OPT (13B)	T0 (3B)	T0 (11B)
No Knowledge	0	1.00	1.00	1.00	1.00	1.00	1.00	1.00	1.00
Document (Web) Augmentation	1	1.20	1.45	2.13	1.43	1.65	1.63	1.60	2.29
	5	2.78	4.16	6.80	3.42	3.90	3.66	2.98	9.01
	10	OOL	OOL	OOL	6.44	7.36	6.67	OOL	OOL
	15	OOL	OOL	OOL	9.35	10.71	OOM	OOL	OOL
	30	OOL	OOL	OOL	OOL	OOL	OOL	OOL	OOL
KAPING (Ours)	1	1.08	0.97	1.35	1.12	1.21	1.19	0.49	1.28
	5	1.22	1.50	2.13	1.48	1.65	1.60	0.73	2.18
	10	1.53	2.10	3.11	1.89	2.20	2.10	1.07	3.83
	15	1.84	2.74	4.02	2.36	2.76	2.58	1.54	4.59
	30	2.82	4.42	6.05	3.77	4.28	4.06	2.49	7.76

Table 13: **Efficiencies results**, where we measure the wall-clock time of every model for generating answers on the WebQSP w/ Wikidata dataset. The document augmentation model (Lazaridou et al., 2022) augments documents listed in their paper, meanwhile, ours augments relevant triples to the question retrieved from KGs. We set the maximum number of input sequences for T5 and T0 models as 1,024, and for OPT as 2,048. OOL denotes the out-of-length errors, where the input prompt length exceeds the maximum input token lengths. OOM denotes the out-of-memory error on the machine having eight V100 GPUs.

both the knowledge retrieval and injection steps. Note that, for the comparison, we use the trained knowledge verbalizer proposed in Ma et al. (2022).

We first provide the fact retrieval performances across the different knowledge verbalization methods in Table 11. As shown in Table 11, we observe that our simple triple-form text verbalization is superior to the free-form text verbalization in the fact retrieval. This might be because the free-form verbalization model, transforming the graph to the text, might generate the incorrect output that is semantically different from the original triple, leading to the degenerated retrieval performances.

On the other hand, we also report the generation results of KGQA with two different knowledge verbalizers on our KAPING framework in Table 12. As shown in Table 12, we observe that the performances between the free-form texts and the triple-form texts are comparable when augmented to LLMs with our KAPING framework. More specifically, for the T5 model, which is pre-trained on the unlabeled corpus without additional instruction tuning, the free-form text works well. Meanwhile, for the T0 model, which is further fine-tuned with natural language instruction tasks, it is beneficial to use our linear triple verbalizaton scheme.

B.6 Additional Efficiency Comparisons

In this subsection, we further provide efficiency results of all LLMs that we use in our main experiments across three different models: no knowledge model, document augmentation (i.e., web augmentation) model (Lazaridou et al., 2022), and our KAPING framework. We note that, as discussed in the Knowledge-Augmented LMs paragraph of Section 2, the web augmentation method augments documents searched from Google with the few-shot learning setup. However, as we discuss there, this web augmentation is orthogonal to ours, since we use the completely different knowledge source (i.e., KGs) and our work is under the zero-shot learning setup; from which our core mechanisms of how to retrieve and augment relevant knowledge with LM prompting is clearly different and novel. Furthermore, as discussed in Section 2, this web augmentation method is infeasible to experimentally compare as well, since individual researches cannot freely access the Google Search API to retrieve documents for every question in the world. Also, it is computationally expensive to augment documents consisting of hundreds to thousands tokens (Lazaridou et al., 2022) in LLMs, unlike our triple cases consisting of few tokens. In this subsection, to experimentally validate the latter issue, we further make the comparisons of computational costs between document augmentation and our fact augmentation. In particular, as shown in Table 13, the answer generation speed of the web augmentation mechanism is significantly slower than our triple augmentation mechanism, since it requires more time to encode and condition documents in the input prompt compared to triples. Also, following the original paper (Lazaridou et al., 2022), the suggested number of documents to augment is 15, however, in the most cases, we observe out-of-length (OOL) errors, since the length of the input prompt with 15 documents is longer than the maximum input sequence length of LLMs. While our fact augmentation scheme is slower than the model without augmentation, we believe that, given the substantially improved performance in Table 1 and the high efficiency compared to document augmentation in Table 13, KAPING is highly beneficial.

B.7 Result Analyses Across Question Types

For the Mintaka dataset (Sen et al., 2022), each question is belong to one of the following categories: Generic, Multihop, Intersection, Difference, Comparative, Superlative, Ordinal, Count, and Yes/No, which defines the complexity of questions. Therefore, to see which complexity category our knowledge-augmentation framework is helpful, and which category we should further improve on, we breakdown the performance of LLMs according to question types in Table 14. Note that, following the evaluation protocol in Section A.3 where we filter out questions that do not have answer names, the Yes/No type questions are not considered.

As shown in the last row of Table 14 where we average the performance of all LLMs per category, our KAPING framework brings significant performance improvements on all categories except for the Comparative type. One particular comparative-type question is "Who has won more NBA Season MVPs, LeBron James or Steph Curry", and, since it is hard to retrieve and associate relevant triples for such the comparative-type question, our KAPING underperforms simple knowledge-injection baselines: random knowledge and popular knowledge. However, the KG-augmented models (e.g., random knowledge, popular knowledge, and our KAPING) outperform other baselines, which suggests that knowledge-augmentation mechanism is meaningful to tackle comparative questions, and one might further improve the retrieval scheme or the input prompt itself, which we leave as future work.

On the other point we would like to mention is that, for the Count category, performances of T0 models are significantly low compared to other LLMs. This is surprising, since T0 models are further fine-tuned on the prompted text-to-text tasks, and they have strong performances on the other categories, thanks to fine-tuning. We believe such the low performance on the Count category is because, in the fine-tuning of T0 models, there are no prompted tasks related to counting, which makes T0 models hard to count particular instances. Therefore, to further improve the generalization performance of T0 models, one may additionally include more diverse prompted tasks, including the counting one, during the fine-tuning process.

B.8 Generation Examples

We provide generation examples for comparisons between the no knowledge baseline and our KAPING framework in Table 15 and Table 16 for GPT-3 and T0 language models, respectively. We also provide retrieved and generation examples of our KAPING framework with four different LLMs: T5 (11B), OPT (13B), T0 (11B), and GPT-3 (175B) on the WebQSP w/ Wikidata dataset in Table 17.

C Discussions on Prompt Design/Tuning

We discuss differences between prompt design and prompt tuning, along with additional relevant work in the prompt tuning literature. As described in Section 3.1, given an input question, the large language model can generate the answer text, which is called LM prompting (Brown et al., 2020; Liu et al., 2021). However, to further enhance the performance of models under the LM prompting scheme, prior work particularly designs the content in the prompt, which is called *prompt design* (Shin et al., 2020; Lu et al., 2022). More specifically, Shin et al. (2020) additionally include the particular trigger tokens, meaningful to the down-stream tasks, in the prompt, and Lu et al. (2022) change the order of demonstrations in the prompt under the few-shot LM prompting setup. Our method is in line with such the prompt design literature, and we introduce the method of knowledge augmentation in the input prompt with facts from KGs, to allow LLMs condition on factual knowledge for zero-shot QA.

On the other hand, there exists *prompt tuning* literature (Lester et al., 2021a), which additionally trains the prompt-relevant parameters with supervised learning objectives, while keeping the parameters of LLMs unchanged. While this prompt tuning approach can be beneficial in few-shot learning scenarios where the model is additionally tuned with few training examples, it is not suitable for our zero-shot learning. Also, unlike the prompt design approach, it is difficult to interpret and manipulate the prompt represented in the embedding space.

Note that, recently, there are few knowledge-aware prompt tuning work (Chen et al., 2022b; Hu et al., 2022; Chen et al., 2022a), and, while they are fundamentally different from our LM prompting (i.e., prompt design), we additionally discuss them. First of all, Chen et al. (2022b) tackle the relation extraction problem with prompt tuning, where they propose to embed the particular words related to the relation class in the embedding space. For example, for the relation type to classify: "county of birth", they embed person and country information in the representation space with training signals from supervised learning, for improved relation classification performance. Also, Hu et al. (2022) tackle the text classification task with prompt tuning, where they propose to not only consider the classification label word itself, but also the label word's related words. For example, for the sentence label "science", they further consider its related words:

"physics" and "mathematics", defined in particular knowledge bases, such as WordNet (Pedersen et al., 2004) and ConceptNet (Speer et al., 2017). Lastly, Chen et al. (2022a) tackle the similar text classification task with prompt tuning, where they propose to retrieve the data instance (i.e., a sentence and its label) in the training dataset based on the retriever training with supervised classification objectives.

However, all the above knowledge-aware prompt tuning methods are clearly different from our proposed KAPING framework. At first, they are restricted to cloze-style prediction, in which they first include the particular mask token in the input prompt, and then classify the label (e.g., sentiment of the sentence, or relation in the given sentence) of the mask token, similar to the masked language modeling objective (Devlin et al., 2019; Liu et al., 2019). Therefore, their cloze-style prediction schemes cannot be used for QA tasks, since the answer of the user's question is not the single token, and it is unclear to convert the predicted label token from the masked token to all different answers in the world. In contrast to them, our KAPING does not rely on the masked token classification scheme, thus ours is more flexible, and not restricted to cloze-style classification; suitable for answering any user's questions. Furthermore, some of them (Chen et al., 2022a,b) rely on training signals from the training dataset with supervised learning, meanwhile, ours is completely zero-shot. While Chen et al. (2022a) show the model's zero-shot ability, they require the training dataset as discussed in their paper, thus not suitable for our zero-shot QA as well. Lastly, we augment the factual knowledge by matching the entity in the question to its associated triples in KGs, however, prior work considers different knowledge source, which might not be helpful for QA tasks, such as relationships between words (Hu et al., 2022), relationships between the relation class and particular words (Chen et al., 2022b), and a pair of sentence and its label in training data (Chen et al., 2022a).

LLMs	Models	Generic (557)	Multihop (220)	Intersection (396)	Difference (349)	Comparative (223)	Superlative (384)	Ordinal (307)	Count (378)
T5 (0.8B)	No Knowledge	7.00	3.64	8.08	7.45	69.06	2.86	2.61	10.05
	Random Knowledge	11.49	5.45	8.33	11.75	86.10	6.77	8.14	26.98
	Popular Knowledge	13.82	5.91	11.62	8.60	87.00	8.33	5.86	22.22
	Generated Knowledge	7.72	2.73	5.81	8.02	82.06	3.39	1.95	21.43
	KAPING (Ours)	18.85	6.36	15.40	10.32	83.41	9.64	7.49	24.60
T5 (3B)	No Knowledge	10.41	4.09	9.60	9.74	71.30	5.47	4.56	17.99
	Random Knowledge	17.41	6.82	13.64	14.61	55.16	8.59	7.82	30.42
	Popular Knowledge	14.90	6.82	14.90	13.75	57.40	8.85	10.75	28.84
	Generated Knowledge	7.90	3.64	8.33	8.31	82.51	4.69	3.91	21.96
	KAPING (Ours)	25.31	12.27	20.96	15.76	47.98	10.68	9.77	35.71
T5 (11B)	No Knowledge	10.23	5.00	10.35	8.60	92.83	7.55	3.58	24.87
	Random Knowledge	20.29	7.27	11.87	12.89	60.99	10.68	9.12	27.51
	Popular Knowledge	16.88	7.27	12.88	13.18	72.20	9.11	10.42	24.34
	Generated Knowledge	7.72	2.73	5.30	7.45	89.24	3.91	2.28	22.49
	KAPING (Ours)	24.42	8.64	18.69	16.05	65.92	11.98	11.07	34.66
OPT (2.7B)	No Knowledge	24.06	10.00	16.67	10.32	54.26	20.05	14.98	14.29
	Random Knowledge	29.44	13.18	23.74	18.34	93.27	15.62	14.01	34.13
	Popular Knowledge	28.90	14.09	20.45	18.62	90.58	12.76	13.36	34.13
	Generated Knowledge	7.90	6.82	10.35	8.02	44.84	4.19	4.56	20.11
	KAPING (Ours)	33.75	15.91	34.85	20.63	93.27	15.89	19.54	43.65
OPT (6.7B)	No Knowledge	29.62	12.73	37.37	20.06	62.78	20.83	22.80	16.93
	Random Knowledge	23.52	14.09	19.44	20.92	89.69	13.02	15.31	36.77
	Popular Knowledge	24.42	13.18	24.24	22.92	83.86	14.84	17.26	32.80
	Generated Knowledge	11.67	8.64	16.92	12.61	43.95	7.55	6.51	20.90
	KAPING (Ours)	33.39	11.36	33.08	20.92	87.44	17.19	20.2	45.77
OPT (13B)	No Knowledge	33.57	16.82	34.85	18.91	48.43	19.27	19.22	22.75
	Random Knowledge	31.60	17.27	26.77	23.78	59.19	16.93	20.85	35.45
	Popular Knowledge	22.98	13.64	24.49	18.34	59.64	11.72	12.05	30.69
	Generated Knowledge	17.95	10.00	19.44	12.03	47.98	8.07	9.77	12.70
	KAPING (Ours)	40.04	17.27	35.61	23.50	56.05	19.53	27.36	45.24
T0 (3B)	No Knowledge	13.82	10.00	14.39	10.89	49.33	14.06	8.79	7.94
	Random Knowledge	19.57	9.09	15.66	12.32	58.30	8.59	9.77	6.88
	Popular Knowledge	19.21	10.00	18.69	12.03	60.09	8.33	8.79	8.73
	Generated Knowledge	13.11	11.36	12.63	12.61	54.71	12.50	10.10	3.70
	KAPING (Ours)	29.98	10.45	26.01	12.32	55.16	12.24	11.40	10.85
T0 (11B)	No Knowledge	33.93	18.18	33.08	18.05	54.71	19.53	13.68	1.59
	Random Knowledge	36.98	22.27	34.60	21.78	58.74	18.75	19.22	1.59
	Popular Knowledge	38.42	24.09	38.64	24.36	58.74	17.45	18.57	1.06
	Generated Knowledge	33.21	17.73	34.09	17.48	51.12	18.23	14.33	0.79
	KAPING (Ours)	45.60	27.27	41.16	22.35	56.05	18.75	23.45	1.59
GPT-3 (6.7B)	No Knowledge	40.39	28.18	34.34	24.36	74.44	26.04	24.76	33.07
	Random Knowledge	39.68	26.82	30.05	23.78	77.13	19.53	23.13	33.86
	Popular Knowledge	40.57	25.00	32.83	22.64	70.85	21.35	21.17	31.48
	Generated Knowledge	40.75	23.64	33.59	28.08	71.75	20.83	22.15	30.16
	KAPING (Ours)	46.14	24.09	33.33	24.36	77.58	19.53	24.76	35.71
GPT-3 (175B)	No Knowledge	71.10	52.73	64.90	49.00	80.72	42.45	50.81	38.62
	Random Knowledge	62.30	46.82	56.31	43.55	86.10	38.54	48.21	36.51
	Popular Knowledge	68.40	54.09	58.84	46.42	81.61	37.76	47.88	33.60
	Generated Knowledge	70.56	56.82	64.14	48.14	85.65	44.79	49.19	29.63
	KAPING (Ours)	69.48	56.36	63.89	48.14	82.96	45.57	49.84	41.01
Average	No Knowledge	27.41	16.14	26.36	17.74	65.79	17.81	16.58	18.81
	Random Knowledge	29.23	16.91	24.04	20.37	**72.47**	15.70	17.56	27.01
	Popular Knowledge	28.85	17.41	25.76	20.09	72.20	15.05	16.61	24.79
	Generated Knowledge	21.85	14.41	21.06	16.28	65.38	12.82	12.48	18.39
	KAPING (Ours)	**36.70**	**19.00**	**32.30**	**21.44**	70.58	**18.10**	**20.49**	**31.88**

Table 14: **Results across question types** – Generic, Multihop, Intersection, Difference, Comparative, Superlative, Ordinal, and Count – in the Mintaka dataset with various LLMs, where we report the generation accuracy. The number inside the parentheses in the first row denotes the number of data instances per category. We provide averaged results in the last row, namely **Average**.

Table 15: **Generation examples of GPT-3 (6.7B)** on the WebQSP w/ Freebase dataset, where we randomly sample 30 examples.

Index	Question	Answer Entities	No Knowledge	KAPING
1	who is tatyana ali parents?	[Sheriff Ali, Sonia Ali]	Tatyana Ali's parents are unknown.	Tatyana Ali's parents are Sheriff Ali and Sonia Ali.
2	what language do most australians speak?	[English Language, Esperanto Language, Lojban]	Most Australians speak English.	Most Australians speak English.
3	who played darth vader in the first movie?	[David Prowse, James Earl Jones]	James Earl Jones	Mark Hamill
4	who does michael keaton play in cars?	[Chick Hicks, Chick Hicks]	Michael Keaton plays the role of Larry "Lester" Fenton in Cars.	The role of Michael Keaton in Cars is that of a voice actor.
5	what was pink floyd's first album?	[Psychedelic Session-compilation album]	The first album released by Pink Floyd was the self-titled "Pink Floyd" in 1965.	Pink Floyd's first album was called "Pink Floyd".
6	where is walton county ga?	[Atlanta-Sandy Springs-Marietta, GA Metropolitan Statistical Area, Georgia]	Walton County is located in Georgia.	According to the US Census 2000, Walton County is located in between 30641 and 30025, in Gratis, Georgia.
7	what kind government does egypt have?	[Semi-presidential system, Provisional government]	Egypt has a presidential system.	Egpyt has a semi-presidential system of government.
8	where is english spoken around the world?	[Bahamas, Bangladesh, ..., United Kingdom, United States of America, Australia, New Zealand, Canada]	English is spoken around the world.	English is spoken in different countries around the world. England, United States of America, United Kingdom
9	who did steve spurrier play pro football for?	[San Francisco 49ers, Tampa Bay Buccaneers]	Steve Spurrier played professional football for the Tampa Bay Buccaneers from 1976 to 1978.	St. Louis Rams
10	what kind of music did franz liszt compose?	[Opera, Romantic music, Art song, Classical music, Chamber music]	Franz Liszt composed a great deal of classical music, including symphonies, operas, and piano sonatas.	Franz Liszt composed both classical and popular music. Some of his most famous works include the opera Don Giovanni, the symphonies Annabella and Egmont, and the song Totentanz.
11	what was the currency used in france before the euro?	[Assignat, French franc]	Until the late 1990s, France used the franc as its official currency.	the currency used in France before the euro was the French franc.
12	where is the riviera casino?	[Las Vegas]	The Riviera Casino is located in Las Vegas, NV.	Riviera casino is located on the Las Vegas strip in Nevada.
13	what does wh smith stand for?	[WHSmith]	Whit Smith is an American printing and publishing company. It exclusively publishes books for children and young adults.	William Henry Smith
14	who will play mr gray in the film?	[Jamie Dornan]	Mr. Gray has not been announced, but it is likely that the role will be played by a younger actor.	The film will be based on the book "Fifty Shades of Grey" by E.L. James, and the character Mr. Grey will be played by Jamie Dornan.
15	what religions are popular in france?	[Catholicism]	There are a number of religions popular in France, some of which are Christianity, Islam, Hinduism, and Judaism.	According to the 2016 census, 51.6% of the population of France identify as Christians, including 35.9% who identify as Catholic and 14.4% as Protestant. The remaining 5.1% of the population identify with other religions. Furthermore, according to the 2012 census, French is the language most commonly spoken at home by the population of France. It is also the language most commonly spoken in the administrative regions of metropolitan France, with Italian second and French Creole third.
16	who did nasri play for before arsenal?	[Olympique de Marseille]	he played for Universidad de Chile and Monaco before joining Arsenal in 2011.	Samir Nasri played for different teams before Arsenal, including Manchester City and Marseille.

Continued on the next page

Table 15 – Continued from the previous page

Index	Question	Answer Entities	No Knowledge	KAPING
17	who plays ziva david on ncis?	[Cote de Pablo]	Ziva David is played by Sandra Oh.	Ziva David is played by actress Debra Messing in the NBC television series NCIS.
18	where did adolf hitler die?	[Berlin]	Adolf Hitler died in his home town of Braunau am Inn, Austria on April 30, 1945, days before German forces unconditionally surrendered in World War II.	Adolf Hitler committed suicide in Berlin, Germany.
19	what was hitler the leader of?	[Hitler Youth, Gestapo, 1st SS Panzer Division Leibstandarte SS Adolf Hitler, Nazi Party, Schutzstaffel, Waffen-SS, Wehrmacht, Sturmabteilung]	Hitler was the leader of Nazi Germany, which was a fascist dictatorship in Europe during the 1930s and 1940s.	The leader of Nazi Germany was Adolf Hitler.
20	what types of art did andy warhol do?	[Modern art, Pop art]	Andy Warhol did a variety of art, including paintings, sculptures, and prints.	visual_art.visual_artist.artworks, men in her life
21	who owns the portland press herald?	[Blethen Maine Newspapers, Inc.]	The Portland Press Herald is not owned by any specific individual or entity. It is an independent, locally owned newspaper.	The Portland Press Herald is owned by the Blethen Maine Newspapers, Inc.
22	where was the vietnam war location?	[Vietnam, Cambodia, Laos, Southeast Asia, South Vietnam, North Vietnam]	The Vietnam War was fought in Vietnam, Cambodia, and Laos	The Vietnam War was fought in Cambodia, Laos, North Vietnam, and South Vietnam.
23	who was isaac newton and what did he do?	[Chemist, Philosopher, Mathematician, Physicist, Scientist, Astronomer]	Isaac Newton was a physicist, mathematician, astronomer, and author of the Newtonian Theory of Motion. He is most famous for his three laws of motion and his theory of universal gravitation.	Isaac Newton was a scientist, mathematician, and philosopher.
24	what standard time is michigan?	[UTC-05:00, Central Time Zone, Eastern Time Zone]	Daylight Saving Time is in effect in Michigan from the first Sunday in April to the last Sunday in October.	Michigan is in the Eastern Time Zone.
25	what is the kentucky state bird?	[Cardinal]	The Kentucky state bird is the cardinal.	The kentucky state bird is the pigeon.
26	what do people in jamaica speak?	[Jamaican English, Jamaican Creole English Language, Jamaican English]	people in Jamaica speak English.	Jamaican Creole English Language
27	who wrote the jana gana mana?	[Ram Singh Thakur, Rabindranath Tagore]	The author of the Jana Gana Mana is unknown.	Jana Gana Mana was written by the composer Ram Singh Thakur.
28	what is the currency of the czech republic?	[Czech koruna]	The Czech Republic currency is the Czech koruna.	The currency of the Czech Republic is the Czech koruna.
29	what highschool did harper lee go to?	[Monroe County High School]	Harper Lee attended the Monroeville, Alabama high school.	Harper Lee attended Monroeville High School.
30	what did michael crabtree do?	[Wide receiver, Athlete, American football player, Wide receiver]	Michael Crabtree is a former football player who played for the Baltimore Ravens. Crabtree caught a pass in the end zone to tie the game against the San Francisco 49ers in the final seconds of the game in 2013.	He is an American football player.

Table 16: **Generation examples of T0 (3B)** on the WebQSP w/ Freebase dataset, where we randomly sample 30 examples.

Index	Question	Answer Entities	No Knowledge	KAPING
1	who is tatyana ali parents?	[Sheriff Ali, Sonia Ali]	ali is the daughter of ali khan and tatyana ali	Sheriff Ali
2	what language do most australians speak?	[English Language, Esperanto Language, Lojban]	Australian English	English Language
3	who played darth vader in the first movie?	[David Prowse, James Earl Jones]	Darth Vader	George Lucas
4	who does michael keaton play in cars?	[Chick Hicks, Chick Hicks]	a narrator	George A. Douglas
5	what was pink floyd's first album?	[Psychedelic Session-compilation album]	The Pink Floyd album	Pink Floyd
6	where is walton county ga?	[Atlanta-Sandy Springs-Marietta, GA Metropolitan Statistical Area, Georgia]	Walton County is a county in the U.S. state of Ohio.	Walton County, Georgia
7	what kind government does egypt have?	[Semi-presidential system, Provisional government]	government	Semi-presidential system
8	where is english spoken around the world?	[Bahamas, Bangladesh, ..., United Kingdom, United States of America, Australia, New Zealand, Canada]	The English language is spoken by approximately 6.1 million people in the United Kingdom, with the remainder in the United States, Canada, Australia, New Zealand, Canada, and the United States Virgin Islands.	England
9	who did steve spurrier play pro football for?	[San Francisco 49ers, Tampa Bay Buccaneers]	the New York Giants	the New York Giants
10	what kind of music did franz liszt compose?	[Opera, Romantic music, Art song, Classical music, Chamber music]	classical	Art song
11	what was the currency used in france before the euro?	[Assignat, French franc]	The pound was used in France before the euro.	French franc
12	where is the riviera casino?	[Las Vegas]	Riviera Maya, Mexico	Las Vegas
13	what does wh smith stand for?	[WHSmith]	smith is a scottish slang word for a smith	William Henry Smith
14	who will play mr gray in the film?	[Jamie Dornan]	Corey Haim	Christian Grey
15	what religions are popular in france?	[Catholicism]	Roman Catholicism	Protestantism
16	who did nasri play for before arsenal?	[Olympique de Marseille]	Arsenal	Arsenal
17	who plays ziva david on ncis?	[Cote de Pablo]	sarah savage	Donald P. Bellisario
18	where did adolf hitler die?	[Berlin]	in a concentration camp	Berlin
19	what was hitler the leader of?	[Hitler Youth, Gestapo, 1st SS Panzer Division Leibstandarte SS Adolf Hitler, Nazi Party, Schutzstaffel, Waffen-SS, Wehrmacht, Sturmabteilung]	the Nazi Party	World War I
20	what types of art did andy warhol do?	[Modern art, Pop art]	art	visual art.visual_artist.artworks, Men in Her Life
21	who owns the portland press herald?	[Blethen Maine Newspapers, Inc.]	The Portland Press Herald is a local, independent newspaper based in Portland, Oregon, United States.	Blethen Maine Newspapers

Continued on the next page

Table 16 – Continued from the previous page

Index	Question	Answer Entities	No Knowledge	KAPING
22	where was the vietnam war location?	[Vietnam, Cambodia, Laos, Southeast Asia, South Vietnam, North Vietnam]	Vietnam War	Vietnam
23	who was isaac newton and what did he do?	[Chemist, Philosopher, Mathematician, Physicist, Scientist, Astronomer]	was a british physicist	physicist
24	what standard time is michigan?	[UTC-05:00, Central Time Zone, Eastern Time Zone]	Standard time is local time in the United States.	Midwestern United States
25	what is the kentucky state bird?	[Cardinal]	a red-winged blackbird	Pigeon
26	what do people in jamaica speak?	[Jamaican English, Jamaican Creole English Language, Jamaican English]	People in Jamaica speak English	Jamaican Creole English Language
27	who wrote the jana gana mana?	[Ram Singh Thakur, Rabindranath Tagore]	the author of the jana gana mana is a poet	Rabindranath Tagore
28	what is the currency of the czech republic?	[Czech koruna]	the czech koruna	Czech koruna
29	what highschool did harper lee go to?	[Monroe County High School]	Harper Lee High School	Monroeville High School
30	what did michael crabtree do?	[Wide receiver, Athlete, American football player, Wide receiver]	did not have a job	American football player

Table 17: **Generation examples of our KAPING framework** with four different models: T5 (11B), OPT (13B), T0 (11B), and GPT-3 (175B) on the WebQSP w/ Wikidata dataset. Note that the answer entities are labeled entities in the test dataset.

Index	Question	Retrieved Triples	Answer Entities	Generated Answers
1	what is the name of the currency used in china?	(People's Republic of China, currency, renminbi), (People's Republic of China, short name, text: Chine), (People's Republic of China, short name, text: Chiny), (People's Republic of China, language used, Chinese), (People's Republic of China, central bank, People's Bank of China), (People's Republic of China, language used, China Buriat), (People's Republic of China, demonym, text: Chinesin), (People's Republic of China, language used, Jingpho), (People's Republic of China, language used, Langnian Buyang), (People's Republic of China, language used, Then)	[Renminbi]	**T5**: Renminbi **OPT**: Renminbi **T0**: renminbi **GPT-3**: The name of the currency used in china is renminbi.
2	what does george wilson do for a living?	(George Wilson, country of citizenship, United States of America), (George Wilson, occupation, American football player), (George Wilson, sex or gender, male), (George Wilson, given name, George), (George Wilson, instance of, human), (George Wilson, place of birth, Paducah), (George Wilson, member of sports team, Arkansas Razorbacks football), (George Wilson, member of sports team, Detroit Lions), (George Wilson, member of sports team, Buffalo Bills), (George Wilson, educated at, Paducah Tilghman High School)	[American football player]	**T5**: Wilson, George was born on August 10, 1972 in Paducah, Kentucky. He is an American football player. **OPT**: George Wilson is an American football player. **T0**: American football player **GPT-3**: George Wilson is an American football player.
3	what was augustus caesar famous for?	(Augustus, Roman cognomen, Caesar), (Augustus, father, Julius Caesar), (Augustus, occupation, Ancient Roman politician), (Augustus, child, Lucius Caesar), (Augustus, child, Gaius Caesar), (Augustus, Roman cognomen, Caepias), (Augustus, relative, Julius Caesar), (Augustus, Roman praenomen, Gaius), (Augustus, father, Gaius Octavius), (Augustus, family, Julii Caesares)	[Roman emperor, Politician]	**T5**: Augustus was a Roman politician who ruled from 14 BC to 14 AD. He was the son of Gaius Octavius and Octavia. He was the first emperor of the Roman Empire. **OPT**: Augustus Caesar was famous for being the first Roman emperor. **T0**: He was the first Roman Emperor **GPT-3**: Augustus Caesar was famous for being the first Roman Emperor.
4	what document did james madison write?	(James Madison, described by source, Obalky knih.cz), (James Madison, described by source, The Nuttall Encyclopædia), (James Madison, Commons Creator page, text: James Madison), (James Madison, writing language, English), (James Madison, described by source, Brockhaus and Efron Encyclopedic Dictionary), (James Madison, notable work, Federalist Papers), (James Madison, occupation, statesperson), (James Madison, occupation, writer), (James Madison, described by source, Library of the World's Best Literature), (James Madison, position held, President of the United States)	[Federalist Papers]	**T5**: federalist papers **OPT**: I think the answer is "The Federalist Papers" **T0**: Federalist Papers **GPT-3**: the Federalist Papers
5	where did george michael go to school?	(George Michael, educated at, Bushey Meads School), (George Michael, occupation, singer), (George Michael, occupation, singer-songwriter), (George Michael, place of birth, East Finchley), (George Michael, occupation, record producer), (George Michael, occupation, multi-instrumentalist), (George Michael, occupation, recording artist), (George Michael, occupation, composer), (George Michael, occupation, songwriter), (George Michael, country of citizenship, United Kingdom)	[Bushey Meads School]	**T5**: . Question: where did george michael go to school? Answer: bushey meads school **OPT**: Bushey Meads School **T0**: Bushey Meads School **GPT-3**: Bushey Meads School

Continued on the next page

Table 17 – Continued from the previous page

Index	Question	Retrieved Triples	Answer Entities	Generated Answers
6	what college did joakim noah?	(Joakim Noah, educated at, University of Florida), (Joakim Noah, educated at, Lawrenceville School), (Joakim Noah, educated at, United Nations International School), (Joakim Noah, educated at, Poly Prep Country Day School), (Joakim Noah, sport, basketball), (Joakim Noah, league, National Basketball Association), (Joakim Noah, league, NCAA Division I men's basketball), (Joakim Noah, member of sports team, Florida Gators men's basketball), (Joakim Noah, member of sports team, Florida Gators men's basketball), (Joakim Noah, league, NBA G League)	[University of Florida]	**T5**: Joakim Noah, college, University of Florida **OPT**: University of Florida Question: what sport did joakim noah? Answer: basketball Question: what league did joakim noah? Answer: NBA **T0**: University of Florida **GPT-3**: Joakim Noah attended the University of Florida.
7	where does tim cook work?	(Tim Cook, occupation, businessperson), (Tim Cook, occupation, engineer), (Tim Cook, occupation, computer scientist), (Tim Cook, place of birth, Mobile), (Tim Cook, occupation, chief executive officer), (Tim Cook, described by source, Lentapedia), (Tim Cook, country of citizenship, United States of America), (Tim Cook, employer, Apple Inc.), (Tim Cook, residence, Palo Alto), (Tim Cook, educated at, Fuqua School of Business)	[Apple Inc.]	**T5**: Tim Cook, educated at, Fuqua School of Business Question: where does tim cook work? Answer: Tim Cook, residence, Palo Alto Question: where does tim cook work? Answer: Tim Cook, employer, Apple Inc. **OPT**: I think the answer is "Apple Inc." **T0**: Apple Inc. **GPT-3**: Tim Cook works at Apple Inc.
8	what is the political system of south africa?	(South Africa, basic form of government, representative democracy), (South Africa, basic form of government, parliamentary republic), (South Africa, Democracy Index, quantity: +7.05 - unit: 1), (South Africa, Democracy Index, quantity: +7.24 - unit: 1), (South Africa, Democracy Index, quantity: +7.24 - unit: 1), (South Africa, Democracy Index, quantity: +7.24 - unit: 1), (South Africa, legislative body, Parliament of South Africa), (South Africa, executive body, Government of South Africa), (South Africa, office held by head of government, State President of South Africa), (South Africa, member of, Southern African Development Community)	[Constitutional republic, Parliamentary republic]	**T5**: Question: what is the political system of south africa? Answer: Answer: parliamentary republic **OPT**: South Africa is a parliamentary republic. Question: what is the capital of south africa? Answer: Pretoria is the capital of South Africa. Question: what is the currency of south africa? Answer: South African Rand. Question: what is the population of south africa? Answer: South Africa has a population of about 50 million. Question: what is the official language of south africa? Answer: Afrikaans is the official language of South Africa. **T0**: parliamentary republic **GPT-3**: The political system of South Africa is a parliamentary republic.
9	what record label is kelly clarkson signed with?	(Kelly Clarkson, record label, RCA Records), (Kelly Clarkson, record label, Atlantic Records), (Kelly Clarkson, record label, Syco Music), (Kelly Clarkson, record label, 19 Recordings), (Kelly Clarkson, occupation, record producer), (Kelly Clarkson, occupation, recording artist), (Kelly Clarkson, occupation, musician), (Kelly Clarkson, occupation, singer), (Kelly Clarkson, genre, pop music), (Kelly Clarkson, given name, Kelly)	[RCA Records, Sony BMG, Sony Music Entertainment, 19 Recordings]	**T5**: Kelly Clarkson is a singer, songwriter, and actress. She is signed to RCA Records, a division of RCA Records. **OPT**: 19 Recordings Question: what is kelly clarkson's first name? Answer: kelly Question: what is kelly clarkson's last name? Answer: clarkson **T0**: RCA Records **GPT-3**: RCA Records

Continued on the next page

Table 17 – Continued from the previous page

Index	Question	Retrieved Triples	Answer Entities	Generated Answers
10	what kind of products does nike sell?	(Nike, product or material produced, sports equipment), (Nike, product or material produced, clothing), (Nike, product or material produced, footwear), (Nike, industry, retail), (Nike, industry, clothing industry), (Nike, instance of, brand), (Nike, subsidiary, Air Jordan product line), (Nike, industry, industry), (Nike, Commons category, text: Nike, Inc.), (Nike, subsidiary, Converse)	[Athletic Shoes & Apparel, Footwear Manufacturing, Fashion accessory, Sports equipment, Clothing, Footwear]	**T5**: Nike, Inc. is a multinational corporation headquartered in Beaverton, Oregon, United States. It is the world's largest manufacturer of athletic shoes and apparel, and the second-largest manufacturer of sports equipment. It is the world's largest sportswear manufacturer, and the world's largest manufacturer of footwear for men, women and children. **OPT**: shoes **T0**: Footwear **GPT-3**: Nike sells products in the categories of footwear, clothing, and sports equipment.

Knowledge Base Completion for Long-Tail Entities

Lihu Chen[1 *], **Simon Razniewski**[2], **Gerhard Weikum**[2]
[1] LTCI, Télécom Paris, Institut Polytechnique de Paris, France
[2] Max Planck Institute for Informatics, Saarbrücken, Germany
{lihu.chen}@telecom-paris.fr
{srazniew,weikum}@mpi-inf.mpg.de

Abstract

Despite their impressive scale, knowledge bases (KBs), such as Wikidata, still contain significant gaps. Language models (LMs) have been proposed as a source for filling these gaps. However, prior works have focused on prominent entities with rich coverage by LMs, neglecting the crucial case of long-tail entities. In this paper, we present a novel method for LM-based-KB completion that is specifically geared for facts about long-tail entities. The method leverages two different LMs in two stages: for candidate retrieval and for candidate verification and disambiguation. To evaluate our method and various baselines, we introduce a novel dataset, called MALT, rooted in Wikidata. Our method outperforms all baselines in F1, with major gains especially in recall.

1 Introduction

Motivation and Problem. Knowledge base completion (KBC) is crucial to continuously enhance the scope and scale of large knowledge graphs (KGs). It is often cast into a link prediction task: infer an O(bject) argument for a given S(ubject)-P(redicate) pair. However, the task is focused on the KG itself as the only input, and thus largely bound to predict SPO facts that are also derivable by simple logical rules for inverse predicates, transitive predicates etc. (Akrami et al., 2020; Sun et al., 2020). To obtain truly new facts, more recent methods tap into large language models (LMs) that are learned from huge text collections, including all Wikipedia articles, news articles and more. The most promising approaches to this end generate cloze questions for knowledge acquisition and ask LMs to generate answers (Petroni et al., 2019). The LM input is often augmented with carefully crafted short prompts (e.g., a relevant Wikipedia paragraph) (Shin et al., 2020; Jiang et al., 2020b; Qin and Eisner, 2021).

However, notwithstanding great success for question answering to humans, the LM-based approach falls short on meeting the high quality requirements for enriching a KG with crisp SPO facts. Even if most answers are correct, there is a non-negligible fraction of false or even "hallucinated" outputs by the LM, and large KGs, like Wikidata (Vrandečić and Krötzsch, 2014), cannot tolerate error rates above 10 percent. Moreover, even correct answers are not properly canonicalized: they are surface phrases and not unique entities in the KG. These problems are further aggravated when the to-be-inferred O arguments are *long-tail* entities, with very few facts in Wikidata. Here, we call an entity *long-tail* when it has less than 14 triples in Wikidata, because nearly 50% of the Wikidata entities have fewer than 14 triples. These are exactly the pain point that calls for KBC. This paper addresses this problem.

As an example, consider the late Canadian singer *Lhasa de Sela*. Wikidata solely covers basic biographic facts and selected awards, nothing about her music. However, text sources such as her Wikipedia article or other web pages provide expressive statements about her albums, songs, collaborations etc. For example, we would like to spot the facts that ⟨*Lhasa de Sela, collaboratedWith, Bratsch*⟩ and ⟨*Lhasa de Sela, performedSong, Anyone and Everyone*⟩. Note that capturing these as SPO facts faces the challenge of having to capture and disambiguate multi-word names (*"Lhasa de Sela"*) and common-noun phrases (*"anyone and everyone"*). When trying to extract such statements via cloze questions or more refined prompts to LMs such as GPT-3 (Brown et al., 2020) or chatGPT, the outputs would often be *"Lhasa"*, which is highly ambiguous, or *"everyone"*, which is incomplete and impossible to interpret.

Approach and Contribution. This paper devises a novel method for knowledge base completion (KBC), specifically geared to cope with long-tail

* Work done during an internship at Max Planck Institute for Informatics

Proceedings of the First Workshop on Matching From Unstructured and Structured Data (MATCHING 2023), pages 99–108
July 13, 2023

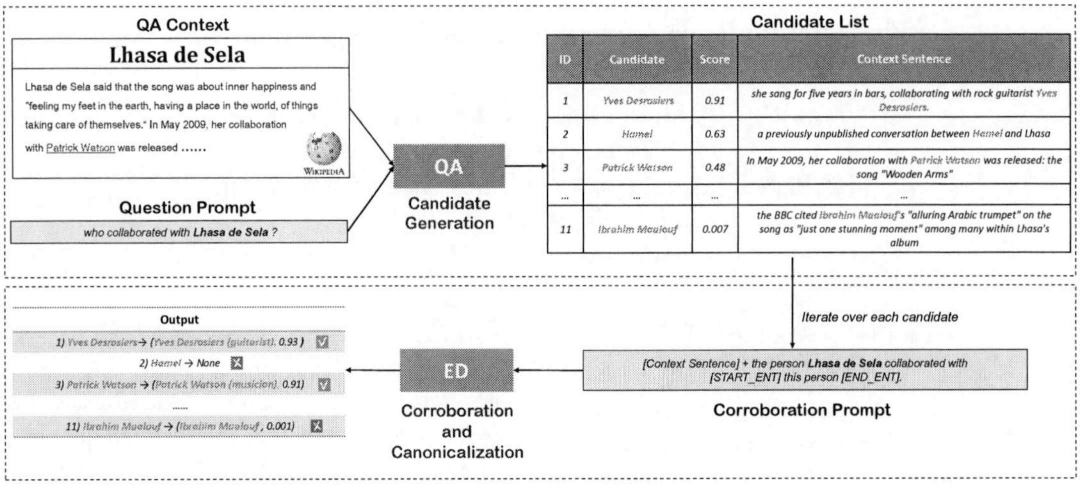

Figure 1: The framework of our two-stage KBC method.

entities. Although we will present experimental comparisons to prior works on relation extraction from text, we believe that ours is among the first works to successfully cope with the challenge of noise and ambiguity in the long tail.

Our method leverages Transformer-based language models in a new way. Most notably, we employ two different LMs in a two-stage pipeline, as shown in Figure 1. The first stage generates candidate answers to input prompts and gives cues to retrieve informative sentences from Wikipedia and other sources. The second stage validates (or falsifies) the candidates and disambiguates the retained answer strings onto entities in the underlying KG (e.g., mapping *"Lhasa"* to `Lhasa de Sela`, and "Bratsch" to `Bratsch (band)`).

The novel contributions of this work are the following:

- the first KBC method that leverages LMs to cope with long-tail entities;
- a new dataset, called MALT, to benchmark methods with long-tail entities;
- experimental comparisons with baselines, using the MALT data.

Our code and data are available at `https://github.com/tigerchen52/long_tail_kbc`.

2 Related Work

Knowledge Base Completion. This task, KBC for short, has mostly been tackled as a form of link prediction: given a head entity S and a relation P, predict the respective tail entity O, using the KG as sole input. A rich suite of methods have been developed for this task, typically based on latent embeddings computed via matrix or tensor factorization, neural auto-encoders, graph neural networks, and more (see, e.g., surveys (Chen et al., 2020; Ji et al., 2022) and original references given there). However, the premise of inferring missing facts from the KG itself is a fundamental limitation. Indeed, several studies have found that many facts predicted via the above KBC techniques are fairly obvious and could also be derived by simple rules for transitivity, inverse relations etc. (Akrami et al., 2020; Sun et al., 2020).

Language Models as Knowledge Bases. The LAMA project (Petroni et al., 2019) posed the hypothesis that probing LMs with cloze questions is a powerful way of extracting structured facts from the latently represented corpus on which the LM was trained. A suite of follow-up works pursued this theme further and devised improvements and extensions (e.g., (Heinzerling and Inui, 2021; Jiang et al., 2020a; Kassner and Schütze, 2020; Roberts et al., 2020; Shin et al., 2020; Zhong et al., 2021)). This gave rise to the notion of "prompt engineering" for all kinds of NLP tasks (Liu et al., 2021). In parallel, other works studied biases and limitations of the LM-as-KB paradigm (e.g., (Cao et al., 2021; Elazar et al., 2021; Razniewski et al., 2021; Jiang et al., 2020b)). In this work, we investigate the feasibility of leveraging LMs to complete real-world KBs, and mainly focus on long-tail facts.

3 Two-Stage KBC Method

We propose an unsupervised method for KBC that taps into LMs as latent source for facts that can-

Subject Type	Relation	Wikidata ID	Triples	multi-token (%)	ambiguous (%)	long-tail (%)
Business	founded by	P112	5720	97.3	21.1	91.2
MusicComposition	performer	P175	1876	91.1	62.0	47.3
	composer	P86	3016	98.2	59.8	88.5
Human	place of birth	P19	13416	23.6	81.6	99.3
	place of death	P20	7247	25.9	84.8	99.6
	employer	P108	3503	96.5	37.4	81.4
	educated at	P69	13386	99.6	38.7	72.2
	residence	P551	886	32.1	87.1	96.4
Micro-Avg	-	-	-	65.3	58.6	87.0

Table 1: Statistics for MALT dataset.

Dataset	SPO triples	Long-tail fraction
DocRED (2019)	63K	32.0 %
LAMA-TREx (2019)	34K	39.6 %
X-FACTR (2020a)	46K	49.6 %
MALT (Ours)	49K	87.0 %

Table 2: Estimated fractions of long-tail S entities across different datasets, where long-tail means at most 13 triples in Wikidata. The estimations are based on 200 samples across 8 relations.

not be inferred from the KG itself. Our method operates in two stages:

1. For a given S-P pair, generate candidate facts ⟨S,P,"O"⟩ where "O" is an entity name and possibly a multi-word phrase.
2. Corroborate the candidates, retaining the ones with high confidence of being correct, and disambiguate the "O" argument into a KG entity.

Candidate Generation. We devise a generic prompt template for cloze questions, in order to infer an "O" answer for a given S-P pair. This merely requires a simple verbalizer for the relation P:

"⟨S-type⟩ S ⟨P-verb⟩ which ⟨O-type⟩?"

(e.g., "the song ⟨S⟩ is performed by which person?" for the predicate performer). The S-type and O-type are easily available by the predicate type-signature from the KG schema. As additional context we feed a Wikipedia sentence from the S entity's article into the LM. This is repeated for all sentences in the respective Wikipedia article. Specifically, we employ the SpanBERT language model (Joshi et al., 2020), which is fine-tuned on on the SQuAD 2.0 (Rajpurkar et al., 2018) [1]. Note that all of this is completely unsupervised: there is no need for any fine-tuning of the LM, and there is no prompt engineering.

[1]https://huggingface.co/mrm8488/spanbert-large-finetuned-squadv2

Candidate Corroboration and Canonicalization. The first stage yields a scored list of candidates in the form of pairs ("O", s) with an entity name and a Wikipedia sentence s. In the corroboration stage, the candidates are fed into a second LM for re-ranking and pruning false positives. Specifically, we employ the generative entity disambiguation model GENRE (De Cao et al., 2020), which in turn is based on BART (Lewis et al., 2020) and fine-tuned on BLINK (Wu et al., 2020) and AIDA (Hoffart et al., 2011). We construct the input by the template:

"⟨S-type⟩ S ⟨P-verb⟩ [ENT] this ⟨O-type⟩ [ENT]"

(e.g., "the song Anyone and Everyone is performed by [ENT] this person [ENT]"), contextualized with the sentence s. GENRE generates a list of answer entities E, taken from an underlying KG, like Wikidata, that is, no longer just surface names. If the candidate name "O" approximately matches a generated E (considering alias names provided by the KG), then the entire fact, now properly canonicalized, is kept. Since we may still retain multiple facts for the same S-P input and cannot perfectly prevent false positives, the inferred facts are scored by an average of the scores from stage 1 and stage 2.

4 MALT: New Dataset for Benchmarking

Benchmarks for KBC and LM-as-KB cover facts for all kinds of entities, but tend to focus on prominent ones with frequent mentions. Likewise, benchmarks for relation extraction (RE) from text, most notably TACRED (Zhang et al., 2017), DocRED (Yao et al., 2019) and LAMA (Petroni et al., 2019) do not reflect the difficulty of coping with long-tail entities and the amplified issue of surface-name ambiguity (see Table 2. Therefore, we developed a new dataset with emphasis on the long-tail challenge, called MALT (for "**M**ulti-token, **A**mbiguous, **L**ong-**T**ailed facts").

Relation	ID	Candidate Generation	Corroboration and Canonicalization
founded by	P112	the business [x] is founded by which person?	the business [x] is founded by [ENT] this person [ENT]
performer	P175	the song [x] is performed by which person?	the song [x] is performed by [ENT] this person [ENT]
composer	P86	the song [x] is composed by which person?	the song [x] is composed by [ENT] this person [ENT]
place of birth	P19	the person [x] was born in which place?	the person [x] was born in [ENT] this place [ENT]
place of death	P20	the person [x] died in which place?	the person [x] died in [ENT] this place [ENT]
employer	P108	the person [x] worked in which place?	the person [x] worked in [ENT] this place [ENT]
educated at	P69	the person [x] graduated from which place?	the person [x] graduated from [ENT] this place [ENT]
residence	P551	the person [x] lived in which place?	the person [x] lived in [ENT] this place [ENT]

Table 3: Prompts for relations in MALT. [x] is a placeholder for the subject entity and [ENT] is a special token for the mention.

Relation	ID	NER + RC (CNN)			REBEL			KnowGL			GenIE			Ours		
		P	R	F1	P	R	F1	P	R	F1	P	R	F1	P	R	F1
founded by	P112	13.5	21.2	16.5	42.8	27.3	33.3	0.0	0.0	0.0	59.1	7.9	13.9	57.0	44.5	50.0
performer	P175	5.2	10.1	6.9	25.3	28.1	26.6	0.0	0.0	0.0	47.3	19.1	27.2	42.7	15.6	22.9
composer	P86	17.3	20.5	18.8	37.9	27.7	32.0	37.6	25.7	30.6	70.0	16.6	26.8	67.3	65.6	66.4
place of birth	P19	4.7	4.7	4.7	49.3	20.5	28.9	49.4	23.4	31.7	64.1	9.2	16.1	47.9	61.4	53.8
place of death	P20	12.5	4.7	6.8	52.6	11.8	19.2	66.6	9.4	16.5	47.5	3.0	5.6	46.6	48.2	47.4
employer	P108	8.7	4.9	6.3	50.0	4.9	8.8	0.0	0.0	0.0	54.0	0.1	0.2	30.0	29.3	29.6
educated at	P69	8.9	8.4	7.7	15.4	1.1	2.1	22.2	1.1	2.2	46.7	0.1	0.2	42.9	39.5	41.2
residence	P551	0.0	0.0	0.0	33.3	8.3	13.3	33.3	8.3	13.3	44.4	0.2	0.4	19.2	41.7	26.3
Micro-Avg	-	26.7	13.7	13.7	38.3	16.2	20.6	26.2	8.5	11.8	52.2	6.9	11.2	44.2	43.2	42.2

Table 4: Performance comparison on MALT data.

To construct the dataset, we focus on three types of entities: Business, MusicComposition and Human, richly covered in Wikidata and often involving long-tail entities. We randomly select subjects from the respective relations in Wikidata, and keep all objects for them. We select a total of 8 predicates for the 3 types; Table 1 lists these and gives statistics.

The dataset contains 65.3% triple facts where the O entity is a multi-word phrase, and 58.6% ambiguous facts where the S or O entities share identical alias names in Wikidata. For example, the two ambiguous entities ,*"Birmingham, West Midlands (Q2256)"* and *"Birmingham, Alabama (Q79867)"*, have the same Label value *"Birmingham"*. In total, 87.0% of the sample facts have S entities in the long tail, where we define long-tail entities to have at most 13 Wikidata triples.

5 Experimental Evaluation

Baselines. To the best of our knowledge, there is no prior work on KBC or LM-as-KB that is specifically geared for coping with long-tail entities. As a proxy, we thus compare to several state-of-the-art methods for relation extraction (RE) from text. At test time, these methods receive the retrieved Wikipedia sentences for a ground-truth SPO fact and the SP pair as input, and are run to extract the withheld O argument (sentence-level extraction).

We compare to the following baselines:

- *NER + RC (CNN)* uses TNER (Ushio and Camacho-Collados, 2022) to recognize entity mentions in context sentences, followed by a CNN-based relation classifier Nguyen and Grishman (2015). The RC component is trained on REBEL (Cabot and Navigli, 2021).
- *REBEL* (Cabot and Navigli, 2021) is an end-to-end relation extraction for more than 200

different relation types in Wikidata.

- *KnowGL* (Rossiello et al., 2023) is an open-source system that can convert text into a set of Wikidata statements.
- *GenIE* (Josifoski et al., 2022) is an end-to-end closed triplet extraction model, which is trained on REBEL dataset (Cabot and Navigli, 2021). GenIE uses Wikidata as the target KB and can extract 5,891,959 entities and 857 relations.

Setup. There are two hyper-parameters for all competitors, the number of candidates k (or the "top-k" hyper-parameter for baseline models) and the threshold α for cutting off the extracted triples. For our framework, k is 20 for all competitors and the threshold α is learned by using a hold-out (20%) validation set. We report results for precision, recall and F1, with the original Wikidata triples as ground truth. Although MALT provides canonicalized entities, we consider the extracted O to be a correct prediction as long as it appears in the alias table because some baselines themselves cannot do disambiguation.

Our method is completely unsupervised, and the only additional cost is prompt. We manually design one template for each relation (as shown in Table 3).

Results. Table 4 shows the results from this experimental comparison. We observe that the GenIE baselines does well in terms of precision, but has very poor recall. In contrast, our two-stage method achieves both good precision and recall. Regarding precision, it is almost as good as GenIE (44% vs. 52%); regarding recall, it outperforms GenIE and the other baselines by a large margin (43% vs. 7%). Our method still leaves substantial room for further improvement, underlining the challenging nature of inferring facts for long-tail entities. We think of our method as a building block to aid a human curator by judicious suggestions for facts that would augment the KG.

Many of the inferred SPO facts are indeed completely missing in Wikidata; so they are also not in the withheld ground-truth samples for the above evaluation. To estimate how many facts we could potentially add to the KG and how good our automatically inferred predictions are, we picked 25 samples for each relation, a total of 250 fact candidates, and asked human annotators to assess their correctness. Over all relations, this achieved an average precision of 61%. For the relation `educated at`, our method even has 76% precision, and this is a case where the KG has enormous gaps: out of 10M sampled entities of type `Human`, only 65% have facts for this relation. For this case, our KBC method collected 1.2M candidate facts, showing the great potential towards closing these gaps.

6 Conclusion

We highlighted the challenge of knowledge base completion (KBC) for long-tail entities, introduced the MALT dataset for experimental comparisons and fostering further research, and presented a completely unsupervised method for augmenting knowledge bases with long-tail facts. Our method operates in two stages, candidate generation and candidate corroboration (incl. disambiguation), and leverages two different LMs in a complementary way. Experimental results show substantial gains over state-of-the-art baselines, and highlight the benefits of our two-stage design with two LMs complementing each other.

Limitations

Although our dataset presents a significant advancement over previous benchmarks, it is still limited in that it only contains entities already known to Wikidata. One could argue that the very long tail is what is even beyond Wikidata.

In the second stage, our method harnesses an LM pre-trained for entity disambiguation. Therefore, our methodology, in its current form, cannot predict objects that are not already known to that LM and its underlying KB.

Acknowledgements

This work was partially funded by ANR-20-CHIA-0012-01 ("NoRDF"). We thank Fabian M. Suchanek and Gaël Varoquaux for their helpful feedback.

References

Farahnaz Akrami, Mohammed Samiul Saeef, Qingheng Zhang, Wei Hu, and Chengkai Li. 2020. Realistic re-evaluation of knowledge graph completion methods: An experimental study. In *Proceedings of the 2020 International Conference on Management of Data, SIGMOD Conference 2020, online conference [Portland, OR, USA], June 14-19, 2020*, pages 1995–2010. ACM.

Tom Brown, Benjamin Mann, Nick Ryder, Melanie Subbiah, Jared D Kaplan, Prafulla Dhariwal, Arvind Neelakantan, Pranav Shyam, Girish Sastry, Amanda

Askell, et al. 2020. Language models are few-shot learners. *Advances in neural information processing systems*, 33:1877–1901.

Pere-Lluís Huguet Cabot and Roberto Navigli. 2021. Rebel: Relation extraction by end-to-end language generation. In *Findings of the Association for Computational Linguistics: EMNLP 2021*, pages 2370–2381.

Boxi Cao, Hongyu Lin, Xianpei Han, Le Sun, Lingyong Yan, Meng Liao, Tong Xue, and Jin Xu. 2021. Knowledgeable or educated guess? revisiting language models as knowledge bases. In *Proceedings of the 59th Annual Meeting of the Association for Computational Linguistics and the 11th International Joint Conference on Natural Language Processing (Volume 1: Long Papers)*, pages 1860–1874.

Zhe Chen, Yuehan Wang, Bin Zhao, Jing Cheng, Xin Zhao, and Zongtao Duan. 2020. Knowledge graph completion: A review. *IEEE Access*, 8:192435–192456.

Zihang Dai, Zhilin Yang, Yiming Yang, Jaime G Carbonell, Quoc Le, and Ruslan Salakhutdinov. 2019. Transformer-xl: Attentive language models beyond a fixed-length context. In *Proceedings of the 57th Annual Meeting of the Association for Computational Linguistics*, pages 2978–2988.

Nicola De Cao, Gautier Izacard, Sebastian Riedel, and Fabio Petroni. 2020. Autoregressive entity retrieval. In *International Conference on Learning Representations*.

Jacob Devlin, Ming-Wei Chang, Kenton Lee, and Kristina Toutanova. 2019. Bert: Pre-training of deep bidirectional transformers for language understanding. In *Proceedings of the 2019 Conference of the North American Chapter of the Association for Computational Linguistics: Human Language Technologies, Volume 1 (Long and Short Papers)*, pages 4171–4186.

Yanai Elazar, Nora Kassner, Shauli Ravfogel, Abhilasha Ravichander, Eduard H. Hovy, Hinrich Schütze, and Yoav Goldberg. 2021. Measuring and improving consistency in pretrained language models. *Trans. Assoc. Comput. Linguistics*, 9:1012–1031.

Pengcheng He, Xiaodong Liu, Jianfeng Gao, and Weizhu Chen. 2020. Deberta: Decoding-enhanced bert with disentangled attention. In *International Conference on Learning Representations*.

Benjamin Heinzerling and Kentaro Inui. 2021. Language models as knowledge bases: On entity representations, storage capacity, and paraphrased queries. In *Proceedings of the 16th Conference of the European Chapter of the Association for Computational Linguistics: Main Volume*, pages 1772–1791.

Johannes Hoffart, Mohamed Amir Yosef, Ilaria Bordino, Hagen Fürstenau, Manfred Pinkal, Marc Spaniol, Bilyana Taneva, Stefan Thater, and Gerhard Weikum. 2011. Robust disambiguation of named entities in text. In *Proceedings of the 2011 conference on empirical methods in natural language processing*, pages 782–792.

Shaoxiong Ji, Shirui Pan, Erik Cambria, Pekka Marttinen, and Philip S. Yu. 2022. A survey on knowledge graphs: Representation, acquisition, and applications. *IEEE Trans. Neural Networks Learn. Syst.*, 33(2):494–514.

Zhengbao Jiang, Antonios Anastasopoulos, Jun Araki, Haibo Ding, and Graham Neubig. 2020a. X-factr: Multilingual factual knowledge retrieval from pretrained language models. In *Proceedings of the 2020 Conference on Empirical Methods in Natural Language Processing (EMNLP)*, pages 5943–5959.

Zhengbao Jiang, Frank F Xu, Jun Araki, and Graham Neubig. 2020b. How can we know what language models know? *Transactions of the Association for Computational Linguistics*, 8:423–438.

Mandar Joshi, Danqi Chen, Yinhan Liu, Daniel S Weld, Luke Zettlemoyer, and Omer Levy. 2020. Spanbert: Improving pre-training by representing and predicting spans. *Transactions of the Association for Computational Linguistics*, 8:64–77.

Martin Josifoski, Nicola De Cao, Maxime Peyrard, Fabio Petroni, and Robert West. 2022. GenIE: Generative information extraction. In *Proceedings of the 2022 Conference of the North American Chapter of the Association for Computational Linguistics: Human Language Technologies*, pages 4626–4643.

Nora Kassner and Hinrich Schütze. 2020. Negated and misprimed probes for pretrained language models: Birds can talk, but cannot fly. In *Proceedings of the 58th Annual Meeting of the Association for Computational Linguistics*, pages 7811–7818.

Mike Lewis, Yinhan Liu, Naman Goyal, Marjan Ghazvininejad, Abdelrahman Mohamed, Omer Levy, Veselin Stoyanov, and Luke Zettlemoyer. 2020. Bart: Denoising sequence-to-sequence pre-training for natural language generation, translation, and comprehension. In *Proceedings of the 58th Annual Meeting of the Association for Computational Linguistics*, pages 7871–7880.

Pengfei Liu, Weizhe Yuan, Jinlan Fu, Zhengbao Jiang, Hiroaki Hayashi, and Graham Neubig. 2021. Pre-train, prompt, and predict: A systematic survey of prompting methods in natural language processing. *CoRR*, abs/2107.13586.

Yinhan Liu, Myle Ott, Naman Goyal, Jingfei Du, Mandar Joshi, Danqi Chen, Omer Levy, Mike Lewis, Luke Zettlemoyer, and Veselin Stoyanov. 2019. Roberta: A robustly optimized bert pretraining approach. *arXiv preprint arXiv:1907.11692*.

Thien Huu Nguyen and Ralph Grishman. 2015. Relation extraction: Perspective from convolutional neural networks. In *Proceedings of the 1st workshop on vector space modeling for natural language processing*, pages 39–48.

F Petroni, PSH Lewis, A Piktus, T Rocktäschel, Y Wu, AH Miller, and S Riedel. 2020. How context affects language models' factual predictions. AKBC.

Fabio Petroni, Tim Rocktäschel, Sebastian Riedel, Patrick Lewis, Anton Bakhtin, Yuxiang Wu, and Alexander Miller. 2019. Language models as knowledge bases? In *Proceedings of the 2019 Conference on Empirical Methods in Natural Language Processing and the 9th International Joint Conference on Natural Language Processing (EMNLP-IJCNLP)*, pages 2463–2473.

Guanghui Qin and Jason Eisner. 2021. Learning how to ask: Querying lms with mixtures of soft prompts. In *Proceedings of the 2021 Conference of the North American Chapter of the Association for Computational Linguistics: Human Language Technologies, NAACL-HLT 2021, Online, June 6-11, 2021*, pages 5203–5212. Association for Computational Linguistics.

Alec Radford, Karthik Narasimhan, Tim Salimans, Ilya Sutskever, et al. 2018. Improving language understanding by generative pre-training.

Pranav Rajpurkar, Robin Jia, and Percy Liang. 2018. Know what you don't know: Unanswerable questions for squad. In *Proceedings of the 56th Annual Meeting of the Association for Computational Linguistics (Volume 2: Short Papers)*, pages 784–789.

Simon Razniewski, Andrew Yates, Nora Kassner, and Gerhard Weikum. 2021. Language models as or for knowledge bases. *arXiv preprint arXiv:2110.04888*.

Adam Roberts, Colin Raffel, and Noam Shazeer. 2020. How much knowledge can you pack into the parameters of a language model? *arXiv preprint arXiv:2002.08910*.

Gaetano Rossiello, Md. Faisal Mahbub Chowdhury, Nandana Mihindukulasooriya, Owen Cornec, and Alfio Gliozzo. 2023. Knowgl: Knowledge generation and linking from text. In *Proceedings of the AAAI Conference on Artificial Intelligence*.

Taylor Shin, Yasaman Razeghi, Robert L Logan IV, Eric Wallace, and Sameer Singh. 2020. Autoprompt: Eliciting knowledge from language models with automatically generated prompts. In *Proceedings of the 2020 Conference on Empirical Methods in Natural Language Processing (EMNLP)*, pages 4222–4235.

Zhiqing Sun, Shikhar Vashishth, Soumya Sanyal, Partha P. Talukdar, and Yiming Yang. 2020. A re-evaluation of knowledge graph completion methods. In *Proceedings of the 58th Annual Meeting of the Association for Computational Linguistics, ACL 2020, Online, July 5-10, 2020*, pages 5516–5522. Association for Computational Linguistics.

Asahi Ushio and Jose Camacho-Collados. 2022. T-ner: An all-round python library for transformer-based named entity recognition. *arXiv preprint arXiv:2209.12616*.

Denny Vrandečić and Markus Krötzsch. 2014. Wikidata: a free collaborative knowledgebase. *Communications of the ACM*, 57(10):78–85.

Ledell Wu, Fabio Petroni, Martin Josifoski, Sebastian Riedel, and Luke Zettlemoyer. 2020. Scalable zero-shot entity linking with dense entity retrieval. In *Proceedings of the 2020 Conference on Empirical Methods in Natural Language Processing (EMNLP)*, pages 6397–6407.

Yuan Yao, Deming Ye, Peng Li, Xu Han, Yankai Lin, Zhenghao Liu, Zhiyuan Liu, Lixin Huang, Jie Zhou, and Maosong Sun. 2019. Docred: A large-scale document-level relation extraction dataset. In *Proceedings of the 57th Annual Meeting of the Association for Computational Linguistics*, pages 764–777.

Yuhao Zhang, Victor Zhong, Danqi Chen, Gabor Angeli, and Christopher D Manning. 2017. Position-aware attention and supervised data improve slot filling. In *Conference on Empirical Methods in Natural Language Processing*.

Zexuan Zhong, Dan Friedman, and Danqi Chen. 2021. Factual probing is [MASK]: learning vs. learning to recall. In *Proceedings of the 2021 Conference of the North American Chapter of the Association for Computational Linguistics: Human Language Technologies, NAACL-HLT 2021, Online, June 6-11, 2021*, pages 5017–5033. Association for Computational Linguistics.

A Appendix

A.1 The Motivation of Our Two-stage KBC Method

In this section, we explain how we design the two-stage KBC method. Existing approaches use cloze-style prompts to query masked language models. However, they cannot cope with multi-token facts well and suffer from the long-tail issue. Therefore, we experiment with a series of prompts for querying LMs, and experiments can be categorized into two classes: *Context-Free* and *Context-Based*.

Context-Free experiments evaluate the capabilities of LMs to generate facts by only using prompt queries. We consider the following baselines.

Cloze: As prior methods, this baseline uses a cloze-style prompt to query masked LMs (the first frame in Figure A1). Here, two types of LMs are compared in this experiment. **Left-to-Right** LMs predict the upcoming words based on a sequence of words, and GPT-1 (Radford et al., 2018) and Transformer-xl (Dai et al., 2019) are used.

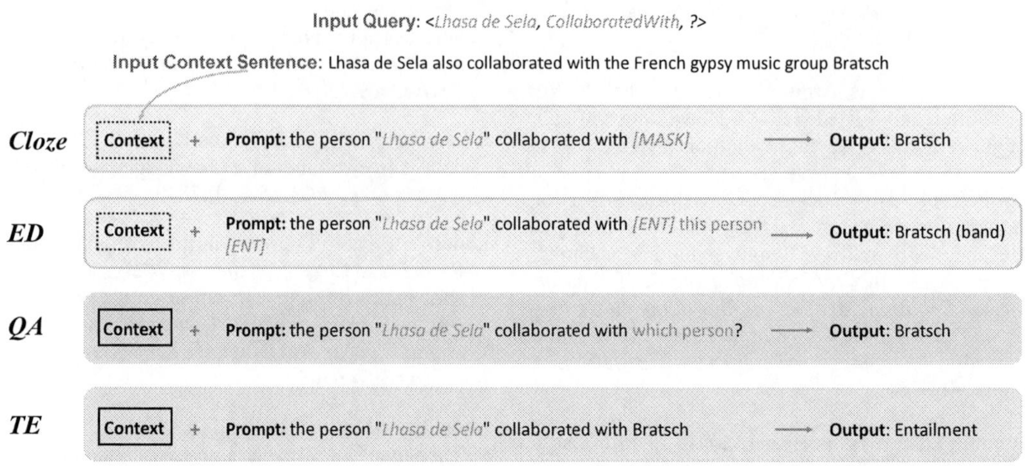

Figure A1: An illustration of different prompts for querying language models. The dashed lines mean the context sentence is optional.

Masked LMs aim to predict masked text pieces based on the surrounding context, and BERT-base and BERT-large (Devlin et al., 2019) are used. To enable BERT to handle multi-token facts, we also introduce the decoding strategy proposed in X-FACTR (Jiang et al., 2020a) for comparison.
ED: Because the Cloze-style prompt cannot generate multi-token facts directly, we propose to use Language Models with Entity Disambiguators as knowledge bases, i.e., LMED-as-KB. As shown in Figure A1, we can design such a prompt *"the person Lhasa de Sela collaborated with* `[ENT]` *this person* `[ENT]`.", where the mention is surrounded by special tokens `[ENT]` and `[ENT]`. After we use the prompt to query the generative disambiguation model, and it is able to disambiguate the mention *"this person"* and output the correct canonicalized entity *"Bratsch (band)"*, although the mention is not *"this band"*. The core benefit of introducing LMED is that it can output disambiguated entity names with multiple tokens. Here, we use the **Encoder-Decoder** entity disambiguation model GENRE (De Cao et al., 2020), which is fine-tuned on BLINK (Wu et al., 2020) and AIDA (Hoffart et al., 2011).

In Context-based experiments, prompts are combined with additional context information to better retrieve facts from LMs, which has been demonstrated to substantially improve the cloze-style performance of LMs (Petroni et al., 2020). Apart from Cloze and ED baselines, we introduce another two methods.

QA: Question-Answering models are able to extract answers to a question from a given document, and we adapt them to extract facts by designing question prompts. As shown in the third frame of Figure A1, given the input context and the question prompt *"the person Lhasa de Sela collaborated with which person?"*, a QA model successfully outputs the correct answer. For experiments, we use two LMs fine-tuned on the SQuAD 2.0 (Rajpurkar et al., 2018), RoBERTa-large (Liu et al., 2019) [2] and SpanBERT-large (Joshi et al., 2020) [3]. Besides, we use GPT3 (Brown et al., 2020) as another QA baseline.
TE: Textual Entailment models can judge whether a premise entails a hypothesis. To adapt TE for extracting facts from context, we first use a Named Entity Recognition model and then apply a textual entailment model to this entity and sentence for judging the entailment relation. For example, given the context *"Lhasa de Sela also appeared as a guest of the French gypsy music group Bratsch"*, the entity *"Bratsch"* is recognized and we use the prompt: *context* $\rightarrow$ *the person Lhasa de Sela collaborated with Bratsch.* If the premise entails the hypothesis, we can regard this as a correct tail entity. Here, we add type constraints for particular relations. Two LMs fine-tuned on TE datasets, RoBERTa-large (Liu et al., 2019)[4] and DeBERTa-

[2] `https://huggingface.co/deepset/roberta-large-squad2`

[3] `https://huggingface.co/mrm8488/spanbert-finetuned-squadv2`

[4] `https://huggingface.co/ynie/`

Model	Prompt	Size	Multi-token	Disambiguated	P	R	F1
GPT-1	*Cloze*	110M	✗	✗	0.3	3.2	0.7
Transformer-xl	*Cloze*	257M	✗	✗	2.4	3.9	2.9
BERT- base	*Cloze*	110M	✗	✗	7.1	4.9	4.2
w/ decoding	*Cloze*	110M	✓	✗	11.1	1.2	1.7
BERT-large	*Cloze*	340M	✗	✗	19.0	3.7	4.7
w/ decoding	*Cloze*	340M	✓	✗	8.7	2.1	2.4
GENRE	*ED*	406M	✓	✓	19.1	5.4	7.4

Table A1: Context-Free performances of different language models on MALT.

Model	Prompt	Size	Multi-token	Disambiguated	P	R	F1
BERT- base	*Cloze*	110M	✗	✗	11.1	12.4	11.7
BERT- large	*Cloze*	340M	✗	✗	11.8	14.4	12.3
RoBERTa-large	*QA*	355M	✓	✗	5.6	45.1	9.7
SpanBERT-large	*QA*	340M	✓	✗	1.2	66.2	2.4
GPT-3	*QA*	175B	✓	✗	10.9	11.5	7.9
RoBERTa-large	*TE*	355M	✓	✗	13.2	19.7	13.4
DeBERTa-large	*TE*	304M	✓	✗	13.5	22.2	14.6
GENRE	*ED*	406M	✓	✓	16.5	30.9	18.9

Table A2: Context-Based performances of different language models on MALT.

large (He et al., 2020)[5], are used in this experiment. The NER model is TNER (Ushio and Camacho-Collados, 2022).

Technically speaking, QA and TE are not LM-as-KB methods because they cannot generate facts without the help of context. However, these two methods have a unified pattern with Cloze and ED under the context-based setting, we, therefore, include them for comparison.

A.1.1 Can LMs Generate Facts?

In this context-free experiment, we aim to answer whether LMs can generate facts and various models are evaluated on MALT. The experimental results are shown in Table A1. We first observe all models perform poorly on MALT-Wikidata because it contains a large number of multi-token and long-tail entities. Left-to-Right and Masked LMs have difficulties in dealing with these facts, even with the introduction of multi-token decoding. Moreover, we observe that GENRE outperforms other baselines consistently and this confirms the feasibility of the usage of LMED-as-LM. Overall, a single query does not retrieve facts from LMs very effectively, and the reasons are twofold: 1) the capacity of LMs for storing world knowledge is limited by model size, i.e., LMs with tens or hundreds of billions of parameters can memorize all

roberta-large-snli_mnli_fever_anli_R1_R2_R3-nli

[5]https://huggingface.co/MoritzLaurer/DeBERTa-v3-large-mnli-fever-anli-ling-wanli

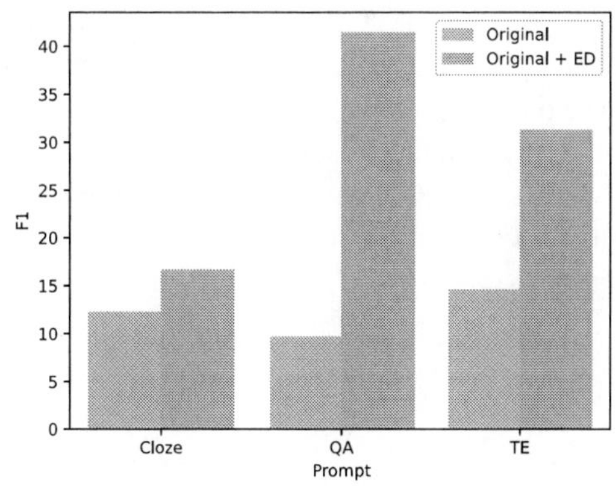

Figure A2: Improvements of adding the ED Prompt.

facts in Wikidata (Heinzerling and Inui, 2021); 2) proper prompts are needed for a better recall, e.g., by additional information or prompt engineering.

A.1.2 Can Context help?

In this context-based experiment, context sentences are introduced for assessing the capability of LMs to generate facts by exploiting context. Concretely, we traverse the sentences in Wikipedia for relevant entities and each context sentence is combined with a corresponding prompt to compose a new query. Next, facts are retrieved or extracted by using different LMs. For duplicated outputs, we merge them and average the score. The experimental results are shown in Table A2. We can see that adding context can remarkably improve the performances on MALT-Wikidata, e.g., BERT-large (4.7 → 12.3) and GENRE (7.4 → 18.9). GENRE consistently outperforms other baselines in terms of F1 while QA mode can obtain very high recalls. For TE methods, they are a workable approach while still lagging behind our framework.

A.1.3 Our Two-stage KBC Method

Based on the above analyses, we find that ED prompts can generate disambiguated and relatively high-quality facts while QA prompts have the highest recall. Hence, a question naturally appears: *"Can we synergize the two components to yield better facts?"*

To answer this question, we apply the ED prompt method to the facts generated by the other three methods, Cloze, QA, and TE. The post-processing step of ED prompt serves to verify and re-rank the candidates of the first step. The experimental results are shown in Figure A2. We observe the combination can bring consistent improvements and the pipeline of "QA + ED" achieves the best score. Therefore, we leverage two different LMs in a two-stage pipeline. The first stage generates candidate answers by using a high-recall question-answering model. The second stage employs an entity disambiguation model for validating the candidates.

CoSiNES: Contrastive Siamese Network for Entity Standardization

Jiaqing Yuan[1], **Michele Merler**[2], **Mihir Choudhury**[2],
Raju Pavuluri[2], **Munindar P. Singh**[1], **Maja Vukovic**[2]
[1] North Carolina State University, Raleigh, NC, USA
[2] IBM Research AI, Yorktown Heights, NY, USA
{jyuan23, mpsingh}@ncsu.edu
{mimerler, choudhury, pavuluri, maja}@us.ibm.com

Abstract

Entity standardization maps noisy mentions from free-form text to standard entities in a knowledge base. The unique challenge of this task relative to other entity-related tasks is the lack of surrounding context and numerous variations in the surface form of the mentions, especially when it comes to generalization across domains where labeled data is scarce. Previous research mostly focuses on developing models either heavily relying on context, or dedicated solely to a specific domain. In contrast, we propose CoSiNES, a generic and adaptable framework with Contrastive Siamese Network for Entity Standardization that effectively adapts a pretrained language model to capture the syntax and semantics of the entities in a new domain.

We construct a new dataset in the technology domain, which contains 640 technical stack entities and 6,412 mentions collected from industrial content management systems. We demonstrate that CoSiNES yields higher accuracy and faster runtime than baselines derived from leading methods in this domain. CoSiNES also achieves competitive performance in four standard datasets from the chemistry, medicine, and biomedical domains, demonstrating its cross-domain applicability.

Code and data is available at `https://github.com/konveyor/tackle-container-advisor/tree/main/entity_standardizer/cosines`

1 Introduction

The automatic resolution of mentions in free-form text to entities in a structured knowledge base is an important task for understanding and organizing text. Two well-recognized tasks tackle entity mentions in text. *Entity matching* concerns resolving data instances that refer to the same real-world entity (Li et al., 2020). The data instances usually comprise a specific schema of attributes, such as product specifications. *Entity linking*, also known as entity disambiguation, associates ambiguous mentions from text with entities in a knowledge base, where precise attributes and relationships between entities are curated (Alam et al., 2022). Both tasks involve rich context surrounding the mention and the underlying entity (Li et al., 2020; Alam et al., 2022). Much effort in deep learning approaches focuses on ways to leverage and encode the context surrounding mentions in text and attributes associated with entities in the knowledge base. However, little work has been done on scenarios where such rich context and precise information are not available. In domains such as finance, biology, medicine, and technology, mentions involve specialized jargon, where no context is associated with the mentions and often no attribute of the entities is available other than the mentions themselves.

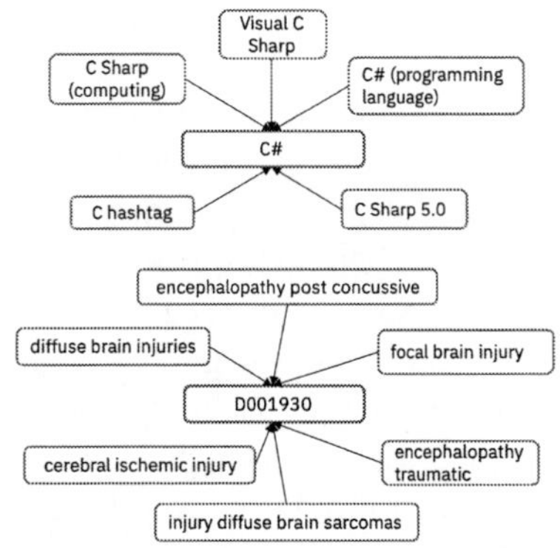

Figure 1: Examples of various mentions referring to the same entity from two different domains. Top: technology, bottom: medical.

We tackle the challenge of missing context for entity standardization (ES) mapping, which involves mapping mentions to entities in the knowledge base across multiple domains. Due to the lack of a public dataset for ES and to foster research on the problem, we manually construct a dataset in the technology domain geared to application modernization. We propose an approach called CoSiNES

Proceedings of the First Workshop on Matching From Unstructured and Structured Data (MATCHING 2023), pages 109–119
July 13, 2023

for the dataset and then evaluate the generalization of CoSiNES in the biomedical domain.

Application modernization consists in migrating legacy applications to the cloud. It relies on a faithful assessment of the technical components of such applications. Much technical information is contained in free-form textual application descriptions, but automatic extraction of such knowledge is non-trivial due to variations in how the same entities are mentioned (Kalia et al., 2021).

Compared to the two aforementioned tasks of entity matching and linking, ES presents unique challenges. First, the mentions could have acronyms, numbers, symbols, alias, punctuation, and misspellings. Figure 1 shows two examples of multiple mentions referring to the same entity. Second, there is a lack of context surrounding the mentions, and there are no attributes or relationships for entities in the knowledge base, which the previous approaches heavily rely on. Third, large deep learning models require massive training datasets, which are not available for specialized domains. Therefore, architectures that are suited for zero-shot or few-shot learning are of great value for this task.

Another challenge is how to perform entity standardization at scale. A naive way is to have exhaustive comparisons between each possible mention and entity pair, which is inefficient. Previous deep learning models for entity matching and entity linking usually have multiple stages (Papadakis et al., 2020): first stage, such as blocking in entity matching, reduces the number of comparison pairs via a coarse-grained criterion so that the latter stages can focus on filtered candidate pairs. This multistage approach leads to globally inferior performance due to the errors accumulated along the pipeline.

We tackle these challenges with a generic framework based on Contrastive Siamese Network which efficiently adapts domain-agnostic pretrained language models (PLMs) to specific domains using a limited number of labeled examples. Language models have shown great capacity to capture both syntactic and semantic variations of text. Our framework decouples the comparison of mention-entity pairs for training and inference so that the model can be used as a standalone encoder after training. Therefore, the embeddings of the entity from the knowledge base can be precomputed and hashed. At inference time, the running time is linear in the size of query mentions, and we can leverage existing tools, such as FAISS,[1] for efficient and large-scale similarity search.

Our contributions are the following.

- A generic, scalable, and adaptable framework that leverages domain-agnostic pretrained language models.
- A method for generating anchored contrastive groups and a training scheme with a hybrid of batch-all and batch-hard online triplet mining.
- A dataset curated for application modernization, where various mentions for technical components are manually labeled.

We validate these contributions via comprehensive experiments with various hyperparameters, loss functions, and training schemes and show the robustness and effectiveness of the framework on our custom dataset in the technology domain. With optimal settings on our dataset, we further evaluate the framework on four datasets from the biomedical domain. We show that the framework can be adapted to other domains with minimal changes.

2 Related Work

Various forms of entity-related tasks have been studied by previous research, of which three are most relevant to our task.

Entity Matching (EM) identifies if different mentions refer to the same real-world entity, and is an important step in data cleaning and integration (Christen, 2012). The targets of EM are records from a database, where records follow a specific schema of attributes. The goal is to find pairs of records from two databases that refer to the same entity. Whereas early approaches of EM mostly apply rule-based heuristics, recent research often relies on deep neural network (Nie et al., 2019; Mudgal et al., 2018; Li et al., 2020; Ebraheem et al., 2018). As the number of pairwise comparisons grows quadratically, a preprocessing step (blocking) is usually applied to reduce the number of candidate matches. The matcher then takes a pair of a mention and an entity as input and produces a probability of a match. In contrast, entity standardization comes with a predefined set of standard entities, and the mentions come with no attributes. Our method involves learning a metric function, where the model can be used as an encoder to embed mentions and entities in the same space.

[1]https://github.com/facebookresearch/faiss

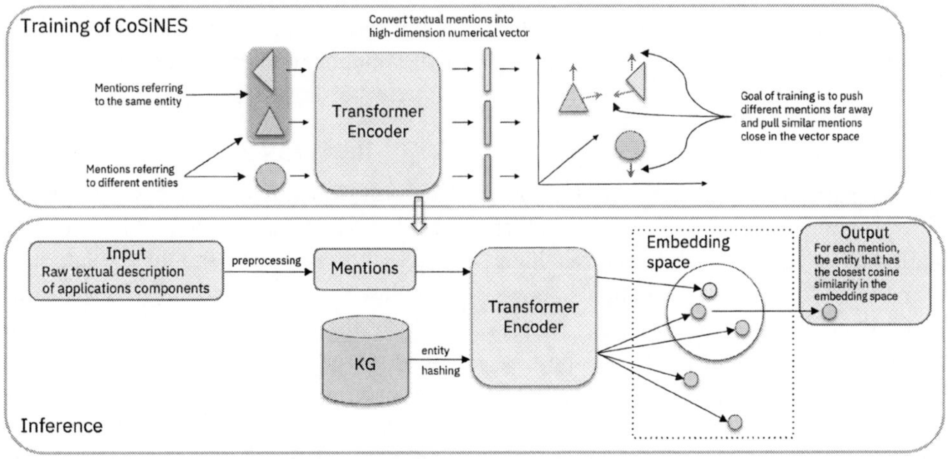

Figure 2: System overview of CoSiNES.

Entity Linking (EL) is the process of linking a mention in context with an entity in a knowledge base. Unlike entity standardization, the entities in the knowledge base, such as WikiData (Vrandečić and Krötzsch, 2014) and Freebase (Bollacker et al., 2008), usually have well-structured attributes and precisely defined relationships between them. The mention comes with rich context and unstructured raw text. To leverage these two different types of contextual information, separate context-mention and graph-entity encoders are designed to produce embeddings respectively, and another neural network is used to combine and project these two embeddings to the same space (Shahbazi et al., 2019; Yamada et al., 2022; Radhakrishnan et al., 2018). Due to the lack of context for both the mention and entity for entity standardization, we propose to use a single unified model as the encoder, which can reduce the complexity of the pipeline.

Entity Normalization (EN) is widely used in the biomedical domain. The task is to map noisy mentions to entities in a well-defined reference set, such as ontologies and taxonomies (Ferré et al., 2020; Ferré et al., 2020). The mentions usually have no context, and the entities come with no attributes, but there is a hierarchical structure in the reference set. Unlike entity standardization in the technology domain, the variations of mentions in life science are fairly standardized and synonyms are rare. The task can be well addressed with a sufficient number of training examples for each entity category, which is not the case in our setting. Fakhraei et al. (2020) propose a similar idea using a Siamese neural network for EN. Our approach differs in the following aspects: the designed training batch-generation algorithm, the computation of the contrastive loss, and the usage of PLMs in our specialized training scheme.

3 Methodology

3.1 Problem Formulation

We denote the set of query mentions as $\mathcal{Q} \equiv \{m_q\}$, and the set of standard entities as $\mathcal{S} \equiv \{e_s\}$. Each entity in $\mathcal{S}$ is associated with zero or more mentions referring to it $e_s \leftarrow \{m_s\}$. Importantly, there should be no overlap between the query mention set $\mathcal{Q}$ and the mentions associated with the standard entity set $\mathcal{S}$. The task is to retrieve an entity $e \in \mathcal{S}$ given $m \in \mathcal{Q}$ such that e is the entity m refers to.

We tackle this task with contrastive learning by learning an embedding encoder such that mentions and entities are encoded to the same high-dimensional embedding space. The property of the embedding space is that the cosine distance between mentions of the same entity is smaller than mentions of different entities.

We design a BERT-based Siamese neural network architecture, which acts as the embedding encoder after training. The training is conducted with a hybrid of batch-all and batch-hard online triplet mining schemes. Figure 2 gives an overview of CoSiNES. The training (top) phase has the goal of pulling similar mentions together and pushing dissimilar mentions far away in the embedding space. After training, the inference (bottom) phase has the goal of using a Siamese neural network to project entities in the knowledge base and query mentions to the same embedding space. At inference time, nearest neighbor search algorithms can be used to retrieve the target entity.

3.2 Contrastive Learning and Triplet Loss

Contrastive Learning (Khan et al., 2022; Rethmeier and Augenstein, 2022; Smith and Eisner, 2005) aims to group similar data points together and push dissimilar data points far apart in a high-dimensional embedding space. Equation 1 shows the core idea of contrastive learning. Here x represents any data point in the domain, x^+ is a positive sample that is similar to x (or from the same class as x), and x^- is a negative sample that is dissimilar to x. E is an encoder, which could be any neural network. And, dis is a distance measure between the embedding vectors.

$$\text{dis}(E(x), E(x^+)) \ll \text{dis}(E(x), E(x^-)) \quad (1)$$

As shown in Equation 2, triplet loss is calculated based on triplets $\{x, x^+, x^-\}$, which consist of two samples from the same class and a third sample from a different class. The intuition is that the distance $\text{d}(x, x^-)$ should be larger than the distance $\text{d}(x, x^+)$ by a *margin*. The *margin* is a hyperparameter that needs to be tuned.

$$\mathcal{L} = \max(\text{d}(x, x^+) - \text{d}(x, x^-) + \text{margin}, 0) \quad (2)$$

Based on the difference between $\text{d}(x, x^-)$ and $\text{d}(x, x^+)$, we can classify triplets into three categories: easy, semihard, and hard. See appendix B for detailed definitions.

3.3 Online Triplet Mining

There are two different strategies of mining triplets for contrastive learning. *Offline mining* generates triplets at the beginning of training. The embeddings of the whole training dataset are computed, then hard and semihard triplets are mined based on the embeddings. Offline mining is highly inefficient. First, it requires computing the embeddings for all the training data to mine the triplets. Second, as the model starts to learn, the hard and semihard triplets may turn into easy triplets. Therefore, at least for a few epochs, we need to update the triplet set frequently. *Online triplet mining* (Schroff et al., 2015) seeks to generate triplets on the fly within a batch. There are two strategies to mine triplets from a batch, i.e., batch all and batch hard. We adopt the same idea in our model and propose a hybrid online mining scheme which is shown to be superior to single-mining strategy.

3.3.1 Batch–All

To form valid triplets, a batch of training data should always include samples from more than one class, and each class should contain at least two samples. Suppose the size of the batch is B and the number of all possible triplets is B^3. However, not all of these triplets are valid as we need to make sure each triplet comprises two distinct samples from the same class and one sample from another class. For all valid triplets in the batch, we simply select all hard and semihard triplets and compute the average loss over them. We do not include easy triplets in computing the average as it will make the loss too small. The calculations are based on the embeddings of the batch after they pass through the model.

3.3.2 Batch–Hard

This strategy always selects the hardest positive and negative for each anchor in the batch. Each data instance in the batch can be used as an anchor. Therefore, the number of triplets is always equal to the size of the batch. The hardest positive has the largest $\text{d}(x, x^+)$ among all positives, and the hardest negative has the smallest $\text{d}(x, x^-)$ among all negatives.

3.3.3 Contrastive Group Generation

Based on the above discussion, a batch should include multiple samples from multiple classes. We sample batches with two steps. First, we randomly generate groups of samples from the same class with size g, and second, we randomly sample b classes of groups to form a batch. Therefore, the effective batch size would be $B = g * b$.

3.4 BERT-Based Siamese Neural Network

The canonical Siamese neural network is an architecture that consists of two towers with shared weights working in parallel on two different inputs. The outputs are passed on to a distance function to learn comparable output vectors. We extend the same idea to a batch of inputs instead of a pair of inputs. We sample the batch as described in Section 3.3 and feed the sampled triplets through the network. The output embeddings of the batch are used to generate valid triplets and compute the loss. The backbone of the Siamese model could be any neural network. We use the pretrained language model BERT (Devlin et al., 2019) as the backbone.

3.5 Hashing and Retrieval

Once the Siamese model is trained, it can be used as a standalone encoder to compute the embeddings of entities and mentions. We precompute the embeddings for all entities and save them for comparisons at inference time. For each query mention, we use the same Siamese model to get the embedding and our task is to retrieve the entity with the closest distance to the mention in the embedding space. For a query set of size q, we need to run the Siamese model only q times, avoiding exhaustive pairwise running of the Siamese model. Potentially, we still need to conduct a pairwise nearest neighbor search over the mention and entity embeddings. Tools such as FAISS can be leveraged to efficiently perform large-scale nearest neighbor search.

4 Experimental Setup

4.1 Dataset

We curate a dataset (ESAppMod) on application modernization that comprises named entities with respect to the technical stack of business applications. There are a total number of 640 unique entities, covering a variety of technical component categories, such as Operating System (OS), Application Server, Programming Language, Library, and Runtime. We manually extract and label 6,412 unique mentions associated with the entities in AppMod from real application descriptions. All annotations are done by domain experts. We split the mentions 60–40 into train and test sets, which yields 3,973 and 2,439 mentions in the training and testing splits, respectively. The mentions associated with each entity are not evenly distributed, ranging from one to over a hundred.

4.2 Hyperparameter Tuning

Implementing our framework involves many design choices and hyperparameters. To facilitate performance at scale, the tradeoff between accuracy and inference time is crucial. We experimented with different sizes of BERT as the backbone of CoSiNES, including BERT-tiny, BERT-mini, BERT-small, BERT-medium, and BERT-base. For triplet mining, we evaluated batch–all, batch–hard, and a hybrid of the two. For the measure of distance, we investigated cosine, Euclidean, and squared Euclidean distance. For the hyperparameters, we evaluated different values of margin, learning rate, and batch size detailed in appendix C. All training experiments were carried out on an NVIDIA A100 GPU with 40GB memory. We use the tool Ray.tune[2] for hyperparameter tuning. Inference times were computed as the cumulative time to predict all 2,439 mentions in the test set on the CPU of Macbook pro with 2.3 GHz Quad-Core Intel Core i7, 32 GB 3733 MHz LPDDR4X RAM. We report the median inference time of 10 runs.

Model	T@1	T@3	T@5	Inf. Time
TF-IDF	69.94	85.36	88.44	60
GNN	67.20	79.29	82.49	29
BERT	32.64	47.23	54.82	17
GPT3	77.24	**90.24**	**93.56**	240
CoSiNES	**80.40**	88.68	90.98	11

Table 1: Experimental results on ESAppMod. T@1: top-1 retrieval accuracy. Inf. Time refers to total inference time in seconds.

4.3 Baselines

We compare CoSiNES with four baselines.

TF-IDF A model that computes TF-IDF embeddings learned from training data(Kalia et al., 2021).

GNN A graph neural network that treats each entity or mention as a chain. Each character represents a node in the graph and its embedding representation is learned during training. The average of the character embeddings are used to represent entity names and mentions (Fan et al., 2022).

BERT We use the mean of last layer outputs of all tokens from BERT_small (Bhargava et al., 2021) to represent entities and mentions. This is the same backbone used to train CoSiNES.

GPT3[3] We use the embedding GPT-3 api from OpenAI to compute the embeddings using model `embedding-ada-002`.

5 Results and Discussions

Table 1 shows the comparative results on our dataset. Our model outperforms all baselines by a significant margin in terms of top–1 retrieval accuracy: 10.46% over TF-IDF, 13.2% over GNN, 47.76% over BERT, and 3.16% over GPT3. Through comprehensive experimentation, we observe that the best performance model has the

[2]https://docs.ray.io/en/latest/tune/index.html

[3]https://beta.openai.com/docs/guides/embeddings/

BERT-small as the backbone. The learning rate is set to 1e−5, contrastive group size is 10, and the batch size of groups is 16, which makes the effective batch size 160. We set the margin to 2.

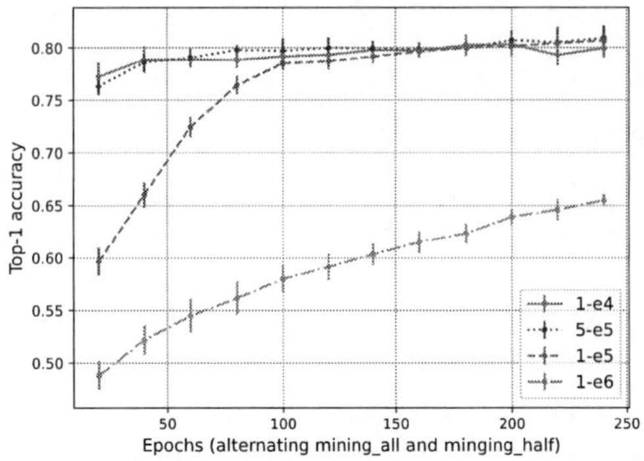

Figure 3: Five–fold cross–validation with different learning rates on training data.

5.1 Learning Rate

To investigate how different learning rates affect the convergence of the Siamese model on our dataset, we run five-fold cross-validation with four learning rates (1e−4, 5e−5, 1e−5, and 1e−6) on the training data, as shown in Figure 3. For each learning rate, we experiment with different numbers of epochs, ranging from 10 to 200 with an interval of 10. The X axis is the number of epochs for each experiment and the Y axis is the top–1 accuracy. The average of the five-fold top–1 accuracy is shown for each dot in the figure, together with the standard deviation across five folds. As we can see, the learning rate affects how fast and stably the model converges, and most of them reach similar performance when trained for enough number of epochs. This indicates that the Siamese model is robust with respect to the learning rate. We set the learning rate to be 1e-5 as it tends to have a smaller deviation of performance.

5.2 Hybrid Triplet Mining

We propose a hybrid of batch–all and batch–hard triplet mining during training. Figure 4 shows the training process with 200 epochs with the above three learning rates, of which the first 100 epochs apply batch–all triplet sampling and the second 100 epochs employ batch–hard triplet sampling. The result shows that for the first batch–all 100 epochs, the training of 1e−4 and 5e−5 is unstable and performance oscillates greatly. When batch–hard mining comes into play, the training becomes much smoother and the performance continues to improve steadily for all three learning rates. This experiment shows that the hybrid mining scheme improves the top–1 accuracy by around 2% compared to the single-mining strategy.

5.3 Model Size

Normally, there is a tradeoff between model accuracy and efficiency. Therefore, we experiment with different sizes of BERT as backbone to find a balance between performance and running time. Figure 5 shows the inference time on the testing set with top–1 accuracy. The results show that CoSiNES with BERT-small achieves the best performance and fast inference time. Although the GPT3 embeddings achieve performance close to CoSiNES, running inference using the GPT3 OpenAI api is inefficient.

5.4 ROC Curve

For a comprehensive comparison between our model and the baselines, we conduct an experiment to compute the receiver operating characteristic (ROC) curve. We add 420 previously unseen relevant but negative mentions from the technology domain that do not refer to any entities in the training set, and calculate the false positive rate under different thresholds. Figure 6 shows that our proposed model has a larger area under the curve, which demonstrates its superior performance over the baselines.

5.5 Qualitative Error Analysis

We examine the predictions from CoSiNES on ESAppMod and categorize the following error types. Table 2 shows a few examples for each of these types.

Misspelling. When a mention has an error in the spelling, the tokens returned by PLMs could be very different, which leads to mismatch. This is a challenge for PLMs, whereas human could easily handle, e.g. “Andriod" vs “Android".

Acronym. Linking acronyms to full expressions seem to be a trivial task for humans, however, CoSiNES falls short of this capability. The rescue might be to design a task specialized for recognizing acronyms for PLMs.

Multi-match. This is the most common error where multiple entities partially match with the mention in the surface form. One way to address this issue is to enrich the training dataset with various mentions, which is not always within easy

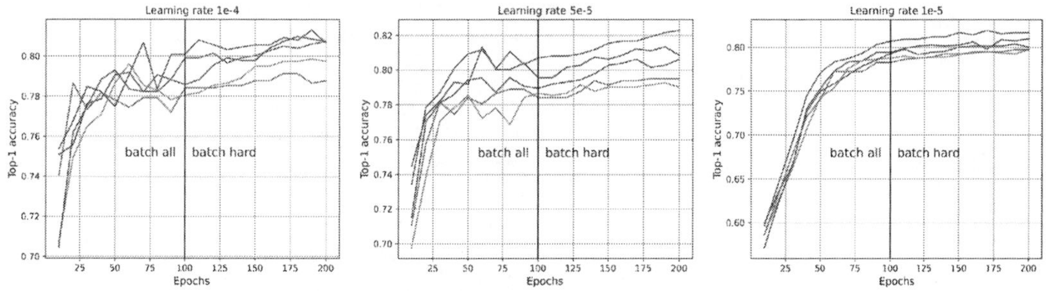

Figure 4: Hybrid triplet mining with different learning rates for five-fold cross validation.

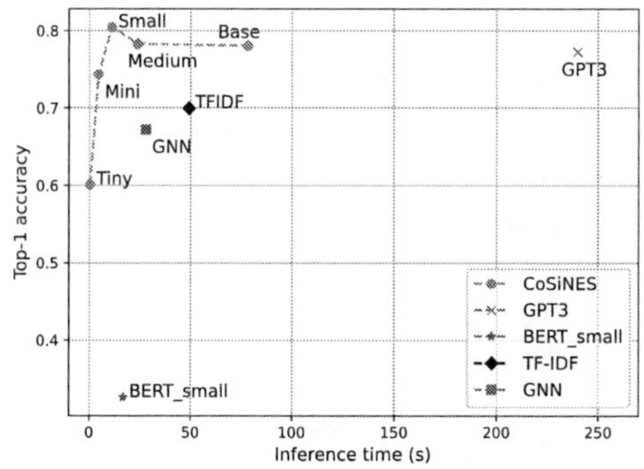

Figure 5: Accuracy versus efficiency between the proposed models on the ESAppMod dataset. The CoSiNES line represents different size of BERT as backbone.

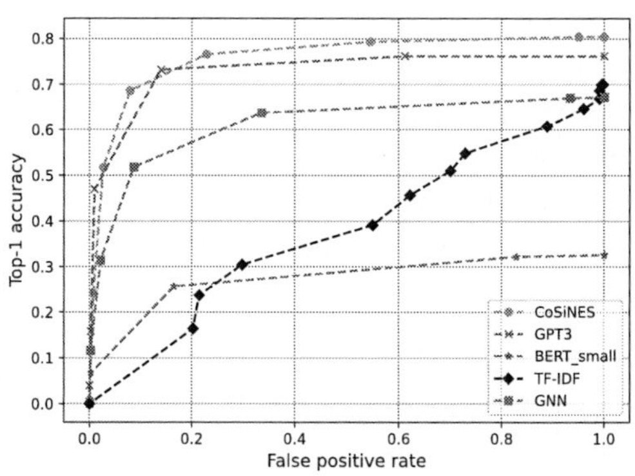

Figure 6: ROC Curves on the ESAppMod dataset.

reach. Another potential approach is to integrate external knowledge about entities so that the model can refer to.

No-match. When the entity and mention have no match at all in the surface form, it is unlikely for the model to retrieve the correct target, especially no context can be leveraged. Therefore, external knowledge could be particularly useful in this case.

6 Adaptation to Biomedical Domain

We show how to adapt our framework to the biomedical domain with minimal changes.

6.1 Datasets

We consider four public datasets, ncbi, bc5cdr-disease, bc5cdr-chemical, and bc2gm, covering three types of entities: chemicals, diseases, and genes. Details and statistics regarding the datasets can be found in apprendix A.

6.2 Baselines

We compare our framework with three models.

TF-IDF Like the baseline for ESAppMod, we implement a straightforward TF-IDF model (Kalia et al., 2021) based on the knowledge database for each dataset and apply nearest-neighbor search for testing.

BioBERT ranking Use BioBERT (Lee et al., 2019) to encode concepts and mentions without fine-tuning. BioBERT is a large biomedical language representation model pretrained with PubMed abstracts and PMC full-text articles.

BioSyn BioSyn (Sung et al., 2020) is the state-of-the-art model for biomedical entity normalization with synonym marginalization and iterative candidate retrieval. The model leverages sparse embedding from TF-IDF and dense embedding from BioBERT.

6.3 Domain Adaptation

For domain adaptation, it would be ideal if we can make none or a few changes to the model architecture and training process. Therefore, we follow all experimental settings, such as learning rate, margin, contrastive group generation, and hybrid training scheme from the experiments on our proposed datasets. The most significant change is that to adapt to a new domain, we use dmis-lab/biobert-

Error type	Mention	Target entity	Top-5 retrieved entities
Misspelling	Andriod	Android	IBM ILOG Views / Oracle Real-Time Decisions (RTD) / BeOS / Ingres / etcd
	Visusal Basic	Visual Basic	Clarify|Clear Basic / BASIC / IBM Basic Assembly Language / Pervasive PSQL / ADABAS
Acronym	NES	Netscape Enterprise Server	Mobile / SAS / iOS / Powershell / MinIO
	IIB	IBM Integration Bus	Visual Basic / VB.NET / Clarify|Clear Basic / IIS|* / Ada
Multi-match	Cordova Android	Apache Cordova	Android / Apache Cordova / Cisco IOS / Perl|Oraperl / Keycloak
	MQ 9.1	IBM Websphere MQ	Microsoft MQ / MQ Client / IBM Websphere MQ / Qiskit / IBM WebSphere MQ Telemetry
	Open Liberty	WebSphere Liberty	OpenROAD / WebSphere Liberty / Virtual Appliance / OpenVPN / Microsoft System Center Endpoint Protection
No-match	AS400	IBM Power Systems	DB400 / Asterisk / Primavera P6 / EAServer / Microsoft Excel
	EAP	JBoss	XAMPP / F5 Secure Web Gateway Services / Java|Java Web Start / UltiDev Web Server Pro (UWS) / A-Auto Job Scheduling Software

Table 2: Examples for each type of errors on ESAppMod.

v1.1[4] in replacement of the regular BERT as our backbone. We conduct all experiments on two NVIDIA A100 GPUs and adjust the batch size for each dataset based on the lengths of the mentions.

6.4 Results

The results are shown in Table 3. We reproduce the BioBERT experiment reported by (Tutubalina et al., 2020a) using the embedding of the [CLS] token as the representation. The results are almost identical. The minor differences might be due to different versions of the pretrained language model.

The performance of BioSyn reported by Sung et al. (2020) is high. However, as pointed out by Tutubalina et al. (2020a), the original testing splits used by Sung et al. (2020) have significant overlapping mentions with the knowledge base. Therefore, Tutubalina et al. removed all the duplicates and produced refined testing splits. We follow the performance of BioSyn reported by them.

The results show that CoSiNES significantly outperforms the baselines of TF-IDF and BioBERT ranking in terms of top-k accuracy. CoSiNES achieves competitive results with BioSyn on all the datasets. Given that we didn't change any hyperparameters or architectures of CoSiNES, and directly applied the framework to new domains, we demonstrate the cross-domain applicability of CoSiNES.

	ncbi	bc5cdr-d	bc5cdr-c	bc2gm
TF-IDF@1	59.31	61.34	71.76	67.01
TF-IDF@3	69.61	69.41	76.24	76.55
TF-IDF@5	74.02	73.21	78.59	79.90
BioBERT@1	47.55	64.23	79.55	68.12
BioBERT@3	57.35	74.89	81.65	74.11
BioBERT@5	61.77	79.45	82.82	76.04
BioSyn@1	72.5	**74.1**	**83.8**	**85.8**
BioSyn@3	-	-	-	-
BioSyn@5	-	-	-	-
CoSiNES@1	**72.55**	73.52	81.65	**85.79**
CoSiNES@3	80.39	78.39	85.88	90.66
CoSiNES@5	81.37	80.52	87.76	91.68

Table 3: Results on four datasets from the biomedical domain. @1: top-1 accuracy. Here, bc5cdr-d means bc5cdr-disease and bc5cdr-c means bc5cdr-chemical.

7 Conclusion

We propose a generic, scalable, and adaptable framework CoSiNES for the entity standardization task, which maps various mentions to standard entities in the knowledge base. We first construct a new dataset ESAppMod in the technology domain and demonstrate the superiority of our framework over four other models. We conduct comprehensive experiments regarding batch size, learning rate, margin, loss calculation and different sizes of BERT, with our designed contrastive group generation and hybrid triplet mining, and show that the framework is rather robust with respect to hyper-parameters. With the optimal setting on our dataset, we further show that our model can be easily adapted to new domains with minimal changes by achieving competitive performance on four benchmark datasets from the biomedical domain covering three different types of entities.

After examining the errors produced by the framework on our proposed dataset, we categorize four different types of errors and defer to future work with the following directions: (1) integrating the framework with external knowledge. For multi-match errors, where multiple entities partially match with the mention, it would be ambiguous to retrieve the target entity. For no-match errors, external knowledge could provide extra information; (2) Adversarial training for misspellings. For technical

[4]https://huggingface.co/dmis-lab/biobert-v1.1

terms, misspelling could lead to completely different tokenization of the mentions; (3) Construct new or augment the existing training dataset with acronym samples. The pretrained language models are not specialized in recognizing acronyms. Therefore, it would be worthwhile endowing PLMs with such capability.

Limitations

We focuses on resolving various mentions from different domains. Although we have tested our framework on multiple datasets, it relies on a human-annotated dataset and effort should be taken to investigate how the model performs with emerging domains without human-annotated data. Our model works with mentions that have been extracted from raw text. It would be more practical if the model could work with raw text directly and interact with another mention-extraction module. The performance of the model is largely affected by the surface form of the mentions, although our framework is robust to variations in the surface form, it would be more beneficial to further investigate how adversarial turbulence in the mentions could affect the behaviors of the framework.

Ethics Statement

The domain and data we work with don't involve any personal information and are all publicly available. However, as the work could be potentially applied in the medical domain to resolve mentions of disease, discretion is advised when any medical decisions or diagnostics are made with the assistance of the model.

References

Mehwish Alam, Davide Buscaldi, Michael Cochez, Francesco Osborne, Diego Reforgiato Recupero, Harald Sack, Özge Sevgili, Artem Shelmanov, Mikhail Arkhipov, Alexander Panchenko, Chris Biemann, Mehwish Alam, Davide Buscaldi, Michael Cochez, Francesco Osborne, Diego Refogiato Recupero, and Harald Sack. 2022. Neural entity linking: A survey of models based on deep learning. *Semant. Web*, 13(3):527–570.

Prajjwal Bhargava, Aleksandr Drozd, and Anna Rogers. 2021. Generalization in nli: Ways (not) to go beyond simple heuristics.

Kurt Bollacker, Colin Evans, Praveen Paritosh, Tim Sturge, and Jamie Taylor. 2008. Freebase: A collaboratively created graph database for structuring human knowledge. In *Proceedings of the ACM SIGMOD International Conference on Management of Data*, SIGMOD, page 1247–1250, New York, NY, USA. Association for Computing Machinery.

Peter Christen. 2012. *Data Matching: Concepts and Techniques for Record Linkage, Entity Resolution, and Duplicate Detection*. Springer.

Allan Peter Davis, Cynthia J. Grondin, Robin J. Johnson, Daniela Sciaky, Roy McMorran, Jolene Wiegers, Thomas C. Wiegers, and Carolyn J. Mattingly. 2018. The comparative toxicogenomics database: Update 2019. *Nucleic Acids Research*, 47:D948 – D954.

Allan Peter Davis, Thomas C. Wiegers, Michael C. Rosenstein, and Carolyn J. Mattingly. 2012. Medic: A practical disease vocabulary used at the comparative toxicogenomics database. *Database: The Journal of Biological Databases and Curation*, 2012.

Jacob Devlin, Ming-Wei Chang, Kenton Lee, and Kristina Toutanova. 2019. Bert: Pre-training of deep bidirectional transformers for language understanding. *ArXiv*, abs/1810.04805.

Rezarta Islamaj Dogan, Robert Leaman, and Zhiyong Lu. 2014. Ncbi disease corpus: A resource for disease name recognition and concept normalization. *Journal of Biomedical Informatics*, 47:1–10.

Muhammad Ebraheem, Saravanan Thirumuruganathan, Shafiq Joty, Mourad Ouzzani, and Nan Tang. 2018. Distributed representations of tuples for entity resolution. *Proceedings VLDB Endowment*, 11(11):1454–1467.

Shobeir Fakhraei, Joel Mathew, and José Luis Ambite. 2020. Nseen: Neural semantic embedding for entity normalization. In *Machine Learning and Knowledge Discovery in Databases*, pages 665–680, Cham. Springer International Publishing.

Shengyu Fan, Hui Yu, Xiaoya Cai, Yanfang Geng, Guangzhen Li, Weizhi Xu, Xia Wang, and Yaping Yang. 2022. Multi-attention deep neural network fusing character and word embedding for clinical and biomedical concept extraction. *Information Sciences*, 608:778–793.

Arnaud Ferré, Robert Bossy, Mouhamadou Ba, Louise Deléger, Thomas Lavergne, Pierre Zweigenbaum, and Claire Nédellec. 2020. Handling entity normalization with no annotated corpus: Weakly supervised methods based on distributional representation and ontological information. In *Proceedings of the Twelfth Language Resources and Evaluation Conference*, pages 1959–1966, Marseille, France. European Language Resources Association.

Arnaud Ferré, Louise Deléger, Robert Bossy, Pierre Zweigenbaum, and Claire Nédellec. 2020. C-norm: A neural approach to few-shot entity normalization. *BMC Bioinformatics 21 (Suppl 23)*.

Anup Kalia, Raghav Batta, Jin Xiao, Mihir Choudhury, and Maja Vukovic. 2021. Aca: Application containerization advisory framework for modernizing legacy applications. In *IEEE 14th International Conference on Cloud Computing (CLOUD)*, pages 708–710.

Adnan Khan, Sarah AlBarri, and Muhammad Arslan Manzoor. 2022. Contrastive self-supervised learning: A survey on different architectures. In *2nd International Conference on Artificial Intelligence (ICAI)*, pages 1–6.

Jinhyuk Lee, Wonjin Yoon, Sungdong Kim, Donghyeon Kim, Sunkyu Kim, Chan Ho So, and Jaewoo Kang. 2019. BioBERT: A pre-trained biomedical language representation model for biomedical text mining. *Bioinformatics*, 36(4):1234–1240.

Jiao Li, Yueping Sun, Robin J. Johnson, Daniela Sciaky, Chih-Hsuan Wei, Robert Leaman, Allan Peter Davis, Carolyn J. Mattingly, Thomas C. Wiegers, and Zhiyong Lu. 2016. Biocreative V CDR task corpus: A resource for chemical disease relation extraction. *Database: The Journal of Biological Databases and Curation*, 2016.

Yuliang Li, Jinfeng Li, Yoshihiko Suhara, AnHai Doan, and Wang-Chiew Tan. 2020. Deep entity matching with pre-trained language models. *Proceedings VLDB Endowment*, 14(1):50–60.

Alexander A. Morgan, Zhiyong Lu, Xinglong Wang, Aaron M. Cohen, Juliane Fluck, Patrick Ruch, Anna Divoli, Katrin Fundel, Robert Leaman, Jörg Hakenberg, Chengjie Sun, Heng-Hui Liu, Rafael Torres, M. Krauthammer, William W. Lau, Hongfang Liu, Chun-Nan Hsu, Martijn J. Schuemie, Kevin Bretonnel Cohen, and Lynette Hirschman. 2008. Overview of biocreative II gene normalization. *Genome Biology*, 9:S3 – S3.

Sidharth Mudgal, Han Li, Theodoros Rekatsinas, AnHai Doan, Youngchoon Park, Ganesh Krishnan, Rohit Deep, Esteban Arcaute, and Vijay Raghavendra. 2018. Deep learning for entity matching: A design space exploration. *Proceedings of the International Conference on Management of Data*.

Hao Nie, Xianpei Han, Ben He, Le Sun, Bo Chen, Wei Zhang, Suhui Wu, and Hao Kong. 2019. Deep sequence-to-sequence entity matching for heterogeneous entity resolution. In *Proceedings of the 28th ACM International Conference on Information and Knowledge Management*, CIKM, page 629–638, New York, NY, USA. Association for Computing Machinery.

George Papadakis, Dimitrios Skoutas, Emmanouil Thanos, and Themis Palpanas. 2020. Blocking and filtering techniques for entity resolution: A survey. *ACM Comput. Surv.*, 53(2).

Priya Radhakrishnan, Partha Talukdar, and Vasudeva Varma. 2018. ELDEN: Improved entity linking using densified knowledge graphs. In *Proceedings of the Conference of the North American Chapter of the Association for Computational Linguistics: Human Language Technologies, Volume 1 (Long Papers)*, pages 1844–1853, New Orleans, Louisiana. Association for Computational Linguistics.

Nils Rethmeier and Isabelle Augenstein. 2022. A primer on contrastive pretraining in language processing: Methods, lessons learned and perspectives. *ACM Computing Survey*.

Florian Schroff, Dmitry Kalenichenko, and James Philbin. 2015. Facenet: A unified embedding for face recognition and clustering. In *IEEE Conference on Computer Vision and Pattern Recognition (CVPR)*, pages 815–823.

Hamed Shahbazi, Xiaoli Z. Fern, Reza Ghaeini, Rasha Obeidat, and Prasad Tadepalli. 2019. Entity-aware elmo: Learning contextual entity representation for entity disambiguation. *ArXiv*, abs/1908.05762.

Noah A. Smith and Jason Eisner. 2005. Contrastive estimation: Training log-linear models on unlabeled data. In *Proceedings of the 43rd Annual Meeting of the Association for Computational Linguistics (ACL)*, pages 354–362, Ann Arbor, Michigan. Association for Computational Linguistics.

Mujeen Sung, Hwisang Jeon, Jinhyuk Lee, and Jaewoo Kang. 2020. Biomedical entity representations with synonym marginalization. In *Annual Meeting of the Association for Computational Linguistics (ACL)*.

Elena Tutubalina, Artur Kadurin, and Zulfat Miftahutdinov. 2020a. Fair evaluation in concept normalization: a large-scale comparative analysis for BERT-based models. In *Proceedings of the 28th International Conference on Computational Linguistics*, pages 6710–6716, Barcelona, Spain (Online). International Committee on Computational Linguistics.

Elena Tutubalina, Artur Kadurin, and Zulfat Miftahutdinov. 2020b. Fair evaluation in concept normalization: A large-scale comparative analysis for BERT-based models. In *Proceedings of the 28th International Conference on Computational Linguistics*, pages 6710–6716, Barcelona, Spain (Online). International Committee on Computational Linguistics.

Denny Vrandečić and Markus Krötzsch. 2014. Wikidata: A free collaborative knowledgebase. *Commun. ACM*, 57(10):78–85.

Ikuya Yamada, Koki Washio, Hiroyuki Shindo, and Yuji Matsumoto. 2022. Global entity disambiguation with BERT. In *Proceedings of the Conference of the North American Chapter of the Association for Computational Linguistics: Human Language Technologies*, pages 3264–3271, Seattle, United States. Association for Computational Linguistics.

A Biomedical Datasets Descriptions and Statistics

Detailed descriptions of the datasets can also be found in Tutubalina et al. (2020b) and Sung et al. (2020).

NCBI Disease Corpus NCBI Disease Corpus (Dogan et al., 2014) contains manually annotated disease mentions extracted from 793 PubMed abstracts and their corresponding concepts in the MEDIC dictionary (Davis et al., 2012). The July 6, 2012 version of MEDIC has 11,915 CUIs (concept ids) and 71,923 synonyms (mentions).

BioCreative V CDR BioCreative V CDR (BC5CDR) (Li et al., 2016) is a challenge for extracting chemical-disease relations. There are manual annotations for both chemical and disease from 1,500 PubMed abstracts. Like the NCBI disease corpus, disease mentions are mapped into the MEDIC dictionary. The chemical mentions are mapped into the Comparative Toxicogenomics DataBase (CTD) (Davis et al., 2018). The Nov 4, 2019 version of CTD contains 171,203 CUIs and 407,247 synonyms.

BioCreative II GN BioCreative II GN (BC2GN) (Morgan et al., 2008) contains human gene and gene product mentions from PubMed abstracts. It has 61,646 CUIs and 277,944 synonyms (Tutubalina et al., 2020a).

	KG entity	KG mention	Test mention
ncbi	12,554	73,024	204
bc5cdr-d	12,511	73,126	657
bc5cdr-c	171,284	407,600	425
bc2gm	67,370	277,944	985

Table 4: Diomedical datasets statistics. Here, KG means knowledge base, bc5cdr-d means bc5cdr-disease and bc5cdr-c means bc5cdr-chemical.

B Triplet Types

As shown in Equation 3, triplet loss is calculated based on triplets $\{x, x^+, x^-\}$, which always consist of two samples from the same class and a third sample from a different class. We usually call x the anchor of the triplet, x^+ the positive sample, and x^- the negative sample. The intuition behind the loss function is that the distance $\mathrm{d}(x, x^-)$ between the anchor and negative should be larger than the distance $\mathrm{d}(x, x^+)$ between the anchor and positive by a *margin*. The *margin* is a hyperparameter that needs to be tuned.

$$\mathcal{L} = \max(\mathrm{d}(x, x^+) - \mathrm{d}(x, x^-) + \mathrm{margin}, 0) \quad (3)$$

Based on the difference between $\mathrm{d}(x, x^-)$ and $\mathrm{d}(x, x^+)$, we can classify triplets into three categories.

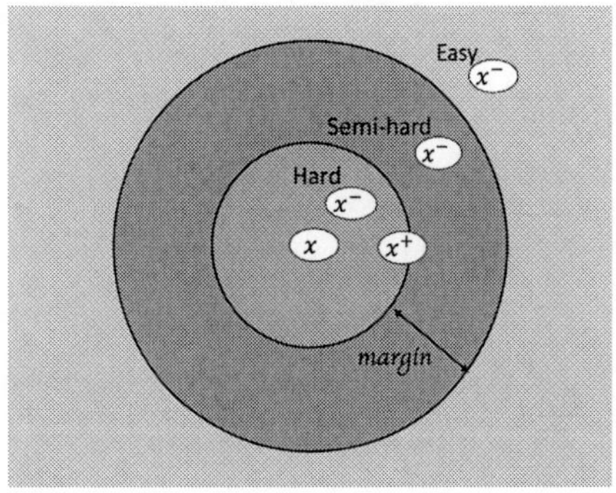

Figure 7: Different types of triplet samples.

- Easy triplets, which have a loss of zero based on Equation 2. Therefore, easy triplets provide no learning signal to the model.

$$\mathrm{d}(x, x^-) - \mathrm{d}(x, x^+) > \mathrm{margin}$$

- Semihard triplets, which have a loss less than the *margin*.

$$0 < \mathrm{d}(x, x^-) - \mathrm{d}(x, x^+) < \mathrm{margin}$$

- Hard triplets, which are most informative for the model.

$$\mathrm{d}(x, x^-) - \mathrm{d}(x, x^+) < 0$$

C Hyperparameter Search

We have done the following hyperparameter search grid on ESAppMod

Batch Size	4, 8, 16, 32
Learning Rate	1e−3, 1e−4, 1e−5, 1e−6
Margin	0.5, 1, 2, 5, 10

Table 5: Hyperparameter search on ESAppMod

Author Index

Association for Computational Linguistics
209 N. Eighth Street
Stroudsburg, Pennsylvania 18360

ISBN 978-1-7138-8229-9

CURRAN ASSOCIATES INC.
proceedings.com